Lecture Notes in Computer Science 11079

Commenced Publication in 1973
Founding and Former Series Editors:
Gerhard Goos, Juris Hartmanis, and Jan van Leeuwen

More information about this series at http://www.springer.com/series/7410

Manel Medina · Andreas Mitrakas
Kai Rannenberg · Erich Schweighofer
Nikolaos Tsouroulas (Eds.)

Privacy Technologies and Policy

6th Annual Privacy Forum, APF 2018
Barcelona, Spain, June 13–14, 2018
Revised Selected Papers

 Springer

Editors
Manel Medina
Universitat Politècnica de Catalunya
Barcelona, Spain

Erich Schweighofer
University of Vienna
Vienna, Austria

Andreas Mitrakas
ENISA
Maroussi, Greece

Nikolaos Tsouroulas
Telefónica
Madrid, Spain

Kai Rannenberg
Goethe University Frankfurt
Frankfurt am Main, Germany

ISSN 0302-9743 ISSN 1611-3349 (electronic)
Lecture Notes in Computer Science
ISBN 978-3-030-02546-5 ISBN 978-3-030-02547-2 (eBook)
https://doi.org/10.1007/978-3-030-02547-2

Library of Congress Control Number: 2018960436

LNCS Sublibrary: SL4 – Security and Cryptology

This Springer imprint is published by the registered company Springer Nature Switzerland AG
The registered company address is: Gewerbestrasse 11, 6330 Cham, Switzerland

Foreword

As the Annual Privacy Forum (APF) marks its sixth edition, the role that ENISA has played in bringing together the seemingly opposing notions of privacy and information security is going through a transformation phase. In the aftermath of large-scale attacks that aimed at disclosing personal data at a massive scale, ENISA has looked into ways to engage with a broader audience and set up a network of like-minded professionals, with a view to promote suitable policies and recommendations. This year's edition of the APF innovates by seeking to bring along industry, so as to complement the policy and research components of this conference and achieve a better outreach.

From May 25, 2018, the protection of personal data and privacy of individuals turned a corner in the EU, as the long-awaited General Data Protection Regulation (GDPR) 2016/679[1] came into effect following a long legislative process. In a practical demonstration in support of fundamental individual rights and of those who govern, the EU has legislated the GDPR, to paraphrase Dworkin[2]. This is a robust piece of legislation with direct application to all EU Member States. The GDPR is expected to have far-reaching consequences for service providers established within the EU but importantly also for those who reside beyond its borders. The GDPR provides a comprehensive framework for the protection of personal data in the EU and beyond.

Compared with the legal framework of the past 20 years in the EU, the GDPR introduces *inter alia* an enhanced approach to governance, accountability, the role of data protection officers, data breach notifications, a risk-based approach, security measures, consent giving and fines, thereby providing a sound future-proof legal framework to the benefit of data subjects. Notions such as privacy by default and design and the right to be forgotten open up new possibilities in the meaningful protection of liberties and individual rights in practice.

It goes without saying that the long-standing contribution of ENISA in terms of analysis and recommendations on security measures to support personal data protection and privacy is likely to expand yet further. ENISA regularly issues actionable recommendations to shaping technology according to data protection and privacy provisions, and addressing privacy and personal data protection requirements through technology. More recently, ENISA published suitable reports seeking to translate legal obligations to technical approaches, in particular with regard to the security of personal data processing[3,4], privacy and data protection by design[5], privacy-enhancing

---

[1] https://eur-lex.europa.eu/legal-content/EN/TXT/?uri=uriserv:OJ.L_.2016.119.01.0001.01.ENG.

[2] Ronald Dworkin, Taking Rights Seriously, Harvard University Press, 1977.

[3] https://www.enisa.europa.eu/publications/handbook-on-security-of-personal-data-processing.

[4] https://www.enisa.europa.eu/publications/guidelines-for-smes-on-the-security-of-personal-data-processing.

[5] https://www.enisa.europa.eu/publications/privacy-and-data-protection-by-design.

technologies (PETs)[6], personal data breach notifications[7], as well as proposing mechanisms for user empowerment (transparency and control) in digital environments[8]. The GDPR is likely to give new impetus to the policy work spearheaded by ENISA in the area of security measures for personal data protection and privacy. With the prospect of a renewed mandate, ENISA is looking forward to better meeting expectations also among the GDPR stakeholders.

In terms of spearheading the sound output and outreach of APF 2018, the important contributions of the Polytechnic University of Catalonia (UPC) and Telefónica as co-organizers along with all organizational contributors, sponsors, speakers, committee members, and chairs and participants are hereby acknowledged.

June 2018   Udo Helmbrecht
                                                      Executive Director, ENISA

---

[6] https://www.enisa.europa.eu/publications/pets-evolution-and-state-of-the-art,
https://www.enisa.europa.eu/publications/pets-maturity-tool.

[7] https://www.enisa.europa.eu/topics/data-protection/personal-data-breaches/personal-data-breach-notification-tool.

[8] https://www.enisa.europa.eu/news/enisa-news/taking-rights-seriously-gdpr-starts-applying-today,
https://www.enisa.europa.eu/publications/enisa-position-papers-and-opinions/enisa2019s-position-on-the-general-data-protection-regulation-gdpr/view.

Preface

For professionals in personal data protection and privacy, and well-informed laypeople alike, 2018 will be conspicuously marked as the year in which the General Data Protection Regulation (GDPR) started applying. Stakeholders in GDPR increasingly come to realize that to comply with the new regulatory framework an interdisciplinary approach is likely to yield better outcomes than any method rooted in any single discipline alone. Legal, organizational, technical, and policy experts need to first come together and then come to terms with the new framework and the challenges it poses to individuals as well as, the private and the public sectors alike.

The Annual Privacy Forum (APF) hosts a distinguished set of expertise that seeks to allow for unfettered discussions and exchange of views. This year inevitably the GDPR took the lion's share of attention and this trend is likely to continue in the years to come. Since its launch, the APF has sought to bring together the seemingly complementary interests of privacy and information security with the goal of presenting a balanced view. Individual rights, however, need protection measures that are as important on cyberspace as they are in the physical world to remain meaningful and serve their purpose for citizens and society. Information security presents a broad framework of measures to render rights meaningful in the information age. The interaction between policy and academic experts has grown and it has currently expanded to include private sector representatives. As policy is giving way to implementation, it is expected that this interaction will grow yet further.

This year the APF benefited from a large number of submitted papers to select. Therefrom, a small number of papers were accepted, those that better address the main disciplinary drivers in privacy and personal data protection. The areas addressed in this year's APF include:

- Legal aspects, seeking to identify aspects open to interpretation in law
- Compliance and assessment of requirements from legislation as it impacts citizens, businesses, and the public sector
- Technical analysis and technical modeling available to meet compliance requirements
- Privacy implementation, describing practical approaches to meet privacy objectives

The papers presented in the proceedings are organized in thematic areas as follows: The first thematic area covers technical analysis and techniques.

In the paper presented by Peter Story, Sebastian Zimmeck, and Norman Sadeh, "Which Apps have Privacy Policies," an analysis of over one million Google Play Store apps, smartphone app privacy policies, and practices is carried out. The absence of privacy policies makes it difficult for users, regulators, and privacy organizations to evaluate apps. Exploratory data analysis of the relationship between app metadata features and app, links to privacy policies was carried out first, and applied to a logistic regression model to predict the probability that individual apps will have policy links.

Another view is presented in the paper by Stefan Schiffner, Bettina Berendt, Triin Sill, Florian Schaub, Kim Wuyts, Robert Riemann, Seda Guerses, Achim Klabunde, Norman Sadeh-Koniecpol, Jules Polonetsky, Massimo Attoresi, Gabriela Zanfir-Fortuna, and Martin Degeling, entitled: "Towards a Roadmap for Privacy Technologies and the General Data Protection Regulation: A Transatlantic Initiative." This paper reports on a workshop regarding the deployment, content, and design of the GDPR that brought together diverse EU- and US-based stakeholders. Five themes are discussed: the state of the art, consent, de-identification, transparency, and development and deployment practices.

Privacy as an innovation opportunity is tackled by Marc van Lieshout and Sophie Emmert in RESPECT4U — privacy as innovation opportunity. The rights to privacy and to personal data protection seemingly focus on a defensive and protective approach while giving way to constructive interpretation. The proposed model offers a framework of seven privacy principles that help organizations in promoting positive attitudes toward the reconciliation of privacy and innovation: responsible processing, empowering data subjects, secure data handling, proactive risk management, ethical awareness, cost–benefit assessment, transparent data processing.

The next thematic area addresses privacy implementation.

In the paper by Pietro Ferrara, Luca Olivieri, and Fausto Spoto, "Tailoring Taint Analysis to GDPR," a static software analysis is brought under the spotlight. As personal data controllers of sensitive data need to enforce privacy by design and by default, static program analysis can be applied to track how sensitive data are automatically managed by means of software, and if such software could leak some of these data.

Co-authors Maurizio Naldi, Alessandro Mazzoccoli, and Giuseppe D'Acquisto present a paper entitled "Hiding Alice in Wonderland: A Case for the Use of Signal Processing Techniques in Differential Privacy." The transformation of data in statistical databases can be leveraged to hide the presence of an individual. By using recoloring that preserves statistical properties of true data, the presence of the individual can be hidden as it enlarges the range of attribute values for which the presence of the individual of interest cannot be reliably inferred.

In the paper by Severin Engelmann, Jens Grossklags, and Orestis Papakyriakopoulos, "A Democracy Called Facebook? Participation as a Privacy Strategy on Social Media," the issues of notice and consent are debated. This paper carries out an empirical assessment of the participatory privacy strategy designed to democratize social media policy-making and it describes the various components of Facebook's participatory governance system.

The thematic part entitled "Compliance," comprises the following papers.

The paper by Diana Dimitrova and Paul De Hert, "The Right of Access Under the Police Directive: Small Steps Forward," sets out to examine the right of access under Directive 2016/680, which regulates the processing of personal data by EU Member States' law enforcement authorities. The right of access is analyzed in terms of transparency provided to data subjects to allow for harmonized data protection across EU law enforcement agencies.

Co-authors Sushant Agarwal, Simon Steyskal, Franjo Antunovic, and Sabrina Kirrane in their paper "Legislative Compliance Assessment: Framework, Model, and

GDPR Instantiation," discuss compliance assessment tools. In this paper, a modular compliance assessment framework is presented that can support multiple legislations.

The last thematic area presented in the proceedings is on legal aspects.

The paper by Wouter Seinen, Andre Walter, and Sari van Grondelle, entitled, "'Compatibility' as a Mechanism for Responsible Further Processing of Personal Data," addresses the area of further processing of article 6(4) of the GDPR. Data to be processed involves data that have been collected at an earlier stage. This paper discusses consent and the compatibility option that allows data controllers to motivate further processing.

Co-authors Jules Sarrat and Raphael Brun present "DPIA: How to Carry Out One of the Key Principles of Accountability." The authors address the important topic of impact assessments prioritization and ecosystems.

Maria Grazia Porcedda, in her paper entitled "'Privacy by design' in EU Law," tackles the question of how to reconcile the technical understanding of "privacy by design" with the nature of "privacy" in EU law. As privacy concerns two discreet constitutionally protected rights– respect for private and family life, and protection of personal data– the author proposes an approach to identify the essence of the two rights, which rests on identifying first the rights' attributes.

Experts view the application of the GDPR as the starting point of the effort toward affording a better level of protection of the rights to privacy and the protection of personal data. It will be equally important to observe the guidance of Data Protection Authorities (DPAs) and the European Data Protection Board (EDPB), in general as well as when they seek to mitigate the consequences of personal data breaches that are currently on the rise.

So far, each year personal data breaches have been growing in volume and impact on data subjects. Data controllers and data subjects need to be guided in order to meaningfully bring down the adverse consequences experienced so far by all parties involved, except the perpetrators, of course. It is still to soon in the implementation of the GDPR to be able to fully come to terms with the influence that this sweeping piece of legislation is likely to have on the processing of personal data across the EU and beyond. The GDPR will face challenges in the future, with far-reaching consequences for the meaningful protection of rights across the EU. Looking into the future, artificial intelligence is likely to pose questions that will be difficult for present-day legislation to respond to, without resorting to broad interpretations thereof. ENISA has built a track record in making available advice and recommendations on security measures for privacy and personal data protection; it will continue remaining committed to the goal of providing a forum to experts involved and retaining a thought leadership role in this field.

June 2018

Manel Medina
Andreas Mitrakas
Kai Rannenberg
Erich Schweighofer
Nikolaos Tsouroulas

Organization

General Co-chairs

Manel Medina   Universitat Politècnica de Catalunya, Spain
Andreas Mitrakas   ENISA, European Union
Kai Rannenberg   Goethe University Frankfurt, Germany
Erich Schweighofer   University of Vienna, Austria
Nikolaos Tsouroulas   11Paths Telefonica Cybersecurity Unit, Spain

Program Committee

Luis Antunes   University of Porto, Portugal
Athena Bourka   ENISA, European Union
Pompeu Casanovas   UAB, Spain
Valentina Casola   University of Naples Federico II, Italy
Claude Castelluccia   Inria, France
Fanny Coudert   EDPS, European Union
Malcolm Crompton   IIS, Australia
José María De Fuentes   Universidad Carlos III de Madrid, Spain
José-Maria Del-Alamo   Universidad Politécnica de Madrid, Spain
Roberto Di Pietro   Hamad Bin Khalifa University, Qatar
Josep Domingo-Ferrer   Universitat Rovira i Virgili, Spain
Prokopios Drogkaris   ENISA, European Union
Alberto   IT+46, Spain
   Escudero-Pascual
Hannes Federrath   University of Hamburg, Germany
Mathias Fischer   University of Hamburg, Germany
Simone Fischer-Hübner   Karlstad University, Sweden
Lorena González   Universidad Carlos III de Madrid, Spain
   Manzano
Antonio Guzmán   11Paths, Spain
Marit Hansen   Unabhängiges Landeszentrum für Datenschutz
                              Schleswig-Holstein, Germany
Dominik Herrmann   University of Bamberg, Germany
Marko Hölbl   University of Maribor, Slovenia
Walter Hötzendorfer   Research Institute AG & Co KG, Austria
Kristina Irion   University of Amsterdam, The Netherlands
Giuseppe Italiano   University of Rome Tor Vergata, Italy
Christos Kalloniatis   University of the Aegean, Greece
Irene Kamara   VUB/TILT, Belgium
Sokratis Katsikas   Center for Cyber and Information Security, NTNU,
                              Norway

Stefan Katzenbeisser	TU Darmstadt, Germany
Dogan Kesdogan	Universität Regensburg, Germany
Peter Kieseberg	Kibosec GmbH, Austria
Dariusz Kloza	Vrije Universitet Brussel, Belgium
Andrea Kolberger	University of Applied Sciences Upper Austria, Austria
Stefan Köpsell	TU Dresden, Germany
Daniel Le Métayer	Inria, France
Herbert Leitold	A-SIT, Austria
Fabio Martinelli	IIT-CNR, Italy
Alexandra Michota	ENISA, European Union
Chris Mitchell	Royal Holloway, University of London, UK
Maurizio Naldi	University of Rome Tor Vergata, Italy
Sebastian Pape	Goethe University Frankfurt, Germany
Aljosa Pasic	Atos Origin, Spain
Joachim Posegga	University of Passau, Germany
Vincent Rijmen	Katholieke Universiteit Leuven, Belgium
Heiko Roßnagel	Fraunhofer Institut, Germany
Kazue Sako	NEC, Japan
Peter Schartner	Klagenfurt University, Germany
Stefan Schiffner	Uni.lu, Luxembourg
Jetzabel M. Serna Olvera	Universitat Politècnica de Catalunya, Spain
Florian Skopik	AIT Austrian Institute of Technology, Austria
Morton Swimmer	Trend Micro, Inc., Germany
Jozef Vyskoc	VaF, Slovakia
Nathalie Weiler	ETZ, Switzerland
Stefan Weiss	Swiss Re, Germany
Diane Whitehouse	IFIP WG 9.2 on social accountability and ICT
Bernhard C. Witt	it.sec GmbH & Co. KG, Germany
Sven Wohlgemuth	Hitachi, Ltd. Research & Development Group, Germany
Harald Zwingelberg	ULD, Germany

Additional Reviewers

Nicolas Fähnrich	Fraunhofer, Germany
Akos Grosz	Goethe University Frankfurt, Germany
Majid Hatamian	Goethe University Frankfurt, Germany
Nikolaos Tantouris	ENISA, European Union
Stephanie Weinhardt	Fraunhofer, Germany

Organization and Sponsors

Organizers

European Union Agency for Network and Information Security (ENISA) (EU)
European Commission Directorate for Communications, Networks, Content and Technology (DG CONNECT) (EU)
Universitat Politècnica de Catalunya (UPC-BarcelonaTECH) (ES)
Telefónica (ES)

Gold Sponsors

Silver Sponsor

Bronze Sponsor

Partners

Contents

Legal Aspects

Technical Analysis and Techniques

Which Apps Have Privacy Policies?

An Analysis of Over One Million Google Play Store Apps

Peter Story[(⊠)] ⓘ, Sebastian Zimmeck ⓘ, and Norman Sadeh ⓘ

Carnegie Mellon University, Pittsburgh, PA 15213, USA
{pstory, szimmeck, nsli}@andrew.cmu.edu

Abstract. Smartphone app privacy policies are intended to describe smartphone apps' data collection and use practices. However, not all apps have privacy policies. Without prominent privacy policies, it becomes more difficult for users, regulators, and privacy organizations to evaluate apps' privacy practices. We answer the question: "Which apps have privacy policies?" by analyzing the metadata of over one million apps from the Google Play Store. Only about half of the apps we examined link to a policy from their Play Store pages. First, we conducted an exploratory data analysis of the relationship between app metadata features and whether apps link to privacy policies. Next, we trained a logistic regression model to predict the probability that individual apps will have policy links. Finally, by comparing three crawls of the Play Store, we observe an overall-increase in the percent of apps with links between September 2017 and May 2018 (from 41.7% to 51.8%).

Keywords: Privacy · Privacy policy · Smartphone · Smartphone apps

1 Introduction

The Google Play Store makes over a million apps accessible to Android users in the US [29]. Many apps collect location details, contact information, phone numbers, and a variety of other data from their users [20]. Oftentimes, the collected data is not only leveraged for the apps' main functionalities but also for other purposes, most notably, to serve advertisements and for analytics. The notice and choice paradigm prescribes that app developers should notify their users of how they collect, use, share, and otherwise process user information in their privacy policies. The promises contained in

This study was supported in part by the NSF Frontier grant on Usable Privacy Policies (CNS-1330596 and CNS-1330141) and a DARPA Brandeis grant on Personalized Privacy Assistants (FA8750-15-2-0277). The US Government is authorized to reproduce and distribute reprints for Governmental purposes not withstanding any copyright notation. The views and conclusions contained herein are those of the authors and should not be interpreted as necessarily representing the official policies or endorsements, either expressed or implied, of the NSF, DARPA, or the US Government.

© Springer Nature Switzerland AG 2018
M. Medina et al. (Eds.): APF 2018, LNCS 11079, pp. 3–23, 2018.
https://doi.org/10.1007/978-3-030-02547-2_1

these policies are enforceable by privacy regulators and are of interest to privacy-focused organizations and researchers.

In the absence of comprehensive federal legislation in the US, the California Online Privacy Protection Act requires online services that collect personally identifiable information to post a policy.[1] A similar requirement is contained in Delaware's Online Privacy and Protection Act.[2] Further, the Federal Trade Commission's Fair Information Practice Principles call for consumers to be given notice of an entity's information practices before any personally identifiable information is collected [16]. The Children's Online Privacy Protection Act makes policies mandatory for apps directed to or known to be used by children.[3]

The Google Play Store gives app developers the option to include links to their privacy policies on their Play Store pages. However, in three separate crawls of apps we found that only 41.7% (August 28 through September 2, 2017—in the following "First Crawl"), 45.2% (November 29 through December 2, 2017—in the following "Second Crawl"), and 51.8% (May 11 through May 15, 2018—in the following "Third Crawl") have such links. While there appears to be an upward trend, these percents are relatively low, especially, as they include links for apps that are legally required to disclose their practices in privacy policies (most notably, apps that are subject to the Children's Online Privacy Protection Act [15]).

In this study we aim to identify app features that are associated with whether an app links to a privacy policy or not. To that end, we offer the following contributions:

1. We present an in-depth exploratory analysis of features associated with whether apps have privacy policies (Sect. 4). Among other findings, our analysis reveals that only 63.1% of apps which describe themselves as sharing their users' locations link to privacy policies.
2. We design a logistic regression model which quantifies the associations between policy links and other app features (Sect. 5). For example, our model indicates that an app with a developer address in Germany has greater odds of having a policy link than an app without country information.
3. We discuss how our work might be useful to government regulators, privacy organizations, and researchers (Sect. 6). In particular, we provide suggestions about how our techniques can be used to prioritize regulatory enforcement actions, evaluate the relative merits of individual app features, and observe trends over time.

2   Related Work

We are aware of several previous studies examining privacy policy occurrence in the app ecosystem. Our work goes beyond these studies by analyzing orders of magnitude more apps and by employing more scalable analysis techniques. Sunyaev et al.

---

[1] Cal. Bus. & Prof. Code §22575(a).

[2] Del. Code Tit. 6 §1205C(a).

[3] 16 CFR §312.4(d).

analyzed the presence of privacy policies for the most popular health-related Android and iOS apps [30]. In addition to following links from the Play Store, they searched for policies on developers' websites and Google. They found that only 22.7% of the Android apps with the most ratings in the Health and Fitness and Medical categories had privacy policies. Blenner et al. analyzed the privacy polices and practices of a random sample of diabetes-related Android apps [3]. They found that only 19% of apps had privacy policies. Different from these previous studies, we conclude that a substantially higher percent of apps in the Health and Fitness and Medical categories linked to privacy policies from their Play Store pages (45.6% and 45.0%, respectively). Our finding suggests that it is now more common for app developers to link to privacy policies (Sect. 6) than at the time of the previous studies.

Instead of gathering data from the Play Store directly, Balebako et al. interviewed and surveyed US app developers about how they protect the privacy of their users [2]. 57.9% of the developers they surveyed reported hosting a privacy policy on their website. In comparison, we found that 64.0% of apps with US mailing addresses link to privacy policies, which suggests an increase over time. Balebako et al. found a generally positive relationship between company size and whether companies have privacy policies.

In the closest work to ours, Zimmeck et al. analyzed 17,991 free Android apps for features that identify apps with privacy policy links [33]. They found a number of features useful for predicting whether an app has a privacy policy: recent app update, small or large number of installs, Editors' Choice or Top Developer badges, in-app purchase offers, and Entertainment Software Rating Board (ESRB) content ratings [12] appropriate for younger audiences. However, they also found that apps in the Comics, Libraries & Demo, Media & Video, and Personalization categories had particularly low percents of policies. In this report, we not only repeat the analysis of these features,[4] but we go beyond their examination in multiple dimensions. First, we collected the metadata of a much larger set of apps. We also take into account features that were not analyzed by Zimmeck et al., including apps' ESRB content descriptors, prices, and developers' home countries. In addition, we train a logistic regression model which considers all these features together. Further, the repetition of our analysis gave us insight into how the app population changes over time (Sect. 6).

A number of other researchers have performed analyses at the scale of the entire Google Play Store, however, not for purposes of predicting whether apps have privacy policy links. In particular, d'Heureuse et al. used multiple crawling techniques to explore the app ecosystem, including browsing by category, by related apps, and by searching [11]. One notable finding was that only 46% of apps in the Google market were discoverable solely by following links to related apps. However, whether this finding is still true today is unclear. In our First and Second Crawls, we found over a million apps by following links to related apps. By the time of our Third Crawl, only about 179K apps could be found when just this technique was used (Sect. 3). Viennot et al. also used searching techniques to discover apps on the Google Play Store [31].

---

[4] We were unable to consider the Top Developer badge in our analysis because it is no longer displayed on the Play Store [13, 26].

Wang et al. analyzed the privacy characteristics of Play Store apps [32]. However, they did not consider whether apps linked to privacy policies. Different from prior work, we focus on the prevalence of links to privacy policies.

This report is also informed by our earlier work in the field of smartphone app privacy, performed as part of the Usable Privacy Policy Project [28].[5] In particular, Lin et al. used crowdsourcing to detect unexpected uses of data by smartphone apps [25]. Kelley et al. demonstrated that alternate presentations of apps' privacy-related behavior can impact which apps users install [23]. Lin et al. clustered users based on their app privacy preferences [24]. Almuhimedi et al. used nudges to encourage users to customize their smartphone permission settings [1].

3 Methodology

It is our goal in this study to find features that predict the occurrence of privacy policy links for apps. The features we examined were obtained from apps' Play Store metadata and include, among others, the average rating assigned by reviewers, how many times the app was installed, and the Play Store categories the app belongs to.

Starting with a randomly selected app (com.foxandsheep.littlefox), we recursively followed links to related apps. This technique is relatively resource efficient: on a single virtual server,[6] our crawls all completed in less than a week. Our First and Second Crawls used only this recursive technique. However, by the time of our Third Crawl, only about 179 K could be found when just this technique was used. We think this is because Google altered the algorithms which recommend related apps. Consequently, for the Third Crawl we seeded the database with the app identifiers collected by the Second Crawl. Using these techniques, we retrieved the metadata associated with $n = 1, 423, 450$ apps (First Crawl), $n = 1, 163, 622$ apps (Second Crawl), and $n = 1, 044, 752$ (Third Crawl). Unless otherwise noted, all statistics and results described herein refer to the Second Crawl. Also, note that our results refer to the US Play Store.

For each feature, we perform two types of analyses (Sect. 4). First, we evaluate the relative occurrence of the different values of a feature (e.g., for the install count we leverage the install ranges given on the Play Store and evaluate the percent of apps that were installed 1–5 times, 5–10 times, etc.). Second, we examine the relative occurrence of apps with privacy policy links at different feature values (e.g., for apps that were installed 1–5 times, 49.5% have a privacy policy; for apps that were installed 5–10 times, 47.7% have a privacy policy; etc.).

Next, based on the results of our feature analysis, we build and evaluate a logistic regression model for predicting whether apps link to privacy policies from their Play Store pages (Sect. 5).

It is a limitation of our approach that some apps may not have a link to their policy on their Play Store page, but rather provide such a link in another place (e.g., inside their code). However, using privacy policy links on the Play Store as proxies for actual

---

[5] https://www.usableprivacy.org, accessed: May 20, 2018.
[6] Our virtual server had four Intel Xeon E5-2640 CPU cores at 2.50 GHz and 8 GB of RAM.

policies is not unreasonable since regulators requested that app publishers post such links [14, 22], and app store owners obligated themselves to provide the necessary functionality [21]. Furthermore, Zimmeck et al. found that of apps which didn't link to their policy from the Play Store, only 17% of apps provided their policies somewhere else [33]. Also, in order for the notice and choice model to be effective, users should be able to examine an app's privacy policy before they install it. In future work, we will go beyond this assumption by seeking links to privacy policies within the apps themselves using static code analysis.

Another limitation is that our recursive crawling technique may not discover all the apps on the Play Store. However, based on the large number of apps included in our crawls, we estimate that our crawls covered the vast majority of apps that a typical user would encounter.

4 Exploratory Data Analysis of Potentially Relevant Features

We find that 45.2% of apps link to their privacy policy from their Play Store page. We now seek to explore the features that predict such occurrence. In the following we examine two types of features: native Play Store features (Sect. 4.1), such as an app's install range on the Play Store, and ESRB features (Sect. 4.2), such as ESRB content ratings.

4.1 Play Store Features

Country (Fig. 1). While Google does not require that developers display their countries of origin, some post a contact mailing address. With a few steps of pre-processing we were able to determine the countries of 17.2% of apps. First, we extracted the country from each address using the pypostal library.[7] Note that we skip addresses which do not explicitly include a country.[8] We cleaned the data by consolidating abbreviations and alternate spellings of countries using the pycountry library.[9] Further, we wrote custom mappings for all other countries except for those with fewer than 30 associated apps. These 0.2% of apps are shown as "Not Parsed" in Fig. 1. In total we were able to fully extract the countries for 17.2% of apps. The remaining 82.5% of apps either did not have an address on the Play Store or our technique was unable to extract a country from the address that was posted (shown as "Undefined"). Finally, countries associated with fewer than 250 apps were combined in the "Other" category (unless they were already included in the "Not Parsed" category).

---

[7] https://github.com/openvenues/pypostal, accessed: May 20, 2018.

[8] Consequently, the relative frequencies shown in Fig. 1 should be interpreted cautiously. For example, it would not be safe to assume that there are more developers from India than from the US as developers from India may possibly include the country in their address more frequently than developers from the US.

[9] https://bitbucket.org/flyingcircus/pycountry, accessed: May 20, 2018.

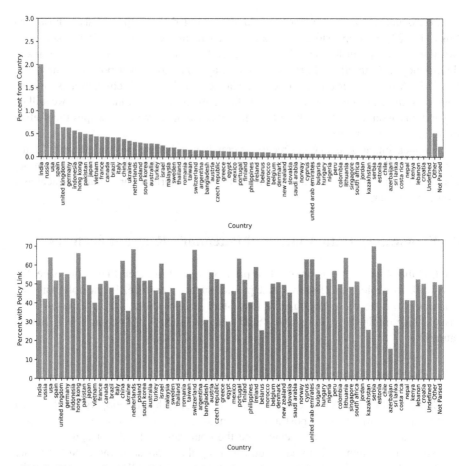

Fig. 1. Percent of apps per country (top) and respective privacy policy percent (bottom).

As Fig. 1 shows, there are many developers publishing apps on the US Play Store from countries other than the US (most notably, from India and Russia). As discussed later (Sect. 5.2), we found that some country features affect the odds of apps having privacy policies.

It should be noted that we were only able to determine the country for 17.2% of apps; this result is based on Google's decision to not require developers to post a mailing address. Also, the addresses which are posted do not have a consistent format, and many addresses are given without country informa- tion. However, the country data we did extract were still salient, since many countries were retained in our logistic regression model.

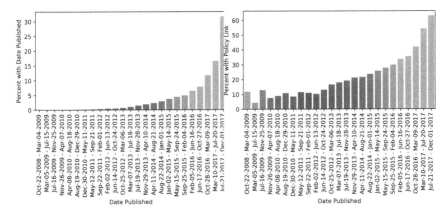

Fig. 2. Percent of apps by date published (left) and respective policy percent (right).

Date Published (Fig. 2). Apps' Play Store pages display the date when its latest version was published. If the app was never updated, it will be the date when it was first released. Figure 2 shows a distribution which is skewed to the left indicating that most apps have been published recently. Similar to earlier results [33] our analysis appears to show that apps published more recently are more likely to have privacy policies.

Editors' Choice. Google assigns Editors' Choice badges to "apps and games with the best experiences on Android" [4]. Just 621 apps have the Editors' Choice badge, of which 93.1% have a privacy policy. As only 45.2% of apps without such badge have privacy policies, it appears to be a strong signal. However, given the small number of apps that have a badge, its impact overall is rather limited.

Install Ranges (Fig. 3). The Play Store does not display the exact number of installs of apps. Instead, at the time of our First and Second Crawls it displayed ranges of installs (e.g., 1–5 installs, 5–10 installs, etc.).[10] Figure 3 shows that the distribution of app install ranges has a long tail. In particular, it should be noted that there are only a few apps with billions of installs. Many of those apps have privacy policies. However, even apps with very few installs often have privacy policies. In fact, beginning with apps having 1–5 installs the percent of apps with policies decreases to a low point at 100–500 installs, then generally increases from there. This finding confirms a trend that was observed earlier: apps with relatively high and low install ranges are more likely to have privacy policies than apps with medium install ranges [33]. A hypothesis provided by Zimmeck et al. was that apps with fewer installs were more recently published and hence more likely to aim for privacy compliance [33].

---

[10] By the time of our Third Crawl, the Play Store had changed the display of the install ranges and started showing only their smallest values, e.g., 1+ installs, 5+ installs, etc.

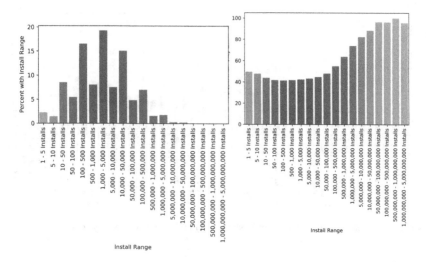

Fig. 3. Percent of apps per install range (left), and respective policy percent (right).

Play Store Category (Fig. 4). Apps on the Play Store are organized by category. A given app can be part of multiple categories. Figure 4 shows how the percent of apps with policies differs by category. In particular, it can be observed that some of the most popular categories—BOOKS_AND_REFERENCE, EDUCATION, and ENTERTAINMENT—are among those with the lowest prevalence of policies. Further, notice that 100% of apps in the FAMILY_ categories have policies. The reason for this complete coverage is Google's management of those categories in the Designed for Families program [17] that requires all apps to have a privacy policy.

Price (Fig. 5). The price of an app is the cost associated with installing that app, without considering in-app purchases. Figure 5 shows that 99.5% of apps are either free or can be purchased for $5 or less. Although there does not seem to be an obvious relationship between an app's price and whether it has a policy, price turned out to be a significant feature in our model (Sect. 5.2).

Rating Count (Fig. 6). Play Store users can rate apps on a scale of one to five (worst to best). The rating count is the number of ratings an app has received. Figure 6 shows that the distribution of rating counts is strongly skewed: most apps have only a few ratings but some have much higher counts. 12.5% of apps have no ratings. Fewer than 9% of apps have more than 1,000 ratings. Figure 6 appears to show that apps become more likely to have privacy policies as their number of ratings increases. Our logistic regression analysis confirmed this observation (Sect. 5.2). The trend seems similar to the trend for install ranges (see Fig. 3).

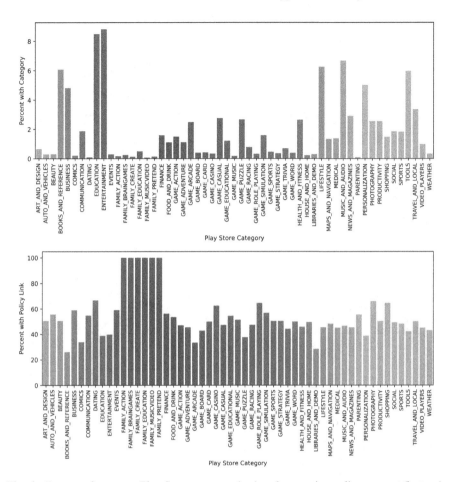

Fig. 4. Percent of apps per Play Store category (top) and respective policy percent (bottom).

Rating Value (Fig. 7). The rating value is the average of all its user ratings. Figure 7 shows the percent of apps with different average rating values. The peaks at 1, 2, 3, 4, and 5 might be caused by apps that have only a few ratings: in those cases, it is more likely that the average rating will be a whole number. While Fig. 7 does not show an obvious connection between rating value and whether apps have policies, our logistic regression analysis actually discovered a nonlinear relationship between the two (Sect. 5.2).

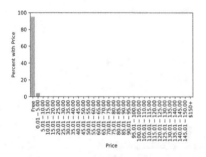
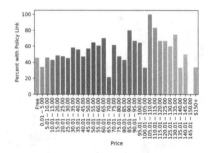

Fig. 5. Percent of apps per price category (left) and respective policy percent (right).

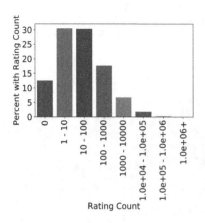
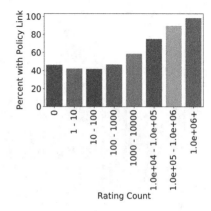

Fig. 6. Percent of apps per rating category (left) and their respective policy percent (right). Note the use of log-scales on the x-axes.

4.2   ESRB Features

Google provides a questionnaire that developers can use to describe the content of their app [18, 19]. The answers to this questionnaire are used to generate an app's ESRB content rating, its ESRB content descriptors, and its interactive elements. All this information is displayed to users on the US Play Store [12].

ESRB Content Rating (Fig. 8). ESRB content ratings define the age categories an app is appropriate for, and every app has exactly one such rating. Figure 8 shows that over 84% of apps in our sample are rated as suitable for EVERYONE. There are comparatively few apps with other ratings. In particular, we found only 44 apps with the ADULTS rating. It can be observed that the UNRATED apps appear to be much less likely to have policies. It is encouraging to see that TEEN-rated apps have the highest policy percent. However, it is also true that many apps rated EVERYONE 10+ do not have policies.

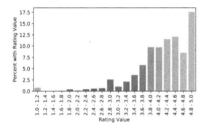 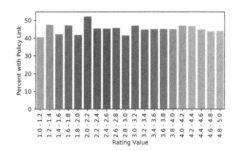

Fig. 7. Percent of apps per average rating category (left) and respective policy percent (right).

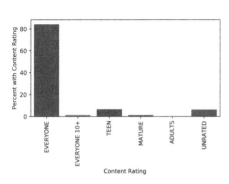 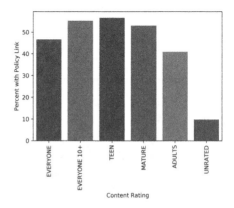

Fig. 8. Percent of apps per ESRB content rating (left) and respective policy percent (right).

ESRB Content Descriptors (Fig. 9). Content descriptors describe app content that is potentially objectionable to certain users. Figure 9 shows the relative frequencies of different content descriptors and how the percent of apps with policies differs by descriptor. Only 12% of apps have one or more content descriptors. The Warning descriptor is by far the most used one.[11]

It also is the content descriptor with the second-lowest policy percent. The Mild Sexual Themes descriptor is only used by one app. Thus, its 0% policy coverage is of very limited relevance.

Interactive Elements (Fig. 10). ESRB interactive elements describe five other characteristics of apps that are of potential interest to users. 18% of apps have one or more interactive element. Our logistic regression analysis found that all interactive elements except Unrestricted Internet were associated with an increase in the odds that an app would have a privacy policy (Sect. 5.2).

---

[11] Note that the full Warning descriptor reads "Warning - content has not yet been rated. Unrated apps may potentially contain content appropriate for mature audiences only."

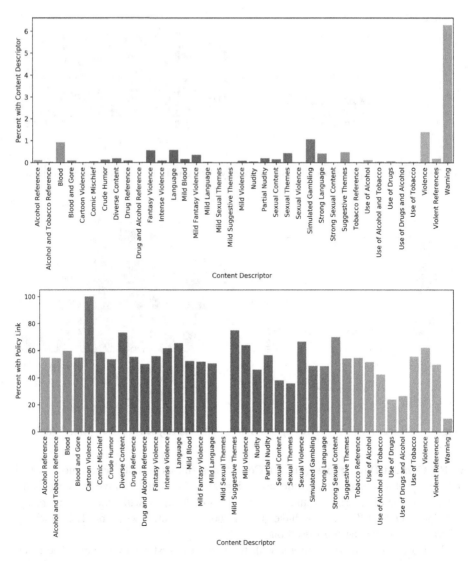

Fig. 9. Percent of apps per ESRB content descriptor (top) and respective policy percent (bottom).

5   Results

In this section we discuss the results of our logistic regression model (Sect. 5.2) as well as some preprocessing steps that affect those results (Sect. 5.1). We begin with the latter.

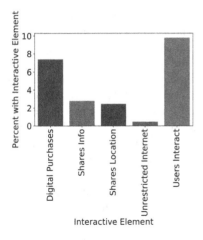 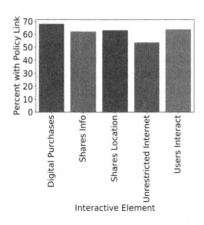

Fig. 10. Percent of apps per interactive element (left) and respective policy percent (right).

5.1 Preprocessing

We performed various data preprocessing steps to improve the performance of our model. Initially, we removed metadata for 8,997 apps as the data were incomplete: the metadata for those apps were missing install ranges. It may be that the Play Store page rendered by Google is sometimes incomplete.

Further, as an app may legitimately not have a rating value given a rating count of zero, we imputed missing rating values with all apps' mean rating value of 4.206.

During the time of our First and Second Crawls, the Play Store represented the number of installs per app in numerical ranges (1–5 installs, 5–10 installs, etc.). We trained models using a categorical representation for these ranges. However, we realized that the coefficients corresponding to the apps with very high install ranges were automatically eliminated by the model during training. This elimination could be the result of the relatively small count of apps with very high install ranges. The automatic removal is problematic because we want the install ranges of such apps to be taken into account when making predictions with our model. To mitigate this problem, we transformed the ranges into a quantitative variable consisting of the ranges' mean values. For example, the 10–50 Installs category became $(50 + 10)/2 = 30$. This quantitative variable was retained by the model. As desired, the install ranges of apps with very high ranges are able to influence the predictions of the model.

We represent each app's publication date as the count of seconds after the currently oldest app on the Play Store was published (October 22, 2008).

5.2 Analysis

Model Description. We designed our model based on scikit-learn (version 0.19.1) [27] using 67% of our data for training and 33% as a held out test set.

Our model achieves the following performance on the test set: accuracy = 67.7%, precision = 65.1%, recall = 61.5%, F1 = 63.2%. The accuracy of our model compares favorably to a baseline of always predicting that an app has a privacy policy, which would lead to an accuracy of 54.8%. We chose to use the SGDClassifier [7] instead of the standard LogisticRegression classifier [6] because stochastic gradient descent was orders of magnitude faster due to the size of our dataset [10]. We trained the SGDClassifier with the log loss function (loss='log'), the L1 penalty (penalty = 'l1'), 1,000 maximum iterations over the training data (max_iter = 1000), and a stopping tolerance of 0.001 (tol = 0.001). We choose the L1 penalty in order to get a sparse set of coefficients. As recommended [9], we ran parameter selection over the alpha parameter. We left the other parameters as the defaults.

We squared and cubed all the quantitative variables (date published, install range, price, rating count, and rating value). Without these transformations, our test accuracy would have been 67.2% instead of 67.7%. Although, the change in accuracy is incremental, the transformations improved interpretability; more variables were eliminated from the model. We chose not to perform log transformations because it would have made the interpretation more complicated: $\log(0)$ is undefined, and date published, install range, price, and rating count can assume zero values.

Note that the SGDClassifier requires that quantitative features be centered and scaled. We used the StandardScaler [8] and performed scaling with

$$\frac{x - \bar{x}}{s} \tag{1}$$

where x is a sample value, $\bar{x}$ is the mean of the training data, and s is the standard deviation of the training data. The values for $\bar{x}$ and s in our training data are displayed in Table 1.

Interpretation of Results. Next, we explain how to interpret our model using the coefficients displayed in Table 2. Features that were eliminated from the model are not included in the table; these features neither increased nor decreased the odds of accurately predicting whether an app has a privacy policy. Note that scaling—as explained previously and shown in the Table 1—must be performed before making predictions using the model. Such scaling is beneficial as the relative sizes of the coefficients can be used to roughly compare the relative importance of the different features.[12]

The goal of our interpretation is to observe how the odds of an app having a privacy policy are affected by modifying one or more features as compared to a baseline app. For interpreting the model, note the following definition of the baseline app.

---

[12] Inherently, scaling has the disadvantage that the intercept cannot easily be interpreted because it is the y-intercept of the scaled variables.

Table 1. Parameters for scaling the logistic regression model's quantitative features. $\bar{x}$ and s are the mean and standard deviation of the training data, respectively. Features eliminated by the model are omitted.

Scaling $\bar{x}$	Scaling s	Feature name
2.480e+08	4.170e+07	date_published_relative
6.323e+16	1.816e+16	date_published_relative^2
1.643e+25	6.253e+24	date_published_relative^3
3.406e+05	1.541e+07	install_range
1.954e−01	3.626e+00	price
1.319e+01	1.151e+03	price^2
3.117e+03	1.598e+05	rating_count
4.205e+00	6.427e−01	rating_value
7.914e+01	2.887e+01	rating_value^3

Table 2. Coefficients of the trained logistic regression model sorted by coefficient size. A negative coefficient indicates that a feature decreases the odds of an app having a privacy policy whereas a positive coefficient indicates an increase in the odds. Odds multipliers are calculated by raising e to the coefficient.

Coefficient	Odds Mult.	Feature Name
-0.329		Intercept
-1.664e+00	÷ 5.280e+00	date_published_relative^2
-7.437e-01	÷ 2.104e+00	category_BOOKS_AND_REFERENCE
-5.399e-01	÷ 1.716e+00	content_rating_UNRATED
-5.399e-01	÷ 1.716e+00	content_descriptor_Warning
-4.856e-01	÷ 1.625e+00	content_descriptor_Use_of_Drugs
-4.270e-01	÷ 1.533e+00	content_descriptor_Sexual_Themes
-3.989e-01	÷ 1.490e+00	category_GAME_ARCADE
-3.501e-01	÷ 1.419e+00	category_LIBRARIES_AND_DEMO
-3.355e-01	÷ 1.399e+00	country_belarus
-3.299e-01	÷ 1.391e+00	category_GAME_ACTION
-2.964e-01	÷ 1.345e+00	content_descriptor_Sexual_Content
-2.574e-01	÷ 1.293e+00	country_ukraine
-2.522e-01	÷ 1.287e+00	category_EDUCATION
-2.367e-01	÷ 1.267e+00	category_GAME_PUZZLE
-2.337e-01	÷ 1.263e+00	price^2
-2.204e-01	÷ 1.247e+00	country_russia
-2.125e-01	÷ 1.237e+00	category_COMICS
-1.950e-01	÷ 1.215e+00	category_ENTERTAINMENT
-1.855e-01	÷ 1.204e+00	category_PERSONALIZATION
-1.805e-01	÷ 1.198e+00	category_GAME_BOARD
-1.682e-01	÷ 1.183e+00	country_vietnam
-1.644e-01	÷ 1.179e+00	rating_value^3
-1.598e-01	÷ 1.173e+00	content_descriptor_Simulated_Gambling
-1.324e-01	÷ 1.142e+00	category_GAME_ADVENTURE
-1.116e-01	÷ 1.118e+00	content_descriptor_Blood
-6.541e-02	÷ 1.068e+00	category_GAME_RACING
-2.583e-02	÷ 1.026e+00	category_MUSIC_AND_AUDIO
-2.540e-02	÷ 1.026e+00	category_ART_AND_DESIGN
-1.856e-02	÷ 1.019e+00	category_SOCIAL
-1.527e-02	÷ 1.015e+00	country_egypt
4.896e-02	× 1.050e+00	price
6.041e-02	× 1.062e+00	country_ireland
6.222e-02	× 1.064e+00	content_descriptor_Intense_Violence
7.402e-02	× 1.077e+00	category_HEALTH_AND_FITNESS
7.622e-02	× 1.079e+00	category_MEDICAL
7.969e-02	× 1.083e+00	category_LIFESTYLE
8.973e-02	× 1.094e+00	category_GAME_CASUAL
9.258e-02	× 1.097e+00	rating_value
1.044e-01	× 1.110e+00	content_descriptor_Mild_Fantasy_Violence
1.062e-01	× 1.112e+00	date_published_relative
1.171e-01	× 1.124e+00	country_france
1.369e-01	× 1.147e+00	country_Other
1.379e-01	× 1.148e+00	category_SPORTS
1.404e-01	× 1.151e+00	category_VIDEO_PLAYERS

Coefficient	Odds Mult.	Feature Name
1.618e-01	× 1.176e+00	category_GAME_SIMULATION
1.810e-01	× 1.198e+00	interactive_element_Shares_Info
2.147e-01	× 1.240e+00	interactive_element_Shares_Location
2.154e-01	× 1.240e+00	install_range
2.199e-01	× 1.246e+00	country_pakistan
2.268e-01	× 1.255e+00	category_PRODUCTIVITY
2.547e-01	× 1.290e+00	country_canada
2.551e-01	× 1.291e+00	country_poland
2.704e-01	× 1.310e+00	country_india
2.867e-01	× 1.332e+00	country_australia
3.131e-01	× 1.368e+00	category_FINANCE
3.256e-01	× 1.385e+00	content_rating_EVERYONE_10_PLUS
3.517e-01	× 1.421e+00	country_germany
3.553e-01	× 1.427e+00	category_TRAVEL_AND_LOCAL
3.822e-01	× 1.465e+00	country_spain
3.919e-01	× 1.480e+00	category_GAME_CASINO
3.986e-01	× 1.490e+00	category_COMMUNICATION
4.052e-01	× 1.500e+00	country_japan
4.339e-01	× 1.543e+00	country_switzerland
4.411e-01	× 1.554e+00	country_israel
4.631e-01	× 1.589e+00	country_united_kingdom
4.759e-01	× 1.610e+00	country_china
5.839e-01	× 1.793e+00	interactive_element_Users_Interact
5.911e-01	× 1.806e+00	content_descriptor_Diverse_Content
6.262e-01	× 1.870e+00	content_descriptor_Language
6.268e-01	× 1.872e+00	country_portugal
6.290e-01	× 1.876e+00	category_BUSINESS
6.397e-01	× 1.896e+00	country_hong_kong
6.578e-01	× 1.930e+00	category_PHOTOGRAPHY
6.854e-01	× 1.985e+00	interactive_element_Digital_Purchases
7.229e-01	× 2.060e+00	content_descriptor_Violence
7.297e-01	× 2.074e+00	category_SHOPPING
7.354e-01	× 2.086e+00	country_netherlands
7.903e-01	× 2.204e+00	country_usa
1.556e+00	× 4.740e+00	rating_count
2.002e+00	× 7.401e+00	category_FAMILY_MUSICVIDEO
2.157e+00	× 8.645e+00	date_published_relative^3
2.505e+00	× 1.224e+01	category_FAMILY_PRETEND
3.004e+00	× 2.016e+01	category_FAMILY_ACTION
6.840e+00	× 9.344e+02	category_FAMILY_CREATE
8.913e+00	× 7.427e+03	category_FAMILY_EDUCATION
1.359e+01	× 7.998e+05	category_FAMILY_BRAINGAMES

- The Undefined country was selected for the baseline app because over 82% of apps have this value, and it can be interpreted as not knowing what country the app is from.
- The ESRB content rating EVERYONE was selected for the baseline app because it is the most common, with over 84% of apps having this rating.
- Before scaling, date_published_relative ranges from 0 to 287,452,800 (corresponding to October 22, 2008 and December 1, 2017, respectively). We selected October 22, 2008 as the publish date for the baseline app, since this is the publish date of the oldest app.
- Before scaling, install_range ranges from 3 to 3,000,000,000. For our baseline app we selected 3 installs, since this is the smallest possible value.
- Before scaling, prices range from $0 (free) to $400. Our baseline app is free, since most apps on the Play Store are free.
- Before scaling, rating_count ranges from 0 to 72,979,974 ratings. Our baseline app has no ratings, since this is the smallest possible value.
- Before scaling, rating_value ranges from 1 to 5. Our baseline app has a rating value of 1, since it is the smallest possible value.
- Our baseline app has no categories, interactive elements, or content descriptors. It also does not have the Editors' Choice badge.

Given this definition, the odds of the baseline app having a privacy policy are 0.412. For details about how these odds were calculated, see Appendix A.1. Suppose we change the country of the baseline app to Germany (country_germany). The new odds can be calculated by multiplying the baseline app's odds by the corresponding odds multiplier from Table 2. This change gives us odds of $0.412 \times 1.421 = 0.585$. Consequently, an app from Germany has greater odds of having a policy than an app from an Undefined country. For an example of changing a quantitative variable, see Appendix A.1.

6   Discussion

Our exploratory data analysis, logistic regression model, and longitudinal analysis (per below) may be helpful to government regulators, privacy organizations, app store operators, and others interested in understanding the state of privacy in the app ecosystem.

6.1   Exploratory Data Analysis

We believe that our analysis of the features associated with apps having privacy policies (Sect. 4) can help regulators prioritize enforcement actions. For example, Fig. 10 shows that only 63.1% of apps which describe themselves as sharing their users' locations link to privacy policies. Although, this percent is higher than the percent for the Play Store as a whole, ideally all apps which share users' locations would have privacy policies. While this finding requires further investigation, it suggests that a number of apps might not be compliant with the General Data Protection Regulation.

6.2   Logistic Regression Model

Our logistic regression model (Sect. 5) yields additional insights. The coefficients of the model, as displayed in Table 2, provide insight into how different features affect the odds of apps having privacy policies. Since the quantitative variables are scaled, the relative sizes of the coefficients can be used to roughly compare the relative importance of the different features. A negative coefficient indicates that a feature decreases the odds of apps having a privacy policy whereas a positive coefficient indicates an increase in the odds. For example, knowing that an app is from the Books and Reference category divides the odds by 2.104 (that is, decreases the odds by approximately 50%), whereas knowing that the app offers in-app purchases multiplies the odds by 1.985 (that is, increases the odds by approximately 100%). Our model eliminated redundant and uninfluential features, which would otherwise serve as noise and obscure the truly meaningful features.

In addition to identifying features that affect the odds of apps having policies our model lends itself to another use case: the model can identify the apps with the highest probability of having policies but which in actuality lack such (that is, false positives). The fact that these apps do not have policies makes them stand out from similar apps. For example, there are many apps with more than 100,000 ratings and millions of installs, which our model predicts would have policies but which actually lack them. As some of these apps are from major companies, the policy absence strikes us as an oversight instead of a lack of knowledge about applicable privacy regulation. In those instances, regulators might find it worthwhile to simply notify the affected companies of their shortcomings to mitigate potential non-compliance with privacy laws and regulations.

6.3   Longitudinal Analysis

Another interesting finding comes from comparing our three crawls. In our First Crawl (August 28 through September 2, 2017), 41.7% of apps had privacy policies. This number increased to 45.2% in the Second Crawl (November 29 through December 2, 2017), and to 51.8% by the time of the Third Crawl (May 11 through May 15, 2018). Further, the number of apps discovered by our crawling techniques decreased over the course of the crawls: $n = 1, 423, 450$ apps (FirstCrawl), $n = 1, 163, 622$ apps (Second Crawl), and $n = 1, 044, 752$ apps (Third Crawl). Notably, only about 179 K apps were originally discovered in the Third Crawl; we seeded the database with the app identifiers collected by the Second Crawl in order to gather the metadata of more apps. One possible explanation for these changes could be Google's curation of apps on the Play Store in between our crawls. After all, Google announced removing apps that collect "Personal and Sensitive Information" but do not have privacy policies [5]. Another possibility could lie in Google's changes to "limit visibility" of certain apps, preventing us from discovering them in our crawl even if they are still present in some form on the Play Store [5]. The sharp decrease in the number of apps discovered by our recursive crawling technique in the Third Crawl shows that Google changed how they recommend related apps. If the increase in the percent of apps with policy links was caused by Google's curation of the Play Store, our findings would show how action by ecosystem managers can have a substantial effect in potentially increasing privacy compliance. Regardless of the explanation, the increase is a step in the right direction as it certainly does not decrease privacy.

7 Conclusion and Future Work

In this study we discussed our exploratory analysis of features associated with apps having privacy policies (Sect. 4), presented our logistic regression model for predicting whether apps actually have privacy policies (Sect. 5), and explained how our work might be useful to government regulators as well as other organizations and individuals interested in privacy (Sect. 6).

Our exploratory analyses yielded novel insights (Sect. 4). Most notably, we discovered that only 63.1% of apps which are described as sharing their users' locations link to privacy policies. By analyzing the metadata of over a million apps, we are able to make conclusions about the privacy landscape in the Android app ecosystem. In our repeated crawls of the Play Store, we discovered possible evidence of Google's actions contributing to an increase in the percent of apps with privacy policies (Sect. 6.3). The coefficients of our logistic regression model show how individual features affect the odds of apps having privacy policies (Sect. 5). The model can also be used to identify apps which stand out from similar apps for not having privacy policies (Sect. 6.2).

A number of areas for future work remain. First, this study focused on the US Google Play Store. It would be worthwhile to perform similar analyses on Play Stores localized for European countries. This would give us insight into how different data protection frameworks affect the prevalence of privacy policies. A longitudinal analysis might even give insight into the effects of new legislation on the privacy landscape. We would welcome the opportunity to engage with European researchers, regulators, privacy organizations, and other parties to perform such comparative analyses.

Second, in the course of conducting our study we observed several examples of privacy policies or parts thereof appearing across seemingly unrelated organizations. In some cases, this repetition of policy language seems to indicate the use of privacy policy generators. However, it sometimes appears that language was simply copied from one policy to another. It would be worthwhile to systematically examine privacy policy reuse across the entire Play Store and beyond. Based on previous work showing a generally positive relationship between company size and whether companies have privacy policies, we hypothesize that smaller organizations may be more likely to reuse policy text [2].

Third, we are working on a large-scale system for comparing the actual practices of apps with the practices described in their privacy policies—using static code analysis and natural language processing, respectively. By analyzing apps' code and privacy policies, our system will automatically flag discrepancies between the two. The system will be a substantial advancement over the work described in this study, because simply knowing whether an app has a privacy policy or not is typically insufficient to determine non-compliance with regulation. In particular, apps that do not collect or share any personally identifiable information are generally not required to have a privacy policy. Also, simply having a privacy policy is insufficient to guarantee compliance, because the privacy policy may not describe all of an app's practices. However, we view our metadata analysis as complementary to this more in-depth analysis; our metadata analysis can help prioritize investigation of the discrepancies flagged by our in-depth analysis.

This study is our first large-scale analysis of the privacy landscape of the Play Store. However, there are still many untapped research opportunities in this area. We plan to use the infrastructure we developed for this analysis for additional large-scale analyses in the future.

A Appendix

A.1 Odds Calculations

Here we provide additional details about how the baseline app's odds were calculated, and how to interpret the model's quantitative variables.

Logistic regression models operate directly in terms of log(odds). For interpretability, log(odds) are easily converted to odds:

$$e^{\log(\text{odds})} = \text{odds} \tag{2}$$

Under the definition of the baseline app in Sect. 4, the log(odds) of the baseline app having a privacy policy can be calculated by substituting the coefficients of Table 2 into the following equation:

$$
\begin{aligned}
\log(\text{odds}(\text{policy} &= \text{True})) \\
&= b_0 + b_{\text{date\_published\_relative}} * \text{date\_published\_relative\_scaled} + \dots
\end{aligned}
\tag{3}
$$

where b_0 is the intercept, $b_{\text{date\_published\_relative}}$ is a feature coefficient, and date_published_relative_scaled is a scaled feature value. Note that the full equation would include terms for all of the coefficients in Table 2. From this equation, we calculate the log(odds) = −0.887 and odds = $e^{-0.887}$ = 0.412 of the baseline app having a privacy policy.

Next, we give an example of changing a quantitative variable. Suppose we start with the baseline app, which has no ratings, and increase the rating_count to 1,000,000. First, we scale rating_count[13] using the coefficients from Table 1:

$$\Delta rating\_count\_scaled = \frac{1,000,000 - rating\_count\_baseline}{S_{rating\_count}} \approx \frac{1,000,000}{1.598 * 10^5} \approx 6.258 \tag{4}$$

---

[13] We can ignore rating_count^2 and rating_count^3 because they were eliminated from the model.

Next, we simply multiply this scaled value by its corresponding coefficient from Table 2 and add it to the log(odds) of the baseline app. This gives us log(odds) = 8.850, or equivalently odds = 6,974. According to our model, an app with 1,000,000 ratings has much greater odds of having a privacy policy than an app with no ratings.

References

1. Almuhimedi, H., Schaub, F., Sadeh, N., Adjerid, I.: Your location has been shared 5,398 times!: A field study on mobile app privacy nudging. In: Proceedings of the 33rd Annual ACM Conference on Human Factors in Computing Systems (2015). https://doi.org/10.1145/2702123.2702210, http://dl.acm.org/citation.cfm?id=2702210
2. Balebako, R., Marsh, A., Lin, J., Hong, J.I., Cranor, L.F.: The privacy and security behaviors of smartphone app developers. In: Workshop on Usable Security (2014). http://repository.cmu.edu/hcii/265/
3. Blenner, S.R., Kollmer, M., Rouse, A.J., Daneshvar, N., Williams, C., Andrews, L.B.: Privacy policies of android diabetes apps and sharing of health information. JAMA **315**(10), 1051–1052 (2016). https://doi.org/10.1001/jama.2015.19426. http://jama.jamanetwork.com/article.aspx?doi=10.1001/jama.2015.19426
4. Bouchard, B., Suzuki, K.: Find great apps and games on Google Play with the editors' choice update, July 2017. https://www.blog.google/products/google-play/find-great-apps-and-games-google-play-editors-choice-update/. Accessed 20 May 2018
5. Clark, B.: Millions of apps could soon be purged from Google Play Store, February 2017. https://thenextweb.com/google/2017/02/08/millions-apps-soon-purged-google-play-store/. Accessed 20 May 2018
6. scikit-learn developers: sklearn.linear model.logisticregression. http://scikit-learn.org/stable/modules/generated/sklearn.linear_model.LogisticRegression.html. Accessed 20 May 2018
7. scikit-learn developers: sklearn.linear model.sgdclassifier. http://scikit-learn.org/stable/modules/generated/sklearn.linear_model.SGDClassifier.html. Accessed 20 May 2018
8. scikit-learn developers: sklearn.preprocessing.standardscaler. http://scikit-learn.org/stable/modules/generated/sklearn.preprocessing.StandardScaler.html. Accessed 20 May 2018
9. scikit-learn developers: Stochastic gradient descent: Tips on practical use. http://scikit-learn.org/stable/modules/sgd.html#tips-on-practical-use. Accessed 20 May 2018
10. scikit-learn developers: Choosing the right estimator (2017). http://scikit-learn.org/stable/tutorial/machine_learning_map/index.html. Accessed 20 May 2018
11. d'Heureuse, N., Huici, F., Arumaithurai, M., Ahmed, M., Papagiannaki, K., Niccolini, S.: What's app?: A wide-scale measurement study of smart phone markets. dl.acm.org. https://dl.acm.org/citation.cfm?id=2396759
12. Entertainment Software Rating Board (ESRB): ESRB ratings guide (2015). https://www.esrb.org/ratings/ratings_guide.aspx. Accessed 20 May 2018
13. Fahey, K.: Recognizing android excellence on Google Play, June 2017. https://android-developers.googleblog.com/2017/06/recognizing-android-excellence-on.html. Accessed 20 May 2018
14. Federal Trade Commission: Mobile privacy disclosures, February 2013. https://www.ftc.gov/os/2013/02/130201mobileprivacyreport.pdf. Accessed 20 May 2018
15. Federal Trade Commission: Children's Online Privacy Protection Rule ("COPPA"), August 2015. https://www.ftc.gov/enforcement/rules/rulemaking-regulatory-reform-proceedings/childrens-online-privacy-protection-rule. Accessed 20 May 2018
16. FTC: Privacy online: a report to congress, June 1998. https://www.ftc.gov/reports/privacy-online-report-congress. Accessed 20 May 2018

17. Google: Designed for families. https://developer.android.com/distribute/google-play/families.html. Accessed 20 May 2018
18. Google: Content ratings for apps & games. https://support.google.com/googleplay/android-developer/answer/188189?hl=en (2017). Accessed 20 May 2018
19. Google: Ratings questionnaire help (2017). https://support.google.com/googleplay/android-developer/topic/6169305?hl=en&ref_topic=6159951. Accessed 20 May 2018
20. Google: Requesting permissions (2017). https://developer.android.com/guide/topics/permissions/requesting.html. Accessed 20 May 2018
21. California Department of Justice: Attorney General Kamala D. Harris secures global agreement to strengthen privacy protections for users of mobile applications, February 2012. http://www.oag.ca.gov/news/press-releases/attorney-general-kamala-d-harris-secures-global-agreement-strengthen-privacy. Accessed 20 May 2018
22. California Department of Justice: Making your privacy practices public, May 2014. https://oag.ca.gov/sites/all/files/agweb/pdfs/cybersecurity/making_your_privacy_practices_public.pdf. Accessed 20 May 2018
23. Kelley, P.G., Cranor, L.F., Sadeh, N.: Privacy as part of the app decision-making process. In: CHI, p. 3393 (2013). https://doi.org/10.1145/2470654.2466466, http://dl.acm.org/citation.cfm?doid=2470654.2466466
24. Lin, J., Liu, B., Sadeh, N., Hong, J.I.: Modeling users' mobile app privacy preferences - restoring usability in a sea of permission settings. In: Proceedings of the Twelfth Symposium on Usable Privacy and Security (2014). http://dblp.org/rec/conf/soups/LinLSH14
25. Lin, J., Sadeh, N., Amini, S., Lindqvist, J., Hong, J.I., Zhang, J.: Expectation and purpose - understanding users' mental models of mobile app privacy through crowdsourcing. In: UbiComp, p. 501 (2012). https://doi.org/10.1145/2370216.2370290, http://dl.acm.org/citation.cfm?doid=2370216.2370290
26. Palmer, J.: After several years of service, the Google Play Top Developer Program is being put to rest, May 2017. http://www.androidpolice.com/2017/05/05/several-years-service-google-play-top-developer-program-put-rest/. Accessed 20 May 2018
27. Pedregosa, F., et al.: scikit-learn: machine learning in Python. J. Mach. Learn. Res. **12**, 2825–2830 (2011)
28. Sadeh, N., et al.: The usable privacy policy project: combining crowdsourcing, machine learning and natural language processing to semi-automatically answer those privacy questions users care about. Carnegie Mellon University Technical Report CMU-ISR-13-119, pp. 1–24, December 2013. http://reports-archive.adm.cs.cmu.edu/anon/isr2013/CMU-ISR-13-119.pdf
29. Statista: Number of apps available in leading app stores as of March 2017 (2017). https://www.statista.com/statistics/276623/number-of-apps-available-in-leading-app-stores/. Accessed 20 May 2018
30. Sunyaev, A., Dehling, T., Taylor, P.L., Mandl, K.D.: Availability and quality of mobile health app privacy policies. J. Am. Med. Inform. Assoc. **22**, e28–e33 (2014). https://doi.org/10.1136/amiajnl-2013-002605. https://academic.oup.com/jamia/article-lookup/doi/10.1136/amiajnl-2013-002605
31. Viennot, N., Garcia, E., Nieh, J.: A measurement study of Google Play. In: The 2014 ACM International Conference, pp. 221–233. ACM Press, New York City (2014). https://doi.org/10.1145/2591971.2592003, http://dl.acm.org/citation.cfm?doid=2591971.2592003
32. Wang, H., et al.: An explorative study of the mobile app ecosystem from app developers' perspective. In: The 26th International Conference, pp. 163–172. ACM Press, New York City (2017). https://doi.org/10.1145/3038912.3052712, http://dl.acm.org/citation.cfm?doid=3038912.3052712
33. Zimmeck, S., et al.: Automated analysis of privacy requirements for mobile apps. In: 24th Network & Distributed System Security Symposium (NDSS 2017). NDSS 2017, San Diego, CA. Internet Society, February 2017

Towards a Roadmap for Privacy Technologies and the General Data Protection Regulation: A Transatlantic Initiative

Stefan Schiffner[1]([⊠]), Bettina Berendt[2], Triin Siil[3], Martin Degeling[4], Robert Riemann[5], Florian Schaub[6], Kim Wuyts[2], Massimo Attoresi[5], Seda Gürses[2], Achim Klabunde[5], Jules Polonetsky[7], Norman Sadeh[8], and Gabriela Zanfir-Fortuna[7]

[1] University of Luxembourg, Esch-sur-Alzette, Luxembourg
Stefan.Schiffner@uni.lu
[2] KU Leuven, Leuven, Belgium
{Bettina.Berendt,Kim.Wuyts,Seda}@kuleuven.be
[3] Cybernetica, Tallinn, Estonia
triin.siil@cyber.ee
[4] Ruhr-Universität Bochum, Bochum, Germany
Martin.Degeling@ruhr-uni-bochum.de
[5] EDPS, Brussels, Belgium
{Robert.Riemann,Massimo.Attoresi,
Achim.Klabunde}@EDPS.europa.eu
[6] University of Michigan, Ann Arbor, USA
fschaub@umich.edu
[7] Future of Privacy Forum, Washington, USA
{julespol,gzanfir-fortuna}@fpf.org
[8] Carnegie Mellon University, Pittsburgh, USA
sadeh@cs.cmu.edu

Abstract. The EU's General Data Protection Regulation is poised to present major challenges in bridging the gap between law and technology. This paper reports on a workshop on the deployment, content and design of the GDPR that brought together academics, practitioners, civil-society actors, and regulators from the EU and the US. Discussions aimed at advancing current knowledge on the use of abstract legal terms in the context of applied technologies together with best practices following state of the art technologies. Five themes were discussed: state of the art, consent, de-identification, transparency, and development and deployment practices. Four traversal conflicts were identified, and research recommendations were outlined to reconcile these conflicts.

1 Introduction

The European Union's General Data Protection Regulation (GDPR), effective as of May 2018, constitutes, intentionally, a big challenge: how to bridge the gap between the fundamental rights it aims to protect including the legal reasoning and instruments proposed to effect such protection on the one hand, and the technologies that threaten

© Springer Nature Switzerland AG 2018
M. Medina et al. (Eds.): APF 2018, LNCS 11079, pp. 24–42, 2018.
https://doi.org/10.1007/978-3-030-02547-2_2

and/or serve to protect these rights including the technological-economic reasoning and practices that give rise to these technologies on the other hand. The GDPR also presents further challenges, such as how to make it work in a worldwide context in which those who control and process personal data are often from legal and social cultures different from those of the EU, with the exact nature of the differences itself a topic of continuing debates. The present paper arose from a workshop under the heading of the second challenge: "Privacy Engineering and the GDPR: A Transatlantic Initiative." For the "EU" and "US" backgrounds that participants represented during the workshop, we found much more unifying than dividing legal and social concerns. The workshop thus constituted the beginning of a transatlantic initiative for drawing a roadmap to address the challenge.[1]

To address the complexity of the questions, we formulated sub-problems, with a view to letting these answer the challenge in conjunction. Five key themes were identified as crucial in the roadmapping process: (1) what is the state of the art in technology; (2) how can consent be meaningful; (3) is de-identification a usable tool; (4) how can processing be transparent and interpretable; (5) what are further challenges given current development and deployment practices?

The challenges concern both the *what* and the *how* of design: the question of what technologies are regulated and/or required by the law, and the question of how the legal requirements can be mapped to software design processes.

Regarding the *what*, GDPR Article 2(1) clearly points out that it applies to all operations (in GDPR terminology, 'processing') performed on any information relating to an identified or identifiable natural person (in GDPR terminology, 'personal data'), whether carried out by automated means or manually. As further explained in GDPR Recital 15, this reflects the principle of technology neutrality – the protection of natural persons should not depend on the techniques used. The natural persons who are identified or identifiable by means of personal data are referred to as 'data subjects' in GDPR terminology. GDPR further conceptualizes a 'controller' as a person who decides why and how personal data is processed and a 'processor' as someone who processes personal data on behalf of a controller.

The GDPR addresses technologies for data processing in two main contexts:

1. GDPR Article 24(1) requires controllers to implement appropriate technical and organisational measures to ensure and to be able to demonstrate that processing of personal data is performed in accordance with the GDPR. This requirement is further specified in other norms of the GDPR: (a) data protection by design – Article 25(1) requires appropriate technical and organisational measures, such as pseudonymization, designed to effect data-protection principles, such as data minimisation, in an effective manner and to integrate the necessary safeguards into the processing. (b) data protection by default – Article 25(2) requires appropriate technical and organisational measures for ensuring that, by default, only personal data that are necessary for each specific purpose of the processing are processed. (c) security of processing – Article 32(1)–(2) require appropriate technical and

---

[1] Cf. also the US National Privacy Research Strategy, https://www.nitrd.gov/cybersecurity/nationalprivacyresearchstrategy.aspx.

organisational measures to ensure a level of security appropriate to the risks presented by processing (accidental or unlawful destruction, loss, alteration, unauthorised disclosure of, or access to personal data transmitted, stored or otherwise processed).
2. By applying certain technical measures, the data processing may be partly or entirely out of the scope of the GDPR. With reference to GDPR Article 11, a controller may process personal data under relaxed terms and conditions if it took measures to sanitize data in such a way that data subjects cannot be identified. Furthermore, the GDPR does not apply to anonymous information (Recital 26). In both cases, the GDPR does not specify which technologies should be considered as appropriate. Nevertheless, the GDPR requires controllers and processors to give due regard to the state of the art when choosing the technologies (GDPR Articles 25(1) and 32(1)).

For both requirements, uncertainty persists over the available technologies, the burden their adoption adds for controller and processor, their actual functionality (protection goals), and their relation to the legal requirements.

Regarding the *how*, mappings from legal requirements to available technologies have been proposed by several authors. Particularly relevant for the present purposes are those that map from GPDR principles, first to the software design process (design patterns) and from patterns to available technologies [1]. However, the spectrum of available technologies is heterogeneous (in readiness and provided functionality) and volatile (frequent innovation and obsolescence of technology). In addition, the mapping sequence stresses a top-down or even waterfall-model design, which neglects actual practices as well as state-of-the-art insights about agile design methods. While there are initiatives to establish and maintain a repository of technologies ([2] and IPEN[2]), this bottom-up view and the needs of an agile design process remain under-researched.

The contribution of this paper is a roadmap outlined via five key themes and four transversal conflict areas. The procedure that led to these themes, the workshop and its discussion groups are described in Sect. 2, and the theme-specific results in Sect. 3. In Sect. 4, we present four transversal conflicts that we have identified through a synopsis of the themes. From these conflicts, in Sect. 5 we then derive conclusions for future research.

2   Background: Transatlantic Initiative and Workshop

Motivated by the GDPR going into full effect in May 2018, the Internet Privacy Engineering Network (IPEN), the Future of Privacy Forum, the KU Leuven (University of Leuven) Computer Science Department/DTAI group, and Carnegie Mellon University's Privacy Engineering Program decided to host a joint workshop in Leuven, Belgium, as a transatlantic initiative. With this November 2017 workshop, we aimed to determine the relevant state of the art in privacy engineering with a focus on those areas where the "art" needs to be developed further.

---

[2] www.engineeringprivacy.eu.

The goal of this initiative was to identify open research and development tasks that are needed to make the full achievement of the GDPR's ambitions possible. Within this thematic scope, we wanted to focus the workshop on those areas most relevant to our envisaged audience. We spread an informal survey in our networks, asking people "for a quick shortlist of the most pressing issues (a) that [they] have encountered in the preparation for adapting [their] data processing to the GPDR in their organisation, (b) that [they] perceive as a gap, or as getting too little attention, in research, whether in [their] particular area or in any other, and that [they] think privacy engineers should focus their attention on."

We received a wide range of insightful input from more than 40 people from academia, industry, civil society and regulators, mostly but not exclusively from computational and legal backgrounds. We grouped the answers into categories and selected those that had garnered most interest. The resulting five themes (see Sect. 3) were described in a call for contributions that was sent out via the same (and additional) channels as the survey, asking potential participants to describe their interests with respect to these themes and to outline how they and the workshop could profit from one another.[3]

This resulted in a group of 105 participants whom we invited to come to the workshop. We were happy to see the intended balances along a number of dimensions, in particular EU/US and academia/industry/civil society/regulators. The program reflected this balance: opening statements by the European Data Protection Supervisor were followed by a keynote presentation and a panel discussion involving researchers, industry and standards bodies representatives. Five breakout groups then worked on the themes and presented their results in the forum.[4]

3 Privacy Engineering and the GDPR: Five Key Themes

In this section we discuss the results of the working groups: (1) what is the state of the art in technology; (2) how can consent be meaningful; (3) is de-identification a usable tool; (4) how can processing be transparent and interpretable; (5) what are the further challenges from development and deployment practices.

3.1 What is the "State of the Art" in Privacy Enhancing Technologies?

The guiding questions of this theme were: How is the state of the art of privacy engineering defined and who defines it? What PET tool boxes can be used for developers, corporate decision makers and supervisory bodies? What data-driven risk assessment frameworks for implementing Privacy by Design in data science and big data analytics already exist? How can these be improved?

The GDPR mandates, in Article 25 on *data protection by design and by default*, controllers of data processing to take into account among others the *state of the art*

---

[3] https://fpf.org/2017/08/30/privacy-engineering-research-gdpr-trans-atlantic-initiative/.

[4] https://fpf.org/wp-content/uploads/2017/08/TransAtlantic-GDPR-Workshop-Agenda-1.pdf.

when defining means for data processing and during the data processing itself. While the state of the art is also mentioned in Article 32 on *security of processing* and in Recitals 78 and 83, a definition comparable to those in Article 4 for e.g. personal data or processing is not given.

Furthermore, the requirement to employ state of the art technologies to protect personal data is not an absolute requirement. According to Articles 25 and 32, it is to be balanced with the "costs of implementation, the nature, scope, context and purposes of the processing as well as the risks [...] and severity for the rights and freedoms of natural persons" posed by the processing.

Controllers and processors in charge to ensure compliance with the GDPR have to determine for their respective means of data processing which state-of-the-art they have to take into account. This is so far a difficult task, because of the missing definition of the state of the art and the unavailability of guidance and case law on this matter and a lack of experience as the GDPR is still new. With no body by law in charge of establishing the state of the art, data controllers, DPAs, self- and co-regulatory bodies, and EU courts will have to determine the minimum requirements case by case.

Technology, and as such the state of the art, are subject of continuous research by public and private actors and evolve in time. As a result, compliance taking into account the state of the art is a moving target. Emerging new technology may increase the risk of data breaches throughout the life time of a product or service. For instance, the availability of faster and cheaper computing resources may allow attackers to break data encrypted in the past much faster. To ensure a constant low risk level of data breaches, the encryption of already encrypted data must be strengthened over time taking into account the current state of the art.

This consideration leads to another set of questions. How can products and services receive security updates, and for how long must updates be provided? How can the controller be sure to not miss out on relevant developments of the state of the art? Who is liable if the controller or processor discontinue their business activity before the end of the product lifetime?

One can also expect interferences with intellectual property law and competition law. For instance, consider a state-of-the-art privacy engineering tool that is proprietary and only offered by a single vendor to competitors under abusive conditions. This situation can be compared to expensive patented pharmaceuticals providing the only cure for certain diseases. Different though here is that those competitors not adopting the state-of-the-art proprietary or non-proprietary privacy enhancing technologies (PETs) may be sued for unfair competition.

To balance the efforts towards data protection and risks for data breaches, but also for privacy risk assessment, the risk must be measured and quantified in the first place. Workshop participants suggested that standardisation and privacy design patterns may simplify this difficult task, which may eventually even enable automated risk assessment. An automation would also benefit the continuous re-assessment of risks throughout the life time of a product or service. Today, different concepts and methodologies exist that make it possible to break down legal high-level requirements to low-level software requirements to be implemented, for example using PETs from common repositories [2]. Participants expressed the need to further streamline, complete and ease such approaches. Without extensive guidance and ready-to-use building blocks, especially small and medium enterprises with no or small research and development teams may struggle to take into account the state of the art.

3.2 Consent

The guiding questions of this theme were: There are detailed parameters for obtaining valid consent under the GDPR and the future ePrivacy Regulation, creating important challenges for sectors such as advertising technology, mobile apps, connected cars, and smart devices. What can engineering contribute, and what should solutions look like?

A data subject's consent is one of six legal bases for data processing defined in GDPR Article 6. In order to be valid under the GDPR, consent must be specific, informed, freely given and unambiguous. Article 7 requires that if data processing is based on consent, the data controller must be able to demonstrate that consent was obtained and freely given by the data subject, that consent declarations need to be clearly separated from other written declarations such as terms of service and must be presented "in an intelligible and easily accessible form, using clear and plain language." Furthermore, Article 7(3) grants the data subject the right to revoke consent at any time and it should be "as easy to withdraw as to give consent." Article 8 further limits the age of consent to age 16 and above, requiring parental consent for children under 16 for the provision of information society services. Data controllers are charged to "make reasonable efforts to verify [...] that consent is given or authorised by the holder of parental responsibility over the child, taking into consideration available technology."

The GDPR requirements for consent pose crucial challenges for privacy engineering. For one, there is a palpable risk that companies will inundate users with consent requests for all data practices to ensure that GDPR consent requirements are met. However, while it plays an integral role in the GDPR, consent is not the only legal basis for data processing. Companies, engineers, lawyers and regulators need to make deliberate decisions about when consent is required and when other grounds for lawful processing suffice. Of particular relevance are contractual relationships (Article 6(1)(b)) and legitimate interests of the data controller or third parties (Article 6(1)(f)), the latter still granting data subjects the right to object, thus opting out of a certain kind of processing. Thus, explicit consent should be used in cases where it is actually required as a legal basis for processing. There is a need for clear guidance and decision frameworks for helping controllers, which may include technology designers, determine on what legal basis for processing to rely on in what situation.

A second challenge is the provision of consent requests in "intelligible and easily accessible form, using clear and plain language." While usability of privacy notices and controls has been studied extensively (e.g., [3]), few ideal solutions exist. Obtaining truly informed user consent remains a challenge, further spurred by the GDPR's important but extensive transparency requirements (Articles 13 and 14). When providing consent prompts and consent-relevant information to data subjects, the level of granularity and specificity of information provided needs to strike a balance between the requirement for clear and plain language, conciseness and the transparency requirements. It is by now widely recognized that consumers rarely read privacy policies and struggle to understand them [4–7]. While they may not reach the same complexity as privacy policies, there is a risk that consent prompts may be stuffed with information in order to satisfy transparency requirements, resulting in yet more dialogs users ignore, and thereby negating the intent of ensuring that obtained consent is informed and an explicit expression of agreement rather than perfunctory. Instead, consent prompts should contain only information directly relevant for informing the consent decision in the given context with more extensive information being available in additional notice layers [3]. Consent prompts should be designed in a user-centric process involving active and extensive user testing. Writing and designing privacy notices and consent prompts should not be an art form but rather follow an evidence-driven process.

Ideally, well-tested and validated consent prompts and user experiences would be shared as best practice design patterns among the community of legal, technical and regulatory privacy professionals. Standardization of consent language and terminology may also be desirable to ensure that legal concepts are adequately represented in language that is clear and understandable to users and data subjects. This would further allow consistent translation of consent-specific text into different languages.

The notion of consent faces a particular challenge in the context of Internet of Things technology, when devices and technology become integrated with the physical environment. In smart homes or other smart infrastructures, one person might set up a device and consent to data collection and processing, but other individuals might also be subject to data collection in a shared physical environment. Future consent solutions will need to become user-centric rather than being focused on specific devices and technology. Can and should consent proliferate across multiple devices of the same user or across different infrastructures in which the user interacts? Can personal devices act as an agent for managing the user's privacy preferences across contexts and "consent" for the user by translating privacy preferences into responses to consent prompts?

A practical challenge is keeping track of user consent to specific data practices and across different entities. What is an appropriate technical record of consent? How should consent with third parties be handled? For example, when third party widgets are presented on a website, is it sufficient if the first part collects user consent or are separate consent records needed for each party collecting information on the website?

A related challenge is the need for companies to accept and respect when users say no to specific consent requests. Consent needs to be bound to a purpose for processing – but how specific must purposes be to be meaningful both for data subjects and organizations?

Questions regarding consent also extend beyond initial consent requests. Once consent has been given (or not), data subjects need to be given opportunities to access data about them, as well as change prior consent indications in order to exercise their right to object (GDPR Article 21). Such ex post controls require closer attention to ensure that they are usable and enable users to effectively review and change their privacy settings and consent expressions.

Article 21(5) states that "data subjects may exercise [their] right to object by automated means using technical specifications." Prior technical privacy specifications, such as P3P [8] or Do Not Track [9], lacked legal basis as well as industry adoption. Article 21(5) creates a legal basis for using and respecting automated technical specifications, but in order to get companies to adopt a certain specification, they may need assurance that a given standard is considered compliant with Article 21(5). Thus, research and development of privacy agent solutions and technical standards needs to be accompanied by legal assessment and possibly certification to facilitate adoption and support of automated privacy management approaches by industry. Certified GDPR compliance for consent technologies would provide a strong incentive for companies to adopt more innovative and more effective consent approaches. Such certification should also be based on actual user testing to ensure that consent prompts and processes are understandable and usable.

3.3   De-identification

The guiding question of this theme was: How can different levels of de-identification techniques be used or further developed to effectively advance the obligations under the GDPR?

Anonymization and pseudonymization are frequent topics among both academics and practitioners, since the GDPR provides several new provisions relating to these topics compared to the earlier Data Protection Directive (Directive 95/46/EC). The GDPR explicitly introduces the term 'pseudonymization' in Article 4 p. 5. If a controller or processor de-identifies personal data, i.e., makes it hard to link such data to an identifiable person, they are permitted to process such "depersonalized" information under relaxed terms according to Article 11 of the GDPR. If they can demonstrate the "depersonalized" information is "anonymous" in terms of Recital 26, the GDPR requirements on data protection do not apply. The Article 29 Working Party (hereinafter "Art. 29 WP") in [10] declares clearly that "anonymised data do fall out of the scope of data protection legislation." Hence, de-identification techniques most likely are an important aspect of GDPR compliance. Nevertheless, the GDPR does not provide guidelines how to achieve de-identification. Due to this lack of implementation guidelines, data controllers and processors who choose the opportunity of using de-identification techniques face a risk of future enforcement action. For this section, we outline the obstacles discussed in our breakout session.

A first obstacle are mismatching terms. We often observe, in discussions among legal and technical experts, that certain terms are used very specifically on one side, but understood very broadly on the other side. De-identification is one example: while the terms "anonymous" and "pseudonymization" used in the GDPR seem to be overarching technology neutral terms for lawyers, technologists tend to treat them as subsets of a broader concept of "de-identification." It was discussed in the group that the GDPR terms "anonymization" and "pseudonymization" do not seem to adequately cover all available de-identification techniques from a technical perspective. PET providers, academics, think tanks and data protection authorities who were represented in the group had very different background knowledge and views on this topic, influenced by different levels of understanding of and access to current state of the art in PETs and privacy engineering skills. Consensus is still a work in progress in this area.

For the rest of this section, we will use the Art. 29 WP definition: "anonymization constitutes a further processing of personal data; as such, it must satisfy the requirement of compatibility by having regard to the legal grounds and circumstances of the further processing." [10] We conclude from this that the terms anonymization and pseudonymization in the GDPR are meant by Art. 29 WP to refer to database sanitization and explicitly not to anonymous communication or other techniques of de-identification (e.g., collecting data in anonymous form, encryption, secret sharing, multi-party computation), even if this may seem counter-intuitive in light of the technology neutrality principle provided for in Recital 15. Despite this, we were able to agree in our discussion group that the terms "anonymous" and "pseudonymization" are used consistently in the GDPR.

However, many participants pointed out that the intended scope of the terms "anonymous" and "pseudonymization" remains unclear. The terms seem to be setting too abstract a goal to be directly implemented in IT practices. Further, it is unclear to which standard the efforts to sanitize data from personal information should be held. In particular, what happens if personal data gets exposed despite sanitization efforts? For practitioners, this uncertainty brings along a risk of legal actions. Hence, there were frequent requests in the discussion group for more guidance on how to achieve compliance with GDPR.

In an attempt to provide such guidance on which tools can be used, Art. 29 WP elaborates on some of the technical means and properties that can be used for achieving anonymization, namely noise addition, permutation, differential privacy, aggregation, k-anonymity, l-diversity and t-closeness. [10] These techniques are evaluated from a qualitative angle. However, from an impact or risk-assessment point of view, this leaves open the question of quantification. How can the level of anonymization be measured, and which level is considered appropriate?

In quantification discussions, it is easy to settle in extreme positions. On one hand, the limitations of current anonymization techniques are often pointed out.

Indeed, it is easy to find proof-of-concept attacks on published databases that were supposed to be anonymised, e.g. [11]. Moreover, when speaking in absolute terms, it is quite likely that there is no method to effectively achieve 100% de-identification of personal data. This could lead to the conclusion that database sanitization is futile.

On the other hand, downplaying the situation by claiming that only a small number of data items have been re-identified in proof-of-concept studies, as e.g. in [12], neglects the nature and motivation of these studies. The aim of studies on de-anonymization is to demonstrate the effectiveness of a certain statistical method, not to mount an actual attack. It needs to be pointed out that an actual attack (1) would often not qualify for a scientific publication and (2) the attacker very likely would rather keep their knowledge private. Hence, deriving attack success rates from published proof of concept attacks is unrealistic.

Either of these extreme positions would lead to less privacy. In the worst case, this leaves no incentive for data controllers and processors to make any efforts in that direction. At the same time, it is clear that even the simple deletion of direct identifiers provides some protection, for example from leaks of small parts of the data or from accidental identification. While the "publish and forget" mentality of the other extreme will not work either, there is a middle ground, as [13] conclude: "the GDPR is compatible with a risk-based approach when contextual controls are combined with sanitization techniques."

3.4   Transparent and Interpretable Processing

The guiding questions of this theme were: How can data mining and machine learning methods be made transparent and interpretable? What exactly should be revealed and how? How can we ensure these methods correspond to GDPR requirements and are understandable to the relevant groups of users?

The requirement that (especially AI-based) decision making or decision support systems provide explanations is as old as expert systems themselves, the value of different types of explanations for different audiences have been studied empirically, e.g. [14], and the call for transparency of algorithms is likewise not new[5]. However, the urgency of these desiderata has increased tremendously with the increase of applications and also in complexity of machine-based or –assisted decisions. The GDPR declares transparency to be a guiding principle of all (personal-data) processing (Article 5(1)(a), [15]), and it requires data controllers to provide specific types of information concerning data held and processing performed, as well as "meaningful information about the logic involved" (Articles 13–15). Further principles, such as accountability (Article 5(2), which requires processes and documentation that ensure and show that and how the data are protected), and rights, such as data portability (Article 20), can enhance transparency and interpretability. Recitals 63 and 71 specify requirements that are related to understandability/interpretability.

There has been intensive discussion in the literature between computer science and law just what it is that the GDPR requires – whether this amounts to a "right to explanation" or something less/else [16, 17], and what the specifics of an "explanation" are [18–20]. Is it general information about how a decision-making system works (the system logic, the data categories), or is it an explanation of individual decisions that such a system makes? Does it include justification of a decision or just the mere facts of the results and its effects? The recent Guideline by the Art. 29 WP [21, p. 26] tends to support the latter perspective as it states that "[the data controller] provides details of the main characteristics considered in reaching the decision, the source of this information and the relevance". But while this might be suitable for conservative credit scoring systems or health related information systems, it seems inapplicable to many big data applications that use a high number of characteristics from various sources and might make not one but many decisions repeatedly. Apart from being difficult to resolve in the individual disciplines, these questions are a clear example of the difficulties of mapping between legal and computational notions.

What does it mean for information to be *meaningful* for achieving transparency and interpretability/understandability? To this question raised by [17], we want to add: Is "more" explanation always "better"? Or is it possible that explanations are vulnerable to the same unreflected big-data assumptions as processing itself? Would people (data subjects as well as other stakeholders such as monitoring agents) just ignore additional inundations of information, as they do with privacy notices [22] and consent prompts (see Sect. 3.2)? Similar arguments are made about breach notices [23], as one indicator of 'the limits of notice and choice' [6]. Could an explanation itself become a leakage

---

[5] E.g. 30 years of EPIC's work: https://www.epic.org/algorithmic-transparency/.

channel that endangers the protection of personal data? It has been observed in privacy-preserving data mining that for example machine-learned rules, which are good candidates for explanations, can do this, e.g. [24].

In addition, an argument like the following could also be made about explanations: "Notices are always a second-best tool because they only *respond* to breaches, not *prevent* them. Moreover, they shift the burden from the responsible parties to the innocent data subject." [23, p.1]. Linking interpretability with intervenability [25] can be a partial remedy here, as it may reduce the burden on the individual by limiting the necessity of awareness to cases in which decision systems produce unexpected results. [26] This line of thinking highlights that transparency and interpretability always need to be seen in the context of all principles of data protection.

Another possible obstacle to being meaningful is an over-emphasis on algorithmic or technological aspects. Data protection by design includes the implementation of "appropriate technical and organisational measures" for implementing the GDPR's principles (Article 25). *How* is the meaningful information actually given to data subjects or other questioning parties? How does this relate to the requirements of accountability? Especially in the computational literature, questions of human-computer interfaces, organisation, and process tend to be disregarded, but we expect this to become one of the key interdisciplinary challenges for effective transparency and interpretability.

Both technical and organisational measures need to support the GDPR requirements to *provide* or *(enable to) obtain* "meaningful information about the logic involved" (Articles 13(1)(f), 14(2)(g), 15(1) (h)). The legal text thus formulates requirements to do something, which however in the computational literature tend to be discussed as non-functional requirements, e.g. "algorithms should be transparent", "systems should be interpretable". How can these be turned into requirements that are functional in the sense of software development? What *exactly* does a socio-technical system need to *do*? In this area, we observe a clear conflict between the need for (or the impossibility of) exactly specified requirements: the legal requirement is intentionally underspecified, but the system designer needs exact specifications. In addition, if we consider interpretability as linked to intervenability, what other functional requirements result from this?

Explanations and interpretability also pose challenges for economic interests because what is meaningful to a data subject may be regarded as a trade secret by the data processor. Data protection authorities would then also need to check for what could be termed "explanation fraud" in analogy with audit fraud as in the recent automobile-exhaust scandal: A system could be designed such that, when prodded for an explanation, it generates an answer that satisfies the legal requirements but that does not accurately reflect the normal workings of the system. When machine learning is employed for explanations (e.g., [27]), what roles will adversarial machine learning and secure learning play?

Future research thus needs to answer the following questions:

- What constitutes a "meaningful" or "sufficiently comprehensive explanation" of an automated decisions process?
- What explanations are suitable for which algorithm and which usage context?

- What are user perspectives on this? Can we find levels of explanations that are understandable for different audiences?
- Can modes of intervention be used to prevent the information overload that we see with privacy notices?
- How can we prevent those explanations from leaking either personal information or intellectual property?

3.5 Challenges Arising from Development and Deployment Practice

The guiding questions of this theme were: How can PETs and data protection by design methodologies be integrated into existing software development approaches (especially agile software development)? With software production and use phases collapsing [28], users are integral to experimentation, developers are users themselves, and usability becomes central. Different requirements may be commensurate, complementary, and contradictory. How can we design and evaluate for users and for a democratic society?

The GDPR requires the implementation of Data Protection by design (DP-by-design) and by default. However, both the open-ended scope of the legal requirement, as well as the challenges associated with incorporating PETs and DP-by-design methodologies into existing software development ecosystem requires further attention from researchers and practitioners.

One concern arising from the integration of DP-by-design in existing software development approaches is situated at the inception phase of this integration, namely the translation between legal obligations and technical requirements. Currently there are some *mismatches between legal and technological terminology and conceptual systems*. Key terms may have entirely different meanings in both fields. For instance, the term 'data owner', often used by developers, has no legal meaning, and concepts such as 'data controller' and 'data processor' are in general unknown by software engineers. A privacy engineering vocabulary and ontology that can be used by all parties involved in the software engineering life-cycle (including DPOs, developers, business owners, product owners, etc.) may help address this matter. Terminological and ontolgical efforts such as those in [29–34] have so far had minor impact due to the prevalence of a legal interpretation of the term 'personal data' without reference to its derivation from actual concepts present in computational views on data. A common vocabulary would be very helpful in evaluating, for example, third parties before service integration, or developing GDPR certification schemes, but is also likely to fall short of addressing contextual aspects of privacy.

Moreover, there is a *discrepancy between the non-functional requirements that are provided and the necessary requirements that need to be functional*. Legal requirements are often vague (on purpose) and can be hard to translate into technical requirements. High level privacy requirements may not be straightforward to implement if they only express qualities to be achieved. These may hence be hard to implement and validate. Developers can be supported through the integration of privacy engineering principles and processes into existing tools. While efforts have been put into improving security usability and process for developers, the same efforts in privacy are only commencing.

The move to service architectures, data centric software development and increased use of machine learning in services introduces further challenges. While companies' current belief regarding (personal) data is "the more, the merrier", the concept of *'big data' clashes with GDPR's data minimization* principle. Hence, changing the mindset in the industry seems to be a prerequisite for an effective privacy engineering practice. Today, for companies, their (data) assets are the main driver for integrating security into software development. This is, however, where security and privacy differ: while security has typically been applied for protecting company assets, privacy requires protecting users and their interests. A cultural change would have to start with, for example, companies and developers seeing themselves as responsible for protecting the data subject's rights. This may, however, put developers in the odd position of resolving conflicting user and organizational requirements. This may sometimes be resolved using design, e.g., Privacy Enhancing Technologies are often designed to address seemingly conflicting requirements, but not always.

The position of the developer may be strengthened through DP-by-design best practices. Concretely, better integration of the Data Protection Impact Assessments with DP-by-design as well as the Development Life Cycle could help surface conflicts and allow organizations to consider technical and non-technical ways to resolve conflicting requirements. Certification efforts may help create common practices and support companies when they have to integrate third party services. Advancing these projects may, for example, require the development of domain specific standards for DPIAs or better clarification of accountability and documentation requirements when it comes to DP-by-design efforts.

The accelerated iterative approach typical in agile development environments can make DP-by-design more challenging than in a typical waterfall model. In agile development the design of the system is frequently updated and hence requires frequent iterations for privacy and security assessment. Agility, however, requires quick software development sprints, while privacy analysis is typically a slow and time-consuming activity. In addition, technical privacy assessments are based on the architectural description of the system, but in agile development there is, generally speaking, no grand design up front, and little, if any, documentation of the system. It might be possible to assess and integrate privacy for each feature in isolation, but when these features are combined (composed), as well as when services from multiple parties are integrated, there is no guarantee that the service itself, or the entire supply chain that underlies it, fulfills all the privacy requirements. This is especially the case due to modular architectures that are favored in current day software ecosystems. These also raise serious challenges to determining and managing responsibility with respect to privacy. If a company, for example, provides a data service that can be integrated by different third parties, it can be challenging to identify all the privacy risks for all the different uses of the data by these third parties.

Guidance for developers and companies to identify who is legally responsible for the system, as well as studies on how to adapt existing ecosystem to fulfill these requirements will be of great value going forward. For certification efforts, the current ecosystem implies that these should not be one-off efforts but certification processes that integrate frequent updates to software and the service ecosystem into their evaluation.

Legacy systems may also give rise to privacy challenges. It may be difficult to apply privacy 'by design' to existing systems, or achieve sufficient protections through add-on privacy solutions. It may be the case that some systems will have to be re-engineered completely to comply with current laws.

One idea is to adopt tools and techniques from other domains which confront similar challenges such as aviation and medicine [35]. Privacy *can* be formulated as a 'safety' problem. In this respect, tools such as failure model effects analysis [36], data flow modelling [30, 37], checklists [38] and risk management practices [39, 40] directly address many of the issues raised earlier in this paper regarding development processes. Industrial experience has shown this approach to be fruitful [30, 41]; however, it must be noted that some techniques, specifically checklists, come with a significant cultural investment if to be applied correctly and have been criticized in privacy circles as being less than sufficient to provide substantive protections.

The challenges associated with integrating DP-by-design into the development are not the only reason that these principles are often neglected in industry. Many companies still struggle with the identification and documentation of their data processing activities. Clearly, as long as a company does not fully understand what data they process and where it all is stored, applying DP-by-design software development practices will not yet be their priority. For this to change, it is import that integration efforts are intensified and are promoted in industry.

4   Four Transversal Conflicts

We subjected the results described in the previous section to a synoptic analysis and identified four areas of conflicts that re-occurred throughout the themes. We will describe these as transversal conflicts here. In the subsequent Sect. 5, we will use them to identify recommendations for future work. We observe the following conflicts:

1. Hard-to-reconcile and sometimes incompatible terminological and conceptual systems in the legal and technology communities.
2. An unreflected big data ideology that is based on the perception that more data is better even if there is no clear use for the collected data. This is in conflict with data minimization, where data is only collected and stored if needed for a certain functionality.
3. Dysfunctional economics of by-design paradigms if they are implemented as waterfall design process.
4. (From 2 and 3:) A tension between functional vs. non-functional requirements. Design processes, regardless of whether waterfall or agile, are focused on functionality; however, privacy and data protection requirements are often formulated in a non-functional fashion. For accountability (to demonstrate compliance) and enforceability, these properties need to be transformed into functionalities. For example, to ensure confidentiality of communication, encryption needs to be applied.

The protection of personal data and privacy is a particular challenge. It not only describes a "quality" of a system (like all non-functional requirements do) and specifies constraints on the system's functionalities (like many non-functional requirements do), but it is a quality that often derives from "not doing" something (again, data minimization is a good example). However, design(er)s are often focused on making a system "do" something, i.e. on the functional requirements. A focus on "doing" seems necessary to implement accountability, but it may lead to an arms race of technologies and counter-technologies that is counter-productive for the original goal (a phenomenon that predates the GDPR, cf. [42] on similar spirals in risk management).

5   Conclusions: From Conflicts to Roadmap

As the individual themes' discussions show, the conflicts sketched in the previous section re-occurred throughout, although not always in the same intensity. It is probably too early to extract solutions for these conflicts; instead, they offer a productive basis for future work.

Conflict 1: Mismatching Terminology. If left untackled, this conflict will lead to inconsistent interpretations of the legal text, which will have a long-term impact on the technological solutions and the debate on what *state of the art* and *appropriate* mean here.

Terminology divergences are unavoidable because they reflect the different needs of the communities, and these differences cannot easily be resolved by an ontology. For example, on one hand, compliance cannot be defined as a by-design notion, since legal terms are always defined in their context. On the other hand, the designer needs to take implementation decisions for which they need to guarantee legality. In many fields, checklists and standards are established to resolve this conflict.

While standardization plays an important role also in IT security, IT protection measures appear to experience disruptive changes (black swan events) in their effectiveness more often than other technologies. As an example, consider the almost instant scalability of attacks: once a protection measure has been broken, the breaking can usually be replicated rather easily. This is intrinsically different from physical safety measures, where even if a weakness is discovered, a second break-in can be as difficult as the first attempt. This observation leads to the need to keep continuously updated and maintained descriptions of the state of the art.

Lastly for the terminology conflict there is also good news: the often troubled cultural conflict between US and EU may be much smaller than claimed. The need for privacy protection is the same, as is the hope for business opportunities; the conflict is mostly in legal traditions how to reach the same or similar goals.

Conflict 2: Compulsive Data Hoarding. While creativity and market needs might inhibit the application of by-design paradigms, compulsive data hoarding without functionality in mind is more ideology-driven. A wider public debate on the cost for society of this data hoarding is needed. This includes a cost-benefit analysis of knowledge and ignorance. This is generally not new as it is often done in medicine, when the decision needs to be taken whether a medical test is needed or not.

Conflicts 3 and 4: Dysfunctional Economics of by-Design Paradigms and (Non)-Functional Requirements. Given that it is very hard, if not impossible, to "bolt on" data protection functionalities post-production, by-design paradigms seem to be obvious and inevitable. However, their adoption falls beyond expectation. We observe that the waterfall-like development cycle, which is assumed for current PbD interpretations, ignores the creative process that is needed to develop new functionalities and matching business models. Prototypes to test the potential markets for a new functionality need to be developed fast and in cost-efficient ways. This market need was answered by the adoption of agile design methods, driven by use cases and functionalities. However, privacy and security properties need to be turned into functionalities.

Here, PETs come into the play. For example, to implement the requirement that personal data must not be accessible for unauthorized parties, data needs to be encrypted and users need to be authenticated for access.

Having said that, even formulating privacy properties into functional requirements might fall short. These functionalities also need to be considered in the frequent test cycles during development in a meaningful way. For the truly functional part of the security user story (e.g. an encrypt function), this can easily be expressed as a feature, and there will be someone who requires and oversees this in the development team. For the intrinsically non-functional parts such as "every data item needs to be minimised in correspondence with its purpose", such a continuously involved stakeholder is often missing, since it is mostly an end-user requirement or even more strongly for the *non*-users that are affected by (the lack of) privacy solutions.

The law now shifts this protection interest from the end-user domain into the domain of the data controller, by creating liabilities and thus financial risk. This is the point where legal compliance comes into play and where this conflict feeds back into conflicts 1 and 2: There is a need to translate legal abstract terminology into positive and implementable software requirements.

6   A Summary Roadmap

With the GDPR now coming into force, this paper offers initial insights on development practices and organisational measures, including product lifespan until its organized obsolescence as well as the handling of data from its collection and processing, and onto final deletion. We outline the following recommendations and avenues for further research based on the four conflicts identified in this paper. Disparities in terminology is a persistent issue, especially in light of both domains evolving independently: on the one hand, the law will remain relatively unchanged, its interpretation will change by case law and legal praxis and, as a result, so will the concepts behind the words. On the other hand, IT products and the technology on which they are based will change more rapidly and so will the language used to speak about this technology. Much needed now is a platform able to continuously map current interpretations of the law at state of the art level. Regarding compulsive data hoarding, it is anticipated that this issue will naturally fade away notwithstanding its many promises in the field. Researchers can support this process by demonstrating the poor utility and high costs of such unstructured and purposeless data collections. Finally, further research is needed in the field of dysfunctional by-design economics and the handling of non-functional requirements. Greater focus should be placed on truly interdisciplinary research that is directly communicating with the work on matching terminology.

Acknowledgments. This work was partially funded by the European Union's Horizon 2020 project grant no. 740829 and 778615, the Luxembourg National Research Fund project PETIT grant agreement no. 10486741, the National Science Foundation grant agreements CNS-1330596 and SBE-1513957, under the Brandeis privacy initiative DARPA, AFRL grant agreement no. FA8750-15-2-0277, the Research Foundation Flanders, the Research Fund KU Leuven, and the KUL-PRiSE research project.

The views and conclusions contained herein are those of the authors and should not be interpreted as necessarily representing the official positions, policies or endorsements, either expressed or implied, of the institutions they are affiliated with, the EDPS, the National Science Foundation, DARPA, the Air Force Research Laboratory or the US Government.

We thank Ian Oliver and Jef Ausloos and the APF reviewers for their valuable input and comments, and all workshop participants for their contributions and stimulating discussions.

References

1. Hoepman, J.-H.: Privacy design strategies. In: Cuppens-Boulahia, N., Cuppens, F., Jajodia, S., Abou El Kalam, A., Sans, T. (eds.) SEC 2014. IAICT, vol. 428, pp. 446–459. Springer, Heidelberg (2014). https://doi.org/10.1007/978-3-642-55415-5_38

2. ENISA: Privacy Enhancing Technologies: Evolution and State of the Art A Community Approach to PETs Maturity Assessment (2016). https://www.enisa.europa.eu/publications/pets-evolution-and-state-of-the-art

3. Schaub, F., Balebako, R., Durity, A.L., Cranor, L.F.: A design space for effective privacy notices. In: Eleventh Symposium on Usable Privacy and Security (SOUPS 2015), Ottawa, pp. 1–17. USENIX Association (2015)

4. President's Council of Advisors on Science and Technology: Big data and privacy: a technological perspective. Report to the U.S. President, Executive Office of the President, May 2014

5. Cranor, L.F.: Necessary but not sufficient: standard mechanisms for privacy notice and choice. J. Telecommun. High Technol. Law **10**, 273 (2012)

6. Cate, F.H.: The limits of notice and choice. IEEE Secur. Priv. **8**(2), 59–62 (2010)

7. Schaub, F., Balebako, R., Cranor, L.F.: Designing effective privacy notices and controls. IEEE Internet Comput. **21**(3), 70–77 (2017)

8. Wenning, R., et al.: The platform for privacy preferences 1.1 (P3P 1.1) specification (2006). https://www.w3.org/TR/2018/NOTE-P3P11-20180830/

9. Fielding, R.T., Singer, D.: Tracking preference expression (DNT) W3C candidate recommendation (2017). https://www.w3.org/TR/2017/CR-tracking-dnt-20171019/

10. Article 29 Working Party. Opinion 05/2014 on anonymisation techniques (2014). WP216. http://ec.europa.eu/justice/data-protection/article-29/documentation/opinion-recommendation/files/2014/wp216_en.pdf

11. Narayanan, A., Shmatikov, V.: Robust de-anonymization of large sparse datasets. In: 2008 IEEE Symposium on Security and Privacy, SP 2008 (2008)

12. Cavoukian, A., Castro, D.: Big data and innovation, setting the record straight: de-identification does work. In: Information and Privacy Commissioner, p. 18 (2014)

13. Hu, R., Stalla-Bourdillon, S., Yang, M., Schiavo, V., Sassone, V.: Bridging policy, regulation and practice? A techno-legal analysis of three types of data in the GDPR. In: Data Protection and Privacy: The Age of Intelligent Machines, p. 39 (2017)

14. Ye, L.R.: The value of explanation in expert systems for auditing: an experimental investigation. Expert Syst. Appl. **9**(4), 543–556 (1995)

15. Article 29 Working Party. Guidelines on transparency under regulation 2016/679 (2016). 17/EN WP260. http://ec.europa.eu/newsroom/article29/item-detail.cfm?item_id = 615250

16. Wachter, S., Mittelstadt, B., Floridi, L.: Why a right to explanation of automated decision-making does not exist in the general data protection regulation. Int. Data Priv. Law **7**, 76–99 (2017)

17. Selbst, A.D., Powles, J.: Meaningful information and the right to explanation. Int. Data Priv. Law **7**(4), 233–242 (2017)

18. Biran, O., Cotton, C.: Explanation and justification in machine learning: a survey. In: IJCAI-17 Workshop on Explainable AI (XAI) Proceedings, pp. 8–13 (2017). http://www.intelligentrobots.org/files/IJCAI2017/IJCAI-17_XAI_WS_Proceedings.pdf#page=8

19. Lipton, Z.C.: The mythos of model interpretability. In: ICML 2016 Workshop on Human Interpretability in Machine Learning (WHI 2016) (2016). http://zacklipton.com/media/papers/mythos_model_interpretability_lipton2016.pdf

20. Edwards, L., Veale, M.: Slave to the algorithm? Why a 'right to an explanation' is probably not the remedy you are looking for. Duke Law Technol. Rev. **16**, 18 (2017)

21. Article 29 Working Party. Guidelines on automated individual decision-making and profiling for the purposes of regulation 2016/679 (2018). 17/EN WP251rev.01. http://ec.europa.eu/newsroom/article29/item-detail.cfm?item_id=612053

22. Obar, J.A., Oeldorf-Hirsch, A., The biggest lie on the internet: ignoring the privacy policies and terms of service policies of social networking services. In: TPRC 44: The 44th Research Conference on Communication, Information and Internet Policy (2016)

23. Cate, F.H.: Information security breaches: looking back & thinking ahead. Technical report Paper 233, Articles by Maurer Faculty (2008). http://www.repository.law.indiana.edu/facpub/233

24. Atzori, M., Bonchi, F., Giannotti, F., Pedreschi, D.: Anonymity preserving pattern discovery. VLDB J. **17**(4), 703–727 (2008)

25. Hansen, M., Jensen, M., Rost, M.: Protection goals for privacy engineering. In: 2015 IEEE Security and Privacy Workshops (SPW), pp. 159–166, May 2015

26. Schmidt , A., Herrmann, T., Degeling, M.: From interaction to intervention: an approach for keeping humans in control in the context of socio-technical systems. In: 4th Workshop on Socio-Technical Perspective in IS development (STPIS 2018) (2018)

27. Ribeiro, M.T., Singh, S., Guestrin, C.: "Why should I trust you?": explaining the predictions of any classifier. In: Proceedings of the 22nd ACM SIGKDD International Conference on Knowledge Discovery and Data Mining, KDD 2016, pp. 1135–1144. ACM, New York (2016)

28. Gürses, S., van Hoboken, J.: Privacy after the agile turn. In: Selinger, E., Polonetsky, J., Tene, O. (eds.) The Cambridge Handbook of Consumer Privacy (Cambridge Law Handbooks, pp. 579–601). Cambridge University Press, Cambridge (2018). https://doi.org/10.1017/9781316831960.032

29. Ding, L., Bao, J., Michaelis, J.R., Zhao, J., McGuinness, D.L.: Reflections on provenance ontology encodings. In: McGuinness, D.L., Michaelis, J.R., Moreau, L. (eds.) IPAW 2010. LNCS, vol. 6378, pp. 198–205. Springer, Heidelberg (2010). https://doi.org/10.1007/978-3-642-17819-1_22

30. Oliver, I.: Privacy Engineering: A Data Flow and Ontological Approach. CreateSpace Independent Publishing, July 2014. 978-1497569713

31. Anton, A.I., Earp, J.B.: A requirements taxonomy for reducing web site privacy vulnerabilities. Requirements Eng. **9**(3), 169–185 (2004)
32. Solove, D.J.: A taxonomy of privacy. Univ. Pennsylvania Law Rev. **154**(3), 477 (2006). GWU Law School Public Law Research Paper No. 129
33. Solove, D.J.: Conceptualizing privacy. Calif. Law Rev. **90**(4), 1087–1155 (2002)
34. Kost, M., Freytag, J.C., Kargl, F., Kung, A.: Privacy verification using ontologies. In: ARES, pp. 627–632. IEEE (2011)
35. Kern, T.: Flight Discipline. McGraw-Hill Education, New York (1998)
36. Card, A.J., Ward, J.R., Clarkson, P.J.: Beyond FMEA: the structured what-if technique (SWIFT). J. Healthc. Risk Manag. **31**, 23–29 (2012)
37. Scandariato, R., Wuyts, K., Joosen, W.: A descriptive study of Microsoft's threat modeling technique. Requirements Eng. **20**(2), 163–180 (2015)
38. Gawande, A.: The Checklist Manifesto. Profile Books (2011)
39. Reason, J.T.: Managing the Risks of Organizational Accidents. Ashgate, Farnham (1997)
40. Pfleeger, S.L.: Risky business: what we have yet to learn about risk management. J. Syst. Softw. **53**(3), 265–273 (2000)
41. Oliver, I.: Experiences in the development and usage of a privacy requirements framework. In: 24th IEEE International Requirements Engineering Conference, RE 2016, Beijing, China, 12–16 September 2016, pp. 293–302. IEEE Computer Society (2016)
42. Power, M.: The risk management of everything. J. Risk Finance **5**, 58–65 (2004)

RESPECT4U – Privacy as Innovation Opportunity

Marc van Lieshout[(⊠)] and Sophie Emmert

TNO, Anna van Buerenplein 1, 2595 DA The Hague, The Netherlands
marc.vanlieshout@tno.nl

Abstract. The right to privacy is enshrined in the European charter of fundamental rights. The right to data protection is a relatively novel right, also
enshrined in the same European charter. While these rights seem to focus on a
defensive and protective approach, they also give rise to a positive and constructive interpretation. The GDPR may act as driver for innovation. Not only
for assuring a better way of dealing with personal data, but including a more
encompassing approach of assuring privacy. RESPECT4U offers a framework
of seven privacy principles that help organisations in promoting this positive
attitude towards the reconciliation of privacy and innovation: Responsible
processing, Empowering data subjects, Secure data handling, Pro-active risk
management, Ethical awareness, Cost-benefit assessment, Transparent data
processing. This paper introduces the background of RESPECT4U, and elaborates the seven principles that form its foundation. Together they demonstrate
that privacy can act as innovation driver.

Keywords: Privacy · Data protection · Innovation
Privacy as innovation driver · Privacy principles · GDPR
Responsible data processing · Empowerment · Transparency

1 Introduction

The General Data Protection Regulation (GDPR) has led to heightened attention for
how organisations process personal data. A relevant driver of this attention stems from
the relatively high fines that organisations face when they are not compliant. These
fines have parachuted the concern for an appropriate processing of personal data to the
Boards of organisations. No single middle-manager can bear responsibility for fines
with an order of magnitude of 2 till 4% of annual turnover. In the slipstream of these
high fines the concern for data breaches and the negative impact of these breaches on
the reputation of an organization adds to the growing awareness for 'doing the things
right'. The GDPR also leads to controllers pushing the responsibility for a compliant
processing backward to the processors they are working with.[1] Controllers are obliged

---

[1] See the blog post of Daniel Solove on this issue: https://teachprivacy.com/the-hidden-force-that-will-drive-gdpr-compliance/; last accessed 2018/04/08.

© Springer Nature Switzerland AG 2018
M. Medina et al. (Eds.): APF 2018, LNCS 11079, pp. 43–60, 2018.
https://doi.org/10.1007/978-3-030-02547-2_3

to work only with processors that meet GPPR-requirements.[2] Uncertainty on how the GDPR will be supervised, how data protection authorities will fill in their role, and how the many open issues within the GDPR need to be understood, feeds criticism on the GDPR as being an instrument that might negatively impact business opportunities in today's data driven economy (London Economics 2017). Losses could amount up to 58 billion UK pounds for the whole of the EU (UK still included). These losses come among others from organisations moving data analytics back to in house processing instead of hiring third party capacity with specific expertise and competences in doing the analytics. So, innovation might be stifled by these organizational responses.

When these negative implications would largely determine the impact of the GDPR in the long run, one might wonder whether the GDPR could play a role in promoting the free flow of data within the EU and in being an instrument in the Single Market Strategy of the European Commission. This is an interesting dispute by itself. Long term economic perspectives of the strategy chosen are based upon presumptions of how market players will react. One reaction one can already observe is an increasing awareness by these market players for the additional requirements posed by the GDPR. Staying in business within Europe means meeting these requirements. The two-staged strategy that is adopted by some big players (such as Google and Facebook) means that they are both looking for alternatives outside the influence of the GDPR while not alienating themselves fully from the European scene.[3]

Whether this approach will be profitable for European citizens ánd for the European economy in the long run is hard to predict yet. At least we can notice the emergence of a consultancy market that focuses on providing advice and supporting organisations in becoming compliant.[4] This by itself is a positive side-effect of the GDPR.

In this paper we would like to argue that the rigid and encompassing implementation of the GDPR has a beneficial impact on the innovative capacity of organisations and will lead to new innovative services. Our approach is conceptual yet. We are not able to provide empirical evidence for our assumptions in this stage. We only are able to develop a 'line of reasoning' that clarifies our position with respect to the potentially beneficial role of privacy as a driver for innovation. Recent events that highlight the detrimental implications of surreptitious use of personal data for political purposes

---

[2] GDPR, art 24(1): "… the controller shall implement appropriate technical and organisational measures to ensure and to be able to demonstrate that processing is performed in accordance with this Regulation.", Art 28 (1) "… the controller shall use only processors providing sufficient guarantees to implement appropriate technical and organisational measures in such a manner that processing will meet the requirements of this Regulation and ensure the protection of the rights of the data subject."

[3] See for instance https://www.privacylaws.com/Publications/enews/International-E-news/Dates/2018/4/Facebook-shifts-15-billion-users-to-avoid-GDPR/ and https://martech-today.com/facebook-well-implement-gdpr-privacy-protections-globally-213545, showing both sides of the coin. Last accessed 2018/05/20.

[4] See for instance https://gdprindex.com/, a website that provides an overview of firms active in providing consultancy services of various kinds.

demonstrate that the overall societal attitude towards these kind of practices is changing and may promote more responsible organisational behaviour.[5]

This paper starts by outlining the distinction between privacy and data protection and will outline how the two concepts can be reconciled in an approach to promote innovation. Then, RESPECT4U is introduced and elaborated. Basically, RESPECT4U captures seven privacy principles that together create a framework to support organisations in combining 'doing the things right' with 'doing the right things'.

2   Privacy and Data Protection: Two Sides of the Same Coin

2.1   Privacy as a Concept

It is a challenge to succinctly define privacy. Many authors have claimed that such a succinct definition simply cannot be provided, given the differences between countries, cultures and civilisations in how issues such as what is considered to be public and what private are evaluated, what role property plays and how politics is organised. One line of reasoning refers back to ancient civilisations, such as the Greek one in which being public meant being able to act as a person (Van der Sloot 2017). The etymological source of the word 'person', from 'per sonare', basically stipulates the ability to be heard. It refers to the habit of actors in the theatres wearing a mask that enabled amplifying the voice. Opposite the public arena we find the private household, the domain of wives and slaves. The root of the word 'private' is the word 'privare', meaning being robbed of something.[6] It was important to be able to act as a public person in ancient times. While the household was shielded off public appearance, this was mainly because of the non-relevance of the household, and not because of respect. In a similar vein were slaves property of their owner. In present times, we consider the home and the body to be sacrosanct (though admittedly, this is not always enacted). We find references to the privacy of the home in the eighteenth century, through the following statement of the English statesman William Pitt the Elderly:

"The poorest man may in his cottage bid defiance to all the forces of the Crown. It may be frail, its roof may shake; the wind may blow through it; the storms may enter; the rain may enter – but the King of England cannot enter; all his forces dare not cross the threshold of the ruined tenement".[7] (Holvast 1986, 11–12)

---

[5] The 'Cambridge Analytica' casus is a clear point in respect. This organisation has acted quite irresponsibly in its strive to influence people's behaviour by illegitimately using knowledge on their postings on social media. While one could question whether 'nudging people' is unethical by itself, the unlawful processing of personal data by Cambridge Analytica is a clear infringement of legal obligations in offering choice and consent to people.

[6] The second meaning given in the dictionary is to liberate. The meaning of 'being robbed' is however also present in the Spanish meaning of the word 'privar'.

[7] The statement was made during a debate in the House of Parliament in 1773 where it was discussed whether the Crown's forces were entitled to search in houses for evidence of the production of cider in order to levy taxes. See https://www.chroniclesmaga-zine.org/blogs/thomas-fleming/defending-the-family-castle-part-i/; last accessed 2018/04/08.

The very physical dimensions of privacy (the home and the body) are complemented by non-physical dimensions. This has two faces: privacy with respect to relations and privacy with respect to information.[8] The last one is a typical dimension that increasingly becomes relevant in modern societies. Large parts of current behaviour is intermediated by digital technologies. Controlling access to these technologies and especially controlling access to one's behaviour that becomes manifest through these digital technologies is a 'natural' extension of this notion of privacy. The emerging lack of control on who should have access to one's behaviour formed the starting point for US based lawyers Samuel Warren and Louis Brandeis to write their seminal paper on the right to be let alone (Warren and Brandeis 1890). Samuel Warren was married to a senator's daughter and his wife was portrayed in a tabloid without her knowing it. In these days, it became possible to photograph a person without that person's consent, due to creating camera's that were lighter and mobile and especially faster in producing the photo. This invasion of privacy was condemned in the article. Their article is still worth reading, for instance for the manner in which technological progress and its impact on society is tackled.

Attention for privacy, or the right to respect for a private life, became one of the focal points in the 1948 Universal Declaration of Human Rights in the aftermath of the Second World War. The Declaration was an attempt to organize universally accepted ethical standards that should help preventing the experienced atrocities of the Second World War, including its devastating infringements upon human rights.

The European Charter of Fundamental Rights, enacted in 2009 through the Lisboan Treaty, reiterates this right to respect for privacy. The Universal Declaration of Human Rights states in article 12: "No one shall be subjected to arbitrary interference with his privacy, family, home or correspondence, nor to attacks upon his honour and reputation." The European Charter of Human Rights formulates in Article 7 that "[e]veryone shall have the right to respect for his or her private life, family life, the home and communications".

While Declaration and Charter coincide in embracing the broader concept of privacy, the European Charter is the first declaration that pays explicit attention to the respect to data protection. Article 8 of the Charter defines a right to the protection of personal data. These data must be processed "fairly for specified purposes and on the basis of the consent of the person concerned or some other legitimate basis laid down by law. Everyone has the right of access to data which has been collected concerning him or her, and the right to have it rectified."

2.2   The Concept of Data Protection

Article 8 of the European Charter for Fundamental Rights characterises a relevant development in dealing with personal data. While the emergence of data processing equipment was only in its infancy shortly after the Second World War, and no direct

---

[8] See (Finn et al. 2013) for an elaboration of seven dimensions of privacy including the right to relational privacy. In this paper we will stick to the four privacy dimensions that are commonly recognized as relevant ones: information privacy, relational privacy, spatial privacy and bodily privacy.

connection between the protection of privacy and the protection of personal data can be inferred from the acceptance of the Universal Declaration of Human Rights, the scenery changed considerably in the decades to come. This heightened attention for the impact of data processing on the respect to the privacy of citizens led to the USA Privacy Act in 1974. This Privacy Act was the direct consequence of a 1973 report of the Department of Health, Education and Welfare on the rights of citizens concerning records made on them.[9] The report recommended that no database should be kept in secret, that individuals should be informed about processing their data in databases, and that a so-called Code of Fair Information Practices should be established. This Code should detail issues such as purpose specification, right to be notified, right to access, right to rectify and the obligation of the processor to assure the quality of the data processed. The OECD adopted the approach of the HEW and the US Privacy Act and initiated the Fair Information Principles in 1980 (updated in 2013, keeping the original principles intact) (OECD 1980). In 1981, the Council of Europe followed suit with Convention 108, "Convention for the Protection of Individuals with regard to Automatic Processing of Personal Data" (Council of Europe 1981). The Convention used the same principles as set out in the OECD Fair Information Principles. It introduced the notion of special categories of data (article 6). Principles such as purpose specification, collection limitation, quality of data, use limitation and storage limitation are key to the Convention (article 5). Right to access, rectification, erasure and presentation of a copy of the data are present in the Convention (article 8), as well as necessary security safeguards (article 7). Being signed by five Member States of the Council of Europe would make the Convention entering into force, implying that these Member States should implement domestic laws reflecting the Convention. The Convention entered into force October 1, 1985, being signed by France, Germany, Norway, Spain and Sweden.[10] Several countries followed suit in the following years. The last signatory yet is Tunesia in 2017, turning the total number of signatories to 51 at this moment in time.

The principles set out in the OECD FIP and Convention 108 were copied into the Data Protection Directive of 1995 for the countries of the than European Community. Being a Directive, many differences in the implementation between Member States exist. This caused confusion and a distorted level playing field, for instance for business organisations that wanted to roll out business propositions over various EU countries. This has led to the harmonisation over countries within the European Economic Area (Member States of EU plus Lichtenstein, Iceland and Norway) by the General Data Protection Regulation (2016/679/EU).

---

[9] See https://epic.org/privacy/hew1973report/ for a web-based version of the report. Last accessed 2018/04/08.

[10] See https://www.coe.int/en/web/conventions/full-list/-/conventions/treaty/108/signatures; last accessed 2018/04/08.

2.3 Innovation Privacy and Data Protection

The previous sections have presented concise overviews of privacy and data protection as concepts. Both deal with the protection of persons, with safeguarding fundamental rights persons may exercise. While infringement of the right to privacy means that some substantive right is infringed (such as the violation of the body, the home, the reputation of a person), an infringement of the right to data protection means that a procedural right is infringed (such as the right to assurance of the quality of the data processed, or the right to be informed about the data processing) (Gellert and Gutwirth 2013). The distinction between the two types of infringements is visible in the Courts dealing with the infringement: in case of privacy one ends up at the Court of Human Rights in Strassbourg, while in case of data protection one ends up at the Court of Justice in Luxembourg.

The procedural rights as formulated in the GDPR are meant to assure the substantive rights to privacy as laid down in the European Charter (and in constitutional laws of European Member States). These rights thus serve an end in themselves but serve another end as well.

Returning to the objective of this paper, the issue to be tackled is thus whether the GDPR in promoting privacy enables or even enforces innovation or whether it hinders or blocks innovation. The rise in organisations offering compliance tools and services indicates that the economic impact of the GDPR is more than the study of London Economics seems to hint at (London Economics 2017). For sure, the GDPR limits specific forms of data processing that at present are at the heart of the business processes of data brokers and data intensive organisations of any kind (financial services, public services, traffic and transport, energy, health care, etc.). The services offered by these organisations may be at odds with the GDPR while they represent business opportunities. But being at odds with the GDPR implies that these business opportunities may confront human rights and may have adverse societal and individual consequences. The challenge to be addressed is the balance between economic growth perspectives for business organisations involved, interesting new services at the expense of potentially societal implications such as discrimination, exclusion and stigmatisation, and societal justice. While we have experienced the rise of practices that emphasize the first part of the balance (economic growth) we now observe the pendulum swinging back to include the other part of the balance as well. We signal a similarity with the (societal) debate that started in the sixties of the past century and that by now has led to heightened attention for including sustainability objectives in industrial and service practices, leading to organisations profiling themselves as being sustainable and green.[11]

The question to be posed is whether the GDPR promotes specific innovative practices and if so, how these could be organised. We have developed a framework, RESPECT4U, that demonstrates how these innovative practices might be identified from a GDPR perspective. We will now turn to this framework.

---

[11] This similarity may be larger than it seems to be at first glance. The GDPR may have a similar impact on business processes: from resistance to embracement and inclusion in the very heart of business activities.

3 RESPECT4U as Innovation Framework

In our work as privacy researchers of a Research and Technology Organisation we see many organisations struggling with the implementation of the GDPR. The requirements the GDPR imposes on organisations are not be underestimated. While this heightened attention for how to responsibly process personal data for sure has a positive impact for the privacy of the data subjects it easily leads to administratively 'ticking the boxes' as a way of coming to terms with the GDPR. This is enforced by uncertainty about how the Data Protection Authorities (DPAs) will fill in their role. While the GDPR explicitly demands the DPAs to be advisory and supportive, next to tracking the 'bad guys', the fines DPAs may enforce easily tips the balance for organisations to remaining on the safe, administrative, side.

This focus on fulfilling legal obligations without additional benefits for organisations may be a dead end in itself. No positive stimulus, no reward, seems to be baked into the legislative approach. On the other hand one can notice a positive undertone in quite a few contributions on the role the GDPR might play in organisational processes concerning how to deal with the data of their customers, clients, patients, students, etc.[12] And this positive tone is not only uttered by 'usual suspects', such as the International Association of Privacy Professionals[13], but by advertisement organisations such as Experian as well.[14] The basic assumption is that the GDPR may have a positive impact upon trust of consumers on how organisations will handle their data. Since the GDPR requires all organisations to implement specific requirements, simply fulfilling these requirements will not easily serve as a Unique Selling Point for organisations. Of course, frontrunners can do so and can offer this as a feature to differentiate themselves at the market place. But in the end, all organisations need to comply. Our position is that it is not so much compliance that is at stake but the manner in which organisations adopt a comprehensive perspective vis-à-vis the role of processing personal data in their business processes, and the manner in which they embed this, communicate it and innovate their services and products taking responsible processing as a starting point. And this is precisely where RESPECT4U enters the scene.

3.1 The Privacy Principles of RESPECT4U

RESPECT4U is an acronym referring to seven privacy principles:

- *Responsible* processing of personal data
- *Empowering* data subjects
- *Secure* data handling
- *Pro-active* engagement of data processes

---

[12] See for instance https://www.computerweekly.com/opinion/Why-Europes-GDPR-privacy-regulation-is-good-for-business; https://www.computerweekly.com/news/252435774/GDPR-will-have-positive-ripple-effect-say-US-consumer-group. Last accessed 2018/04/14.

[13] https://iapp.org/news/a/why-the-gdpr-is-good-for-businesses/. Last accessed 2018/04/14.

[14] https://www.edq.com/uk/blog/8-reasons-why-the-gdpr-can-help-boost-your-business/; last accessed 2018/04/14.

- *Ethical awareness* on (long term) implications
- *Cost and benefit assessment* of responsible data processing
- *Transparency* re. internal organisation and data subject.

The addition '4U' has a specific meaning. It refers to 'U', being the data subject, '2U', being the data subject in relation to another person, '3U', representing 'three is a crowd', and '4U', referring to the crowd of crowds or society at large. RESPECT4U indicates that privacy is not only an individual concern but has its footing in democratic society itself and should also be evaluated on its impact on democracy as a political system (Bennet and Raab 2006).

The seven principles of RESPECT4U capture the obligations of data controllers and processors and meet the rights of data subjects as these are laid down in the GDPR. But it does not stop there. It also asks attention for new challenges ahead, such as those emerging from new data analytics and use of sophisticated machine learning techniques. And it also asks to look at the value perspective of privacy, both from an ethical position and from a more mundane position, looking at costs and benefits.[15] While the acronym presents the various principles in a specific order this is just an artefact of using an acronym that enables an easy manner of organising activities and instruments. It does not include a value judgement regarding the relevance of the principles. Still, the whole process starts with the need to responsibly process personal data. This being followed by attention for empowering data subjects puts emphasis on the relevance of involving data subjects, but that is just coincidentally second. Together, the seven RESPECT4U privacy principles help promoting innovative behaviour of organisations by 'doing the right thing' (safeguarding privacy) in the right manner (data protection). We will now introduce the various principles.

Responsible Processing

The first principle is the principle that organisations are determined to act responsibly with the personal data they process. The current data society has turned (personal) data into the fuel of many business activities.[16] The data ecosystem that has emerged and that embeds data brokers, data analytics organisations, data scrapers, etc., has become extremely complex over the past few years (Stone 2014). There is no need to be naive about the economic value of personal data, the business processes that are yet in place to capitalize on these data and the potentially adverse implications that this may have on the privacy of individuals.[17] But this does not mean that it is a complete lost case. As indicated above, the past has demonstrated that public awareness may have a

---

[15] Costs and benefits do not only relate to financial or monetary aspects, as we will demonstrate further on.

[16] This refers to the famous saying that data is the new oil. Quoted by many, the origin of the quote is not fully known. See https://www.quora.com/Who-should-get-credit-for-the-quotedata-is-the-new-oil. Last accessed 2018/04/14.

[17] The recent uproar concerning the activities of Cambridge Analytica and the role Facebook played is a point in respect.

decisive influence on business activities and business behaviour.[18] The basic principle thus is that organisations are actively willing to promote responsible processing of personal data, and are willing to demonstrate this responsibility.

The GDPR offers a number of instruments that organisations can use for demonstrating accountability. Code of conducts and certification mechanism are novel instruments. The manner in which certification mechanisms will enter the market place, is an open issue.[19] They may play a role in standardizing requirements and ways of working. Certification organisations, such as EuroPriSe[20], are already active on the market and offer GDPR compliant certification procedures. Issues that need to be resolved are the transferability of certificates between countries, and the role DPAs will play as accrediting organisation, next to national accreditation organisation. The same goes for codes of conduct. Various branches are already active in creating branch-oriented code of conducts that in due time will have to be approved by national DPAs. Branch-wide subscribed codes of conduct may promote a positive image among clients and customers.

Another instrument to be used is the Privacy Maturity Model. The Dutch Centre for Information Security and Privacy Protection (CIP) has used the PMM to develop a guideline that helps organisations in scoring how privacy mature they already are.[21] This uses the well-known gradation from ad hoc up to fully organised.[22] The model can be used to score progress on the implementation of the GDPR. Consultancy organisations are developing their own schemes to be put on the market, and add options for fulfilling the GDPR obligations. These are valuable instruments, as long as they are combined with additional instruments.

They may be accompanied by an internal Data Protection Officer who is entitled to supervise internal processes. A DPO may supervise the legitimacy of goals and grounds of data processing within the organisation, and offer support when it comes to fulfilling obligations such as keeping a register of processing operations and performing a data protection impact assessment. The DPOs are the contact point of the organisation with the national DPA in case of issues concerning data protection, including data breaches.

---

[18] Public (and political) awareness concerning the need to change to sustainable production modes has had a decisive influence on the dominant role of becoming and being sustainable. While differences with 'data pollution' we are experiencing today are obvious, both practices share some similarities as well. See for instance the presentation of Van den Hove during a Conference on sustainability organized by EWI Vlaanderen. https://www.ewivlaanderen.be/sites/default/files/rri_sep2016_vandenhoven.pdf. Last accessed 2018/05/21.

[19] We are participating in a research project for the European Commission in which we study the manner in which art 42 and 43 of the GDPR should be understood and should be operationalized. The results of this study are not publicly available yet, as the study has not been completed. Finalization is foreseen for June 2018.

[20] See https://www.european-privacy-seal.eu/EPS-en/Home; last accessed 2018/04/16.

[21] See https://cip-overheid.nl/privacy-baseline; last accessed 2018/04/16.

[22] Initially developed for scoring the maturity of business processes in the Capability Maturity Model (Paulk 2002).

Empowering Data Subjects

The GDPR is focused on offering data subjects more control over their data. After all, the data somehow originate from their activities and behaviour. The GDPR obliges controllers and processors to organise the rights of data subjects. Instead of just indicating to data subjects that their data are safe and appropriate safeguards have been taken – as can be read in current privacy statements – while data subjects have no clue about the kind of data processed and the kind of security safeguards taken, RESPECT4U promotes a more active role by controllers.

Empowering data subjects means they get a real stance in the data processing operations. This starts by being fully informed on what data processing operations are being executed. While this is an obligation, imposed by the GDPR, it can be fulfilled in various manners. We propose to start by the information needs of data subjects and by their basic behavioural predispositions, thus including behavioural economics as a discipline that may be of help.

Concerning the first, the information needs, we build upon the work of Alan Westin, who has executed many surveys investigating privacy preferences of data subjects (Kumaraguru and Cranor 2005). Westin differentiates between three main categories of persons in respect to their privacy attitude: fundamentalists, pragmatists and unconcerned. The fundamentalists have a very critical attitude vis-à-vis organisations, pragmatists adopt a pragmatic attitude and are willing to negotiate with organisations and unconcerned have a relatively relaxed attitude vis-à-vis organisations and trust these organisations to take their interests into account. The main thing to emphasize here is not whether this model captures the intricacies of human behaviour sufficiently, but rather to open up an undifferentiated perspective on the data subject. In our research we have performed similar surveys to understand the impact of perceptions and preferences of persons (Vos et al. 2016; Van den Broek et al. 2017). This has led to the creation of a model in which we change the perspective from privacy as the determinant factor where to focus on towards 'willingness to share' as the predominant feature relevant to take into account. This model is based on insights offered by behavioural economics, presuming that the manner in which people are willing to engage in a negotiation will depend on the offer made, behavioural predispositions and the context. Several experiments show the relevance of the behavioural predispositions and contextual factors (Acquisti 2009, 2016; Jentsch et al. 2012). Many behavioural characteristics influence the privacy attitude (and the willingness to share) of persons. When informing data subjects these differences should be taken into account.

Secondly, next to informing people, it is relevant to determine what kind of control should be exercised by data subjects. Again, we use the differentiation between privacy preferences, attitudes and contextual factors on how to offer control. Overall, people indicate they appreciate the option to control (Vos et al. 2016; Van den Broek et al. 2017). But exercising meaningful control implies that data subjects fully understand the impact of their choices. Once more, given the complexity of the data ecosystem that has been created one cannot presume that these complexities will be understood by all. Using distinct categories of data subjects may help in the way control should be structured. From a number of experiments we performed for commercial organisations we learned that offering meaningful information and control was supportive to the willingness to share. Overall, data subjects were quite open in sharing data for public interest issues (such as crowd management and health issues) as long as they could be sure that their data would only be used for these purposes.[23]

Security

The third privacy principle relates to secure handling of personal data. Three perspectives can be distinguished:

1. The secure storage of data
2. The secure processing of data
3. The secure access to data

The first of these issues is well understood. Encrypted storage of data is part of normal practices. ISO norms (27001) require usage of encryption keys sufficiently strong to prevent data easily be deciphered when hacked or coincidentally released.

The second and the third bullet point are more open to innovative approaches. New cryptographic approaches are under development for the secure processing of data. Homorphic encryption and multiparty computation are techniques that enable processing of encrypted data in encrypted space such that meaningful results still can be derived (Erkin et al. 2012; Bost et al. 2014; Veugen et al. 2015). New techniques are under development that have the algorithms transferred to the data instead of the other way around.[24] Another technique combines polymorphic encryption and pseudonymization (Verheul and Jacobs 2017). While a number of these techniques are embedded in pilot projects, they are not sufficiently mature to be presented as a commercial product. One such product, the IRMA technology, has created its own foundation seeking for interested commercial parties to explore the potential of this novel attribution based credential system, minimizing data that are needed to identify a person in specific situations.[25] All these techniques, while partly still in their infancy, will help organisations to create more secure data processing systems that not only are more secure than current ones but that also directly help in promoting privacy respecting practices.

Pro-active Attitude

The fourth privacy principle relates to the newly introduced principles in the GDPR concerning the data protection impact assessment (DPIA), and data protection by default and design. These principles underscore the risk approach of the GDPR. Identification of risks and presentation of mitigating measures to reduce the risks such that they become manageable (or the risk residue is considered to be acceptable) are crucial elements for controllers in coming to terms with their legal obligations. While several instruments are on the market, helping organizations to perform a data protection impact assessment, the concept of data protection by design is as yet not really understood. The GDPR mentions data minimization as data protection principle and pseudonymization as instrument to achieve data protection by design. But this seems to

---

[23] These experiments were performed for commercial organisations. We cannot support these claims by public data yet. We hope to do so in the near future.

[24] See https://www.dtls.nl/fair-data/personal-health-train/; last accessed 2018/04/15.

[25] See https://privacybydesign.foundation/irma/; last accessed 2018/04/15.

be not more than just an initial (though relevant) step. Using pseudonymization by default in organizing the processing of personal data will definitely have a beneficial impact upon the protection of rights and freedoms of data subjects. But there are more options to be explored.

The DPIA is an instrument that is already part of standard repertoire of many organisations and national DPAs (Wright and De Hert 2012). The focus of DPIA's is on the possible infringements of data processing on the rights and freedoms of individuals. These individuals can be data subjects but they can also be persons affected by the processing without having their personal data processed. This is a consequence of profiling. Having profiles introduces the risk of being victimized by proxy, for instance because a specific profile has a geographic basis and an individual living in the specific geographic location is considered to fit to the profile. These kinds of risks need to be taken into account when performing a DPIA. One of the major challenges for identifying the level of risk is whether the risk should be seen as a high risk or as an ordinary risk. Though the GDPR adopts the basic approach of risk being a function of frequency of occurrence and level of impact, it hardly details how a high risk should be defined.[26] It is rather obvious that the engineering approach of risk, that is based upon industrial tests of components of instruments, will not work in determining the likelihood of occurrence of an infringement of rights and freedoms, let alone the determination of the impact when an infringement occurs. Within the research organisation we are working in, PhD students work on how the engineering approach of a risk can be reconciled with a legal and societal perspective.[27] This work is quite relevant given the heightened attention for risk in the GDPR, and the fact that through risk the protection of persons with respect to the processing of their data has direct links with the notion of the right to privacy and the avoidance of infringements on rights and freedoms of data subjects. Concerning data protection by design, Ann Cavoukian has pioneered in offering a set of privacy by design principles (Cavoukian 2011). This approach has meanwhile been taken a step further by privacy engineers. They have organised themselves in a network and they have started working on the elaboration of so-called privacy strategies and privacy patterns (Colesky et al. 2016; Danezis et al. 2014).[28] The work of Colesky and others focuses among others on various strategies to streamline the data process itself. This leads to four design patterns: Minimize, Separate, Abstract, and Hide. It has hooks towards data subjects (Inform and Control) and to organisations (Demonstrate and Enforce). The strategies are being translated in patterns that in the end should yield

---

[26] The Article 29 Working Party has produced guidelines fort his identification but these guidelines are also not decisive and leave many items open (such as the definition of 'systematic' and 'large-scale'). The GDPR indicates that a list will be developed that may contain processing operations in need of a DPIA and a list of operations not in need of a DPIA, but it may take some time before such a list has been concluded. (Art29WP 2018)

[27] Our research organization, TNO, collaborates with the Radboud University and Tilburg University in the Privacy & Identity Lab, PI.lab, on digital privacy and electronic identity issues. The PI.lab brings together researchers of various disciplinary backgrounds in order to create a multi-disciplinary approach of privacy in current day data processing. See https: www.pilab.nl; last accessed 2018/04/16.

[28] See IPEN, International Privacy Engineering Network https://edps.europa.eu/data-protection/ipen-internet-privacy-engineering-network_en; last accessed 2018/04/15.

viable products to be used by whoever is interested. This final steps is still under construction, though for specific patterns tools are already available.[29]

Ethical Awareness

Privacy is related to human dignity, to exercising autonomy, to mastering your own destination. The risks that will be identified in a DPIA are risks relating to the infringement of these rights and freedoms. The freedom to behave autonomously, for instance. Awareness for these infringements is growing, for a number of reasons. For one, the practice of nudging that prominently came to the fore in the Facebook-Cambridge Analytica case, might indicate a kind of landslide concerning the legitimacy of these practices.[30] The results of the empirical research into the personality features of the participants has been made public and are part of scientific literature (Youyou *et al.* 2015). It is the application of the results in specific contexts (endangering the right of persons to freely determine whom they should vote for) that led to societal uproar, leading to Congressional hearings in the USA and a public hearing in the European Parliament.[31]

These ethical concerns have been fed by the discussion on the ability to explain the logic of automated decision making. This is another issue that relates to the GDPR but has its own dimensions as well. Having machine learning techniques that are essentially non-deterministic implies that the logic of these algorithms can be explained up to some degree of understanding (such as "the weights used within the algorithm will vary with the input offered") but this does not lend any credibility to the outcome of the algorithm ("now you belong to a specific category; this may change however in the future, depending on new calculations"). This may lead to quite unsettling disputes, especially concerning outcomes that may have legal consequences or have a significant impact upon persons. The emergence of the Internet of Things with its impact upon automatic decision making by systems fed by sensor data (in automated driving, in household energy systems) will contribute to the need for ethical decision making as well (Hildebrandt 2015).

Other concerns relate to bias in data and bias in the algorithms used. Critical reviews have been published that demonstrate how biased data will reproduce the initial bias in its outcome and as such may have adverse selection consequences for groups of individuals that unluckily fall under these biases (EOP 2016). The reports also demonstrate the problem of being aware of what kind of biases might sneak into datasets.

Societal issues concerning how outcomes of data analyses may lead to ethical choices that have an impact upon the autonomy of persons are also demonstrated. One

---

[29] See the literature on for instance k-anonymity and trusted third parties that play a role in organizing these patterns. (Barker *et al.* 2009; Palmer *et al.* 2000).

[30] See   e.g.   https://www.nytimes.com/2018/03/19/technology/facebook-cambridge-analytica-explained.html   and   https://www.washingtonpost.com/business/understanding-the-facebook-cambridge-analytica-story-quicktake/2018/04/09/; last accessed 2018/04/16.

[31] See   https://www.washingtonpost.com/news/the-switch/wp/2018/04/10/transcript-of-mark-zuckerbergs-senate-hearing/?utm_term=.cf7c8e3ff87c and https://www.independ-ent.co.uk/news/uk/politics/mark-zuckerberg-eu-parliament-house-commons-uk-hearing-fa-cebook-data-a8361066.html; last accessed 2018/05/21.

such case relates to predictive policing. The Chicago police uses data analytics to predict gun violence. Having determined potential criminals the police pay a visit to the criminals-to-be that they will be observed in order to prevent gun violence to occur (Saunders *et al.* 2016). Another pilot has been run in the Dutch city of Eindhoven in which sensor technology was used to predict uproars in a street where youngsters came together during weekends to party. The focus was on the stifling effect these interventions may have and the ethical concerns related to these stifling effects (Galic 2016).

Finally, more 'mundane' ethical issues relate to unfair treatment, discrimination, exclusion and stigmatization as a consequence of data processing. The data processing itself may be fair but the impact may have these kinds of consequences. The complexity of present-day data ecosystems makes it more difficult to keep control over parameters that determine group profiling and consequences thereof (Van der Hoven *et al.* 2012). Coping with these ethical issues may introduce the need for ethical impact assessments and may lead to inclusion of ethical principles in designing data processing systems. This is a field of expertise that receives quite some attention in engineering disciplines, and is also known as value sensitive design (Steen and Van der Poel 2012; Van der Hoven and Manders-Huits 2009).

Costs-Benefits Assessment

Usually privacy and data protection are seen as cost factors: the organization needs to make costs for the implementation of security measures and for becoming compliant with the GDPR. Systems need to be adapted, personnel need to be trained, procedures need to be developed, implemented, maintained and supervised. Especially for small organisations, the legal expertise needed to fully understand the requirements to fulfil is not present in the organization itself, and needs to be acquired through third parties. This is costly, time consuming and when direct benefits are absent, a hurdle to overcome, in a fast-moving consumer market where new releases of products may take no longer than three months after the last one.

Balancing costs and benefits is confronted with a number of difficulties: costs can be calculated in hard coins, such as investments to be made, while benefits may be soft (increase in trust in the organization) and longer term oriented. Analyses of previous cases demonstrated that losses (in stock market value, for instance) were usually limited to a couple of days or weeks, and usually rather modest in scale (Acquisti *et al.* 2006).

Again, the Facebook/Cambridge Analytica casus may be a turning point in history, though that is at this moment in time hard to predict.[32]

Privacy is also studied in its impact on economy as a societal subsystem (Acquisti *et al.* 2016; LSE 2010). Acquisti *et al.* (2016) demonstrate that it is still pretty hard to come to conclusive arguments with respect to the economic value of privacy. The economic theory of privacy becomes more nuanced now more empirical relations have been investigated by various scholars. Apart from issues on micro-economic behaviour (see above), the existing information a-symmetry between data subjects and the

---

[32] The bankruptcy of Cambridge Analytica demonstrates that consequences of social condemnation may be severe. See https://www.reuters.com/article/us-cambridge-analytica-bank-ruptcy/cambridge-analytica-files-for-chapter-7-bankruptcy-idUSKCN1IJ0IS; last accessed 2018/05/21.

organisations processing their data leads to systems imperfections that have an impact on the innovative capacity of these data systems. To overcome this hurdle, increased transparency and investing in trust relations are key.[33]

Transparency
The last privacy principle relates to transparency. It connects transparency to trust, an essential ingredient of the relation between an organization and its clients. Studies have demonstrated the positive relation between information transparency and consumer purchasing attitudes (Baduri and Ha-Brookshire 2011) and on value chain partners (Eggert and Helm 2003). Information transparency is a concept that needs to be understood in terms of what information in what circumstances in what form to what participants for what purposes is enfolded (Turilli and Floridi 2009). The studies we performed demonstrate that people highly appreciate transparency as part of control options (Van den Broek *et al.* 2017). The transparency promoted by the GDPR may help in promoting trust in the processing of personal data by organisations and may thus have a positive impact upon service uptake. This relation is however not a strict linear one, in the sense that more transparency always positively impact upon trust. Trust online unfolds in a dialectic relation in which too much transparency may lead to a world that becomes too familiar and that may have negative consequences, for instance when transparency makes apparent that shared values and perspectives are absent (Keymolen 2016). Again, this indicates the relevance of connecting the data subject to the purposes and goals that are connected to the processing of personal data and to include user preferences in these goals and purposes.

Another perspective of transparency emphasizes the internal transparency within organizations. This implies that organizations include all personnel in its privacy policy and implement responsibilities, roles and rules in a transparent manner. One way to promote this is by appointing Privacy Champions within your organization and using them as the ambassadors of a privacy respecting approach.[34]

4   Conclusions

The seven privacy principles of RESPECT4U embed a perspective on organizational approaches to privacy that promotes privacy as a positive driver for innovation and for businesses. It refers to a number of instruments and tools organisations might implement in order to meet the requirements of the GDPR in a systematic and structured manner. Organisational measures, such as indicated in the Responsible and Transparency principle are complemented with technical measures such as indicated in the Security principle. Technical measures are also embedded in the Pro-active principle that promotes a comprehensive approach towards privacy by design/default. Technical measures as promoted in the Security principle can be implemented to achieve a proper

---

[33] See http://blogs.lse.ac.uk/mediapolicyproject/2016/07/27/the-economics-of-privacy/; last accessed 2018/04/16.

[34] See https://privasee.blog/2015/11/18/do-you-have-privacy-champions-in-your-organisation/; last accessed 2018/04/16.

realisation of privacy by design/default. The Empowerment and Transparency principle focus on understanding how consumers/citizens might be helped best in offering tools to help them exercising their rights and understanding what is done with their data. Our perspective in this respect is that it will help promoting the willingness to share data, or the willingness to remain engaged in receiving business or public offers that may be beneficial to them. In the Ethical principle we have outlined some issues that will lead to innovative practices but that also will shed light on potential show-stoppers. Cost and benefits, as last principle, will help understanding the potential business benefits of embedding privacy strategies in organisational and service oriented processes and will also demonstrate pitfalls and barriers.

All in all, the framework intends to overcome a too narrow perspective on data protection and the obligations as put forward by the GDPR. It focuses on privacy as the societal value to be respected and data protection (or, more precisely: the protection of persons with regard to the processing of their data) as the inroad to this societal value. Many of the measures proposed through any of the RESPECT4U privacy principles are oriented on fulfilling obligations of the GDPR. But in their entirety and in the combination of these principles with the measures that are aimed at furthering a better understanding of behaviour of data subjects, and understanding ethical concerns on – future – data processing activities (such as with AI), they go beyond mere compliance and offer an encompassing perspective on responsible processing of personal data, aimed at safeguarding privacy while promoting beneficial services.

The challenges to realise the real innovative potential of privacy are manifold. It requires a multi-disciplinary and multi-layered attitude. Multi-disciplinary, since it is necessary to integrate legal, technological, organizational and societal perspectives on privacy. Multi-layered since it runs from purely organizational activities to understanding behaviour and implications on a more generic level. RESPECT4U outlines an agenda that might help in coping with the various challenges in a coherent and encompassing manner. It enables the identification of practical tools and approaches that can

directly be implemented by organisations. Thirdly, it can also simply be used as a pictorial that enables discussing the 'privacy stakes' for an organisation in an inspiring manner.[35]

References

Article 29 Working Party: Guidelines on Data Protection Impact Assessment (DPIA) and determining whether processing is" likely to result in a high risk" for the purposes of Regulation 2016/679, wp248rev.01. http://ec.europa.eu/newsroom/article29/item-de-tail.cfm?item_id = 611236. Accessed 15 Apr 2018

Acquisti, A., Friedman, A., Telang, R.: Is there a cost to privacy breaches? an event study. In: ICIS 2006 Proceedings, p. 94 (2006). http://aisel.aisnet.org/icis2006/94. Accessed 16 Apr 2018

---

[35] The RESPECT4U white paper outlines the basic elements of the RESPECT4U privacy principles. See https://pilab.nl/research/respect4u.html/; last accessed 2018/05/21.

Aquisti, A.: Nudging privacy – the behavioral economics of privacy. In: IEEE Privacy & Security, November/December, pp. 72–75 (2009)

Acquisti, A., Taylor, C., Wagman, L.: The economics of privacy. J. Econ. Lit. **54**(2), 442–492 (2016)

Barker, K., et al.: A data privacy taxonomy. In: Sexton, A.P. (ed.) BNCOD 2009. LNCS, vol. 5588, pp. 42–54. Springer, Heidelberg (2009). https://doi.org/10.1007/978-3-642-02843-4_7

Baduri, G., Ha-Brookshire, J.E.: Do transparent business practices pay? Exploration of transparency and consumer purchase intention. Cloth. Text. Res. J. **29**(2), 135–149 (2011)

Bennet, C.J., Raab, C.D.: The Governance of Privacy. The MIT Press, Cambridge/London (2006)

Bost, R., Popa, R.A., Tu, S., Goldwasser, S.: Machine learning classification over encrypted data. Crypto ePrint Archive (2014). https://eprint.iacr.org/2014/331.pdf

Cavoukian, A.: Privacy by Design – The 7 Foundational Principles (2011). https://ipc.on.ca/wp-con-tent/uploads/Resources/7foundationalprinciples.pdf

Colesky, M., Hoepman, J.-H., Hillen, C.: A critical analysis of privacy design strategies. In: IEEE Security and Privacy Workshops (SPW) (2016). https://doi.org/10.1109/spw.2016.23

Council of Europe: Convention for the Protection of Individuals with regard to Automatic Processing of Personal Data. Strassbourg (2013)

Danezis, G., et al.: Privacy and Data Protection by Design – from policy to engineering. ENISA (2014)

De Vos, H., et al.: 16244 – PIME - A1602, Guidelines on inclusion of users' perception and attitude on offering control and choice with respect to health data and health data services, EIT PIME Deliverable 2 (2016)

Eggert, E., Helm, S.: Exploring the impact of relationship transparency on business relationships: a cross-sectional study among purchasing managers in German. Ind. Mark. Manag. **32**(2), 101–108 (2003)

Executive Office of the President: Big Data: A Report on Algorithmic Systems, Opportunity and Civil Rights, US Presidency (2016)

Erikin, Z., Veugen, T., Toft, T., Lagendijk, R.L.: Generating private recommendations efficiently using homomorphic encryption and data packing. IEEE Trans. Inf. Forensics Secur. **7**(3), 1053–1066 (2012)

Finn, R.L., Wright, D., Friedewald, M.: Seven types of privacy. In: Gutwirth, S., Leenes, R., De Hert, P., Poulett, Y. (eds.) Data Protection: Coming of Age. Springer, Dordrecht (2013). https://doi.org/10.1007/978-94-007-5170-5_1

Jentsch, N., Preibusch, S., Harasser, A.: Study on monetizing privacy – an economic model for pricing personal information. ENISA (2012)

Galic, M.: Covert surveillance of privileged consultations and the weakening of the legal professional privilege. Eur. Data Prot. Law Rev. **4**, 602–607 (2016)

Gellert, R., Gutwirth, S.: The legal construction of privacy and data protection. Comput. Law Secur. Rev. **29**, 522–530 (2013)

Hildebrandt, M.: Smart Technologies and the End(s) of Law. Edward Elgar Publishing, Cheltenham, Northampton (2015)

Keymolen, E.: Trust on the line – a philosophical exploration of trust in the networked era. Erasmus University, Rotterdam (2016)

Kumaraguru, P., Cranor, L.F.: Privacy Indexes: A Survey of Westin's Studies, CMU-ISRI-5-138, Carnegie Mellon University (2005)

London Economics: Study on the Economic Benefits of PET; Study for the European Commission, DG Justice, Freedom and Security. EC, Brussel (2010)

Paulk, M.: Capability maturity model. In: J.-J. Macinaik (ed.) Encyclopedia of Software Engineering, Wiley Online Library (first published 2002). https://onlineli-brary.wiley.com/doi/book/, https://doi.org/10.1002/0471028959. Accessed 15 Apr 2018

Palmer, J.W., Bailey, J.P., Faraj, S.: The role of intermediaries in the development of trust on the www: the use and prominence of trusted third parties and privacy statements. J. Comput.-Mediat. Commun. **5**(3) (2000). https://doi.org/10.1111/j.1083-6101.2000.tb00342.x. Accessed 15 Apr 2018

Stone, M.: The new (and ever-evolving) direct and digital marketing ecosystem. J. Direct, Data Digit. Mark. Pract. **16**(2), 71–74 (2014)

Saunders, J., Hunt, P., Hollywood, J.S.: Predictions put into practice: a quasi-experimental evaluation of Chicago's predictive policing pilot. J. Exp. Criminol. **12**(3), 347–371 (2016)

Steen, M., Van der Poel, I.: Making values explicit during the design process. IEEE Technol. Soc. Mag. **31**(4), 63–72 (2012)

Turilli, M., Floridi, L.: The ethics of information transparency. Ethics Inf. Technol. **11**(2), 105–112 (2009)

Youyou, W., Kosinski, M., Stillwella, D.: Computer-based personality judgments are more accurate than those made by humans, PNAS (2015). https://doi.org/10.1073/pnas.1418680112. Accessed 15 Apr 2018

Van den Broek, T., Ooms, M., Friedewald, M., Van Lieshout, M., Rung, S.: Privacy and security – citizens' desires for an equal footing. In: Friedewald, M., Burgess, J.P., Cas, J., Bellanova, R., Preissl, W. (eds.) Surveillance, Privacy and Security, pp. 15–35. Routledge, Abingdon, Oxon/New York, (2017)

Van der Hoven, M.J., Lokhorst, G.J., Van de Poel, I.R.: Engineering and the problem of moral overload. Sci. Eng. Ethics **18**(1), 153–155 (2012)

Van der Hoven, J., Manders-Huits, N.: Value sensitive design. In: Berg Olsen, J.K., Pedersen, S.A., Hendricks, V.F. (eds.) A Companion to the Philosophy of Technology, Wiley Online, Chapter 86, https://doi.org/10.1002/9781444310795.ch86. Accessed 16 Apr 2018

Verheul, E., Jacobs, B.: Polymorphic encryption and pseudonymisation in identity management and medical research. NAW **5/18**(3), 168–72 (2017)

Veugen, T., De Haan, R., Cramer, R., Muller, F.: A framework for secure computations with two non-colluding servers and multiple clients, applied to recommendations. IEEE Trans. Inf. Forensics Secur. **10**(3), 445–457 (2015)

Wright, D., De Hert, P. (eds.): Privacy Impact Assessment, Law, Governance & Technology Series, vol. 6. Springer, Heidelberg (2012). https://doi.org/10.1007/978-94-007-2543-0

Privacy Implementation

Tailoring Taint Analysis to GDPR

Pietro Ferrara[1]([⊠]), Luca Olivieri[1], and Fausto Spoto[2]

[1] JuliaSoft SRL, Verona, Italy
{pietro.ferrara,luca.olivieri}@juliasoft.com
[2] Università di Verona, Verona, Italy
fausto.spoto@univr.it

Abstract. Static analysis is the analysis of software at compile time without executing it. Its goal is to explore all execution paths without needing specific inputs to drive the execution. Thanks to its wide coverage, this approach, and in particular taint analysis, has been widely applied to detect security vulnerabilities like SQL injections and XSS. The European General Data Protection Regulation requires all controllers of sensitive data to enforce an approach based on privacy by design and by default. In such context, verification and testing techniques can be applied to check if the system implementation follows the constraints identified at design time. Therefore, static program analysis might be applied to track how sensitive data is automatically managed by a software, and if such software could leak some of this data.

In this paper, we formalize and discuss how taint analysis can be extended and augmented in order to detect potential unintended leakages of sensitive data. Starting from the specification of how sensitive data is retrieved and it could be leaked, and what types of leakages are allowed by the privacy policy established by the controller of sensitive data, we apply standard taint analysis to detect potential leakages, we reconstruct the flow to check if the flow is allowed or not, and we report full details about all the flows not allowed by the privacy policy. This approach has been implemented on the Julia static analysis, and we report some promising experimental results on the OWASP WebGoat benchmark.

Keywords: Static analysis · Taint analysis · GDPR compliance

1 Introduction

The European General Data Protection Regulation[1] (GDPR) was adopted by the European Parliament on April 27, 2016, and will be enforced from May 25, 2018. Its main goal is to "lay down rules relating to the protection of natural persons with regard to the processing of personal data and rules relating to the free movement of personal data" (Article 1). This regulation imposes that the controller of sensible data adopts an approach based on the concepts of privacy by design and by default. The European Commission provided various guidelines to drive the process of GDPR compliance[2]:

---

[1] https://eur-lex.europa.eu/legal-content/EN/TXT/?uri=celex%3A32016R0679.
[2] https://ec.europa.eu/info/law/law-topic/data-protection/reform/rules-business-and-organisations/obligations/what-does-data-protection-design-and-default-mean_en.

© Springer Nature Switzerland AG 2018
M. Medina et al. (Eds.): APF 2018, LNCS 11079, pp. 63–76, 2018.
https://doi.org/10.1007/978-3-030-02547-2_4

Companies/organisations are encouraged to implement technical and organisational measures, at the earliest stages of the design of the processing operations, in such a way that safeguards privacy and data protection principles right from the start ("data protection by design"). By default, companies/organisations should ensure that personal data is processed with the highest privacy protection (for example only the data necessary should be processed, short storage period, limited accessibility) so that by default personal data isn't made accessible to an indefinite number of persons ("data protection by default").

The scope of GDPR is extremely broad, and ranges from very high level organizational to deep technical procedures. This paper focuses on a relatively small and precise aspect of the regulation, that is, the automatic treatment of personal data in software. In this context, a controller of personal data should make the best effort to ensure that software processes data in the *right* way *w.r.t.* the GDPR policy (i.e., a rather standard privacy policy establishing what kinds of sensitive data might disclosed to what kinds of leakage points) of the organization identified during the design of the system. Here the main question is: how could we (hopefully automatically) check if software manages personal data correctly w.r.t. the constraints identified at design time? What tools and approaches could help?

Static analysis has been widely applied to prove various software properties, automatically [7–9]. Its main idea is to create a mathematical model of the executions of a program and to *statically* prove (*i.e.*, without executing the code) some properties on such model. A sound static analysis creates a model that covers all possible executions. Therefore, it can prove that all possible executions of the program under the analysis satisfy the given property.

Absence of runtime errors, correct synchronization between parallel threads, absence of security vulnerabilities such as SQL injection and cross-site scripting (XSS) are just some notable examples of properties that can be proven with static analysis. Here, the scientific literature is extremely broad. In particular, information flow analysis targets privacy properties since several decades, and taint analysis has been already applied for this goal. However, such analyses normally only detect if there exists a data flow from a source of personal data to a leaking point. That is, they do not tell which type of personal data flows and along which path.

This article describes an extension of standard taint analysis that proves if software complies to a given GDPR policy. Section 2 introduces background (static analysis, information flow, taint and privacy analysis); Sect. 3 introduces the configuration of the analysis, which reflects what is already required by the same GDPR compliance process; Sect. 4 presents how the configuration is used to instrument the taint analysis engine, how information is extracted from the results of that analysis, and how a GDPR report is built from this information. We have implemented a prototype in the Julia static analyzer [25] and applied it to the analysis of WebGoat, the motivating example introduced below and used throughout the article to show how our approach works on real-world software.

1.1 WebGoat: Motivating Example

WebGoat version 6.0.1 (the last released legacy version[3]) will be the motivating example throughout this article. It "is a deliberately insecure web application maintained by OWASP[4] designed to teach web application security lessons"[5]. Since WebGoat is a web application designed to expose various security flaws, it is a particularly good target to test and show the results of various security and privacy analysis. In addition, it is a relatively small application (about 20KLOCs of Java code), hence the results of the analysis can be manually checked.

WebGoat contains two critical points interesting from a GPDR perspective:

- class org . owasp.webgoat.session . Employee represents an employee and holds sensitive data, such as name, surname, SSN, credit card number, etc...;
- the lesson class WsSAXInjection asks the user to add or change her password, and therefore deals with this sensitive data.

Moreover, WebGoat contains many standard leakage points, such as standard DB interactions or logging calls. However, we focus on two kinds of leakage:

- into a database, through some standard APIs such as java, sql, PreparedStatement and Connection, and
- into the Internet, through some standard APIs such as java, .net, URL or the Apache Element Construction Set library. This is a library that generates elements for a variety of markup languages. WebGoat uses it to build HTML pages, then sent and rendered.

2 Background

This section introduces background about information flow static analysis, its industrial application to the detection of various security vulnerabilities (such as SQL injection and XSS) and its current extensions to privacy properties.

2.1 Static Analysis

The goal of static analysis is to prove, statically (*i.e.*, without executing the code), various program properties [28]. While dynamic analysis, including testing, explores only a portion of the program, that reachable from some given inputs, static analysis can explore all possible executions. During the last decades, many different approaches have been introduced to develop static analyzers. Model checking [6], type systems [23], data and control flow analyses [18, 21], and abstract interpretation [7, 8] are the most notable and successful examples. In particular, sound static analysis guarantees

---

[3] The source code can be found at https://github.com/WebGoat/WebGoat-Legacy/releases/tag/v6.0.1.

[4] The Open Web Application Security Project, available at the web address https://www.owasp.org/index.php/Main_Page.

[5] https://www.owasp.org/index.php/Category:OWASP_WebGoat_Project.

that, if a property is proven on a program, then *all* possible executions of the program respect the given property. For instance, if a sound static analyzer proves that a program does not contain an SQL injection, then there exists no execution leading to an SQL injection.

Static program analysis has been widely applied to detect bugs in industrial software. Historically, its first application was to detect potential runtime errors in safety critical embedded software for avionics. In this context, various industrial static analyzers [1, 2, 4, 19] have been formalized, implemented and applied to real-world code. During the last decade, various research efforts [25, 27] have targeted the automatic detection of various kinds of injections and XSS vulnerabilities, achieving a relevant impact on industrial software.

2.2   Information Flow and Taint Analysis

Information flow analyses "can prove that a program cannot cause supposedly non-confidential results to depend on confidential input data" [10]. They check if private input (such as sensitive data or user-controlled input) flows explicitly (that is, through assignments) or implicitly (through conditions) to a public channel (such as the Internet or an SQL query execution routine). A lattice structure defines different (hierarchical) levels of private and public channels, allowing to check rather complicated policies.

This concept has been around for more than four decades and produced an impressive amount of scientific and industrial results. As explained by Sabelfeld and Myers [24]:

> The standard way to protect confidential data is (discretionary) access control: some privilege is required in order to access files or objects containing the confidential data. Access control checks place restrictions on the release of information but not its propagation. (...) To ensure that information is used only in accordance with the relevant confidentiality policies, it is necessary to analyze how information flows within the using program; because of the complexity of modern computing systems, a manual analysis is infeasible. (...) This analysis must show that information controlled by a confidentiality policy cannot flow to a location where that policy is violated.

Many analyses (mostly focused on specific type systems) tracking both implicit and explicit flows have been formalized and developed, with JFlow [20] being probably the most notable tool. However, they achieved relatively little industrial impact mostly because of false alarms generated by implicit flows and limited scalability. For this reason, taint analysis [12, 27], introduced more than a decade ago, relaxes standard information flow analysis by considering only explicit flows, hence reducing the number of false alarms; and using only one level of *taintedness* (that is, data can only be public or private) to improve performance. Hence the analysis checks if there is an explicit information flow from an untrusted *source* to a trusted *sink*, without intermediate *sanitization*. This generic schema has been instantiated to several critical security vulnerabilities in the OWASP Top 10 list [22], such as

– SQL injection, where sources are methods returning user's inputs, sinks are methods executing SQL queries, and sanitizers are methods escaping the input;
– cross-site scripting, where sinks are instead methods executing the given data; and
– redirection attacks, where sinks are instead parameters of methods opening an Internet connection.

Taint analysis achieved impressive industrial results, detecting many vulnerabilities in real-world software (and in particular web servers) and achieving amazing results in terms of recall and precision [5], in comparison to other (usually pattern-based) approaches. In addition, several approaches have recently applied static taint analysis to Android applications [3], a context where privacy leaks are particularly relevant.

2.3 Privacy Analysis

Recent research extends static and dynamic taint analysis to detect privacy leaks in mobile applications [11, 15]. It tries to overcome two main limitations of taint analysis. Namely, it tries to devise (i) a source sensitive analysis that allows different types of taintedness and not only a unique public/private layer; and (ii) a finer-grained tracking of sensitive data; for instance, the first eight digits of an IMEI number identify the manufacturer of the device and do not contain any information about the serial number of the device. Hence, they can be freely divulged.

3   Configuration of the GDPR Analysis

This section introduces the configuration that must be provided in order to specify a static analysis for GDPR. In particular, this configuration must specify (i) what types of sensitive data and leakage points exist; (ii) how sensitive data can be accessed and leaked; and (iii) a GDPR policy that specifies the data flows that are allowed or forbidden.

3.1   Categories of Sensitive Data and Leakage Points

Not all types of sensitive data and leakage points are equal. For instance, name and surname of a person are probably sensitive data, but social security number and credit card number are definitely more critical data from a privacy perspective. Similarly, leaking sensitive data into a log could be problematic, but it is rather more dangerous to leak the same data into an insecure Internet connection. Hence, the configuration of a GDPR analysis must include a categorization of sensitive data and leakage points. Formally, it must define sets SD (Sensitive Data) and LP (Leakage Point) of the interesting categories of sensitive data and leakage points, respectively.

Sensitive Data
Password
Address
CreditCard
Name
Surname
Phone
Salary
SSN

Leakage Point
Internet
DB

Sensitive Data	Leakage Point
Address	→ DB
Name	→ DB
Surname	→ DB
Phone	→ DB
Salary	→ DB
SSN	→ DB

(a) Sensitive data and leakage points categories.

(b) Specification of a GDPR policy.

Type	Member	Sensitive Data category
Field	WsSAXInjection.password	Password
Field	Employee.ccn	CreditCard
Field	Employee.firstName	Name
Field	Employee.lastName	Surname

(c) APIs accessing sensitive data (sources).

Type	Member	Parameter	Sensitive Data category
MethodParameter	URL.<init>	arg 0	Internet
MethodParameter	PreparedStatement.setString	arg 1	DB
MethodParameter	ecs.html.B.<init>	arg 0	Internet

(d) APIs leaking data (sinks).

Fig. 1. Configuration of a GDPR analysis for WebGoat.

Motivating Example. Figure 1a reports the categories of sensitive data and leakage points that we consider interesting for a GDPR analysis of WebGoat. They have already been informally discussed in Sect. 1.1. In particular, column A of Fig. 1a reports the categories of data considered as sensitive, while its column B specifies that the only interesting leakage points are in categories Internet or DB.

3.2 Specification of Sensitive Data and Leakage Points

Once the interesting categories have been fixed, one needs to specify how sensitive data is read and leaked at the statements of the program. If on the one hand such information needs to be manually specified, on the other hand the GDPR compliance process requires to know how sensitive data could be accessed and leaked by the software.

In this section, we will denote by St the set of statements.

Sensitive Data. The question of how a program can read sensitive data is equivalent to asking how software can read data programmatically. This can happen through method calls returning a value, or by reading fields, both in the code of the application (for instance through method calls that access a database) and in the code of the libraries. Formally, the sensitive data specification SDSpec is a partial function that relates statements to a sensitive data category: SDSpec: St → SD.

Leakage Points. The specification of leakage points reduces to how data might be passed to components outside the bounds of the main application, programmatically. In this case, this might happen by writing a field, or passing a value to a parameter of a method call. However, this applies only to components in the libraries, since the application itself can leak data only by calling APIs of external libraries. Similarly to sensitive data, the leakage points specification LPSpec is formalized by a partial function LPSpec: St $\rightarrow$ LP.

Motivating Example. Figure 1c and d report (a part of) the specification of sensitive data and leakage points for WebGoat, respectively. In particular, many fields of class Employee are tagged with the appropriate category of sensitive data (for instance, Employee.ccn returns sensitive data in category CreditCard) and field WsSAXInjection.password is tagged as Password. The leakage points java . sql . PreparedStatement.setString and Statement.executeQuery are tagged as DB (since data passed to those methods will be stored into a database); several other APIs that disclose data into the net are tagged as Internet, such as the constructor of java . net . URL, methods for handling cookies or Apache ECS elements (for instance, the class B that represents a bold text in an HTML page). The full specification includes 12 kinds of statements as sensitive data and 58 as leakage point (46 are in the ECS library).

3.3   GDPR Policy

The last part of the configuration of a GDPR analysis is the specification of a privacy policy. As discussed in the introduction, the GDPR obliges the controller of sensitive data to identify, since the design phase, what type of data it manages, and how. Hence, the GDPR policy specifies what categories of sensitive data are allowed to be disclosed to what categories of leakage points. This is represented as a set of pairs relating sensitive data categories to leakage points categories. Formally, GDPRPolicy = $\wp$(SD $\times$ LP).. For instance, the pair (Name, DB) specifies that the GDPR policy allows names to be stored into a database.

Motivating Example. Figure 1b reports a GDPR policy for the analysis of WebGoat, that we consider as a sensible formalization of what is allowed in such a program. In particular, the policy specifies that address, name or surname of an employee can be stored into a database, as well as passwords. However, it is not allowed to store credit card numbers into a database and no sensitive data should ever be leaked into the Internet.

4   Static Analysis for GDPR

This section describes how the configuration in the previous section is used to tune a taint analysis and extract information from it, useful for GDPR purposes.

4.1   Sources and Sinks

Taint analysis requires to specify a set of sources and sinks (Sources and Sinks, respectively, see Sect. 2.2). They are statements in St that access sensitive data or leak information, respectively. These sets can be derived from the configuration of a GDPR analysis, that specifies SDSpec and LPSpec as shown in Sect. 3.2. Namely, let sdspec $\in$ SDSpec and lpspec $\in$ LPSpec be the specification of sensitive data and leakage points, respectively. Taint analysis will be performed with Sources = dom (sdspec) and Sinks = dom(lpspec) (where dom is the domain of a function). There is no specification of sanitizers (as common in taint analysis) since, typically, different types of sensitive data require different sanitizers. Hence, the user must evaluate the report described in Sect. 4.4, to remove false alarms.

4.2   Taint Analysis

After a taint analysis is performed, one obtains (i) all calls to leakage points that might pass a tainted parameter: these are the potential leaks of sensitive data; and (ii) for each program point, the variables and (abstract) heap locations[6] that might be tainted.

The result of a taint analysis is a function St $\rightarrow$ $\wp$(LocalVar$\cup$HeapLoc) that, for each statement, returns the set of heap locations (HeapLoc) and local variables (LocalVar) that might be tainted there (that is, might contain sensitive data) during an execution of the program. That result can be combined with the specification LPSpec of the leakage points to infer where leaks might occur. This is expressed by a function leaks(taint, lpspec) $\in$ $\wp$(St).

4.3   Flow Reconstruction

The taint analysis described in the previous section merges all sources of sensitive data, for scalability. Hence, it cannot identify the source of sensitive data that flows into a leakage point. As observed in Sect. 2.2, existing approaches that track more than one Boolean taintedness flag do not scale to industrial software (that is, up to 100KLOCs or even 1MLOCs). Therefore, they cannot be considered as industrially viable solutions. Moreover, in any case they do not provide the flow (sequence of statements) that tainted data follows from a source to a sink.

To overcome such limitations, for each statement detected as potential leak, our analysis performs a backward flow reconstruction that, according to the semantics of program statements, looks for the origin of tainted data. The result of such reconstruction is one or more (because of conditional statements) flow graphs, that is, potentially interprocedural execution paths. The set of such flow graphs is denoted as FlowGraph.

For most statements, the backward reconstruction is straightforward and just amounts to following assignments backwards. The only operations that require careful processing are:

---

[6] How to abstract heap locations is an orthogonal problem that has been deeply investigated by the static analysis research community. We refer the interested reader to [13, 17] for more details.

- heap access. When the backwards flow reconstruction reaches an access to a heap location that returns sensitive data, it must continue with all potential writers of that (abstract) heap location, backwards. This is achieved by using the same heap abstraction described in Sect. 4.2;
- method call. When the backwards flow reconstruction reaches a method call that returns sensitive data, it must continue with all possible methods that might be called there and might return sensitive data. For that, it relies on the static call graph of the program, that approximates the callers/callees relation in a program[7].

It is possible that this flow reconstruction fails, because of a very large number of alternatives that must be followed backwards. This is particularly true when heap accesses with many writers are followed. As a result, there might be leaks for which no flow graph gets reconstructed.

Formally, we represent the backward flow rebuilder by a partial function flowRebuilder : (TaintRes × St) → $\wp$(FlowGraph). We assume that functions source : FlowGraph → St and sink : FlowGraph → St are defined on flow graphs, to return the source and the sink of the flow, respectively.

4.4 GDPR Report

Algorithm 1 GDPR report construction

1: **procedure** GDPRREPORT(sdSpec, lpSpec, GDPRpolicy, program)
2:    res ← taint(program, dom(sdSpec), dom(lpSpec))
3:    flows ← ∅
4:    unknown ← ∅
5:    **for** l ∈ leaks(res, lpSpec) **do**
6:        **if** (res, l) ∈ dom(flowRebuilder) **then**
7:            flows ← flows ∪ flowRebuilder(res, l)
8:        **else**
9:            unknown ← unknown ∪{l}
10:   unexpectedFlows ← ∅
11:   **for** f ∈ flows **do**
12:       **if** (source(f), sink(f)) ∉ GDPRPolicy **then**
13:          unexpectedFlows ← unexpectedFlows ∪ {f}
14:   **return** (unexpectedFlows, unknown)

After the flow reconstruction, it is possible to generate a report for the user of the GDPR analysis. It tells if the program satisfies the GDPR policy (Sect. 3.3) and shows the unexpected flows, in case of non-compliance.

---

[7] The construction of the static call graph is an orthogonal problem that has been widely investigate by the static analysis community. We refer the interested reader to [16, 26] for more detail.

Algorithm 1 builds the report. It requires the specification of the sources of sensitive data sdSpec ∈ SDSpec and of leakage points lpSpec ∈ LPSpec, of a GDPRpolicy ∈ GDPRPolicy and of a program ∈ Program. It runs the taint analysis with such sources and sinks (line 2). For each leak (line 5), it reconstructs and collects in flows the flows of sensitive data, by using the backward rebuilder (line 7); moreover, a set unknown collects the leakage points for which the flow reconstruction fails (line 9). Then (line 11) the algorithm checks if each flow is allowed by the GDPR policy (line 12); if not, the flow is collected into a set unexpected Flows. At the end, the algorithm returns unexpected Flows and unknown. The returned information will tell the user about (i) the potential flows of sensitive data that are not allowed by the desired GDPR policy and therefore need to be corrected; and (ii) the potential leakage points for which no flow could be reconstructed and that consequently need manual inspection, to determine if they are real issues or false alarms.

4.5   The Result of the Analysis of the Motivating Example

A prototype of the analysis described in this article has been implemented in the Julia analyzer [25]. Julia already contains an industrial implementation of taint analysis [12], widely applied to the detection of security vulnerabilities such as SQL injection and XSS [5]. It also contains a heap abstraction and the construction of a static call graph (both components are used by the taint analysis). We applied it to WebGoat with the specifications of sensitive data, leakage points and GDPR policy from Sect. 3.

Our GDPR analysis spots two flows of sensitive data that are not allowed by the GDPR policy (see Fig. 2a). The first flow is from the credit card number of an employee to the database; it occurs many times in classes that update the employee's profile. An example is in Fig. 2b: the credit card number is retrieved by calling Employee.getCcn() (that returns the value of the tainted field Employee.ccn, see Fig. 1c); it is then passed to method setString of a java . sql . PreparedStatement (method setString is tagged as a sink in the leakage point specification in Fig. 1d). In particular, line 207 of CrossSiteScripting. Up− dateProfile contains the code ps . setString (10, employee.getCcn()). The other flow is different and more complex. It involves the disclosure of a password into the Internet, in particular, into an HTML component. Fig. 2c reports this flow.

The access of sensitive data and its leakage occur at line 166 and 165 of class WsSAXInjection, respectively.

```
165: return new B(HtmlEncoder.encode("You have changed the password for userid "
166:    + changer.getId() + " to ' " + changer.getPassword() + " ' "));
```

GDPR Report

꩜ Flows not allowed

    ▦ CreditCard -> DB

       At line 341 of file UpdateProfile.java
       At line 207 of file UpdateProfile.java
       At line 189 of file UpdateProfile.java
       At line 194 of file UpdateProfile.java
       At line 161 of file UpdateProfile.java
       At line 142 of file UpdateProfile.java
       At line 138 of file UpdateProfile.java
       At line 63 of file UpdateProfile_i.java
       At line 111 of file UpdateProfile_i.java
       At line 243 of file UpdateProfile.java
       At line 247 of file UpdateProfile.java
       At line 299 of file UpdateProfile.java
       At line 184 of file UpdateProfile.java

    ▦ Password -> Internet

       At line 165 of file WsSAXInjection.java

(a) The GDPR report.

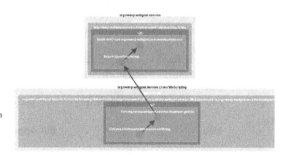

(b) A flow of a credit card number into the DB.

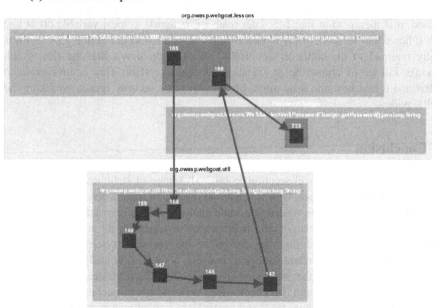

(c) A complex flow from a password into an HTML element.

Fig. 2. GDPR report of WebGoat.

As pointed out by the flow graph, the password is passed to HtmlEncoder.encode, that returns the sensitive data. Below is a code snippet with only the statements identified by the flow graph in Fig. 2c:

```
140:  public static String encode(String s1)
141:  {
142:      StringBuffer buf = new StringBuffer();
            ...
145:      for (i = 0; i < s1.length (); ++i)
147:              char ch = s1.charAt(i );
148:
149:              String  entity  = i2e.get(new Integer((int) ch ));
                    ...
159:                              buf.append(ch);
            ...
168:      return buf.toString ();
169:  }
```

The flow graph explains that sensitive data is passed to the beginning of this method; it is then read at line 145, later read and assigned to local variable ch at line 147; it flows into variable entity at line 149; it is appended to buf at line 159; and it is finally returned to the callee at line 168. This example shows that the flow graph provides full detail about the propagation of sensitive data. This is invaluable to understand if and how the flow might be a problematic security breach, violating the GDPR policy.

5 Conclusion

This article describes a novel solution to take advantage of static analysis inside the process of GDPR compliance. GDPR is a broad regulation that involves many different aspects of data security. We argued that static analysis plays a relevant role in building tools that identify how sensitive data is processed in ways that do not comply to the GDPR policy identified during the design of the software system. The solution leverages many well-known and studied techniques, notably, taint analysis. It augments them in order to (i) allow the user to specify the policy, (ii) reconstruct how sensitive data flows in the program, and (iii) check which flows do not respect the GDPR policy. We formalized the approach in detail and applied it to a standard benchmark, WebGoat, often used to show the effectiveness of static analyses for security. A prototype has been implemented in the Julia static analyzer.

As future work, we are currently working at front-ends to present the results of the analysis: plugins for various IDEs (such as Eclipse and IntelliJ IDEA) and dashboards for the results. We have already studied various levels of reporting, targeting distinct actors of the GDPR compliance process [14]. Each actor will deserve his front-end view of the results.

References

1. Absint. https://www.absint.com/
2. Grammatech. https://www.grammatech.com/
3. Arzt, S., et al.: Flowdroid: precise context, flow, field, object-sensitive and lifecycle-aware taint analysis for android apps. In: Proceedings of PLDI 2014. ACM (2014)
4. Blanchet, B., et al.: A static analyzer for large safety-critical software. In: Proceedings of PLDI 2003. ACM (2003)
5. Burato, E., Ferrara, P., Spoto, F.: Security analysis of the OWASP benchmark with Julia. In: Proceedings of ITASEC 2017 (2017)
6. Clarke Jr., E.M., Grumberg, O., Peled, D.A.: Model Checking. MIT Press, Cambridge (1999)
7. Cousot, P., Cousot, R.: Abstract interpretation: a unified lattice model for static analysis of programs by construction or approximation of fixpoints. In: Proceedings of POPL 1977. ACM Press (1977)
8. Cousot, P., Cousot, R.: Systematic design of program analysis frameworks. In: Proceedings of POPL 1979. ACM Press (1979)
9. Cousot, P., Cousot, R.: Abstract interpretation: past, present and future. In: Proceedings of CSL-LICS 2014. ACM (2014)
10. Denning, D.E., Denning, P.J.: Certification of programs for secure information flow. Commun. ACM **20**(7), 504–513 (1977)
11. Enck, W., et al.: Taintdroid: an information-flow tracking system for realtime privacy monitoring on smartphones. ACM Trans. Comput. Syst. **32**(2), 5 (2014)
12. Ernst, M.D., Lovato, A., Macedonio, D., Spiridon, C., Spoto, F.: Boolean formulas for the static identification of injection attacks in Java. In: Davis, M., Fehnker, A., McIver, A., Voronkov, A. (eds.) LPAR 2015. LNCS, vol. 9450, pp. 130–145. Springer, Heidelberg (2015). https://doi.org/10.1007/978-3-662-48899-7_10
13. Ferrara, P.: Generic combination of heap and value analyses in abstract interpretation. In: McMillan, K.L., Rival, X. (eds.) VMCAI 2014. LNCS, vol. 8318, pp. 302–321. Springer, Heidelberg (2014). https://doi.org/10.1007/978-3-642-54013-4_17
14. Ferrara, P., Spoto, F.: Static analysis for GDPR compliance. In: Proceedings of ITASEC 2018 (2018)
15. Ferrara, P., Tripp, O., Pistoia, M.: Morphdroid: fine-grained privacy verification. In: Proceedings of ACSAC 2015. ACM (2015)
16. Grove, D., DeFouw, G., Dean, J., Chambers, C.: Call graph construction in object oriented languages. In: Proceedings of OOPSLA 1997. ACM (1997)
17. Hind, M.: Pointer analysis: haven't we solved this problem yet? In: Proceedings of PASTE 2001. ACM (2001)
18. Kildall, G.A.: A unified approach to global program optimization. In: Proceedings of the 1st Annual ACM SIGACT-SIGPLAN Symposium on Principles of Programming Languages. POPL 1973. ACM, New York (1973)
19. Mathworks: Polyspace. https://www.mathworks.com/products/polyspace.html
20. Myers, A.C.: JFlow: practical mostly-static information flow control. In: Proceedings of POPL 1999. ACM (1999)
21. Nielson, F., Nielson, H.R., Hankin, C.: Principles of Program Analysis. Springer, New York (1999)
22. OWASP: Top 10 project 2017, March 2018. https://www.owasp.org/index.php/Category:OWASP_Top_Ten_Project

23. Pierce, B.C.: Types and Programming Languages, 1st edn. The MIT Press, Cambridge (2002)
24. Sabelfeld, A., Myers, A.C.: Language-based information-flow security. IEEE J. Sel. A. Commun. **21**(1), 5–19 (2006)
25. Spoto, F.: The Julia static analyzer for Java. In: Rival, X. (ed.) SAS 2016. LNCS, vol. 9837, pp. 39–57. Springer, Heidelberg (2016). https://doi.org/10.1007/978-3-662-53413-7_3
26. Tip, F., Palsberg, J.: Scalable propagation-based call graph construction algorithms. In: Proceedings of OOPSLA 2000. ACM, New York (2000)
27. Tripp, O., Pistoia, M., Fink, S.J., Sridharan, M., Weisman, O.: TAJ: effective taint analysis of web applications. In: Proceedings of PLDI 2009. ACM (2009)
28. Wikipedia: Static program analysis. https://en.wikipedia.org/wiki/Static_program_analysis

Hiding Alice in Wonderland: A Case for the Use of Signal Processing Techniques in Differential Privacy

Maurizio Naldi[✉], Alessandro Mazzoccoli, and Giuseppe D'Acquisto

Department of Civil Engineering and Computer Science,
University of Rome Tor Vergata, Via del Politecnico 1, 00133 Rome, Italy
maurizio.naldi@uniroma2.it

Abstract. A transformation of data in statistical databases is proposed to hide the presence of an individual. The transformation employs a cascade of spectral whitening and colouring (named recolouring for brevity) that preserves the first- and second-order statistical properties of the true data (i.e. mean and correlation). A measure of practical indistinguishability is introduced for the presence of the individual to be hidden (the Impact Factor), and the transformation is applied to a toy model for the case of correlated data following a Gaussian copula model. It is shown that the Impact Factor is a multiple of what would be achieved with noise addition: the proposed recolouring transformation significantly enlarges the range of attribute values for which the presence of the individual of interest cannot be reliably inferred.

Keywords: Privacy · Statistical databases · Differential privacy
Noise addition · Correlation

1 Introduction

Privacy in statistical databases is a compelling issue, since answers to queries about aggregate characteristics of the database entities have to be provided, while protecting the information concerning any specific individual.

Several measures have been proposed to protect an individual's data (or even its presence) while providing a useful response to the query. Among them, noise addition is one of the most prominent, consisting in simply adding noise to the actual data, so that the response does not carry the exact value. The technique, first tested by Spruill [20], has spawn many variants (see the reviews by Brand in [2] and Domingo-Ferrer, Sebé, and Castellá-Roca in [4] as well as [15]), differing for the type of noise added (uncorrelated as in [22,23] vs correlated as in [3]) and for the operations performed on the data (just addition vs linear [11] or nonlinear transformation [21]).

A special case for the addition of noise is related to the choice of the Laplace model for the distribution of noise (rather than the straightforward Gaussian

© Springer Nature Switzerland AG 2018
M. Medina et al. (Eds.): APF 2018, LNCS 11079, pp. 77–90, 2018.
https://doi.org/10.1007/978-3-030-02547-2_5

choice). By adding Laplace noise, we obtain what has been named differential privacy, which at the same provides a definition of quantifiable privacy and a way to guarantee it (see the introducing paper by Dwork [5], the subsequent survey in [6], and its re-examination in 2011 [7]). In differential privacy, the level ϵ of privacy guaranteed to an individual is measured through the extent to which its inclusion in a database changes the database response to a query. However, the disclosure of aggregate data under the differential privacy scheme is not immune from problems. For example, though the choice of the level of privacy may be chosen in an optimal way [17], through a synthetic dataset McClure and Reiter have questioned the use of the differential privacy level as a measure of the statistical disclosure risk, showing that the probability of an intruder uncovering true values may be significant even for high levels of differential privacy [14]. This happens in particular when the individual's position is eccentric with respect to the bulk of the database population [18]. On the other hand, allowing multiple queries, which worsens the level of differential privacy and erodes the privacy budget, may require the addition of large quantities of noise [10,19]. In the presence of multiple queries, optimization of the noisy response has been sought after to preserve differential privacy while maintaining an adequate accuracy for the database response to be useful [12]. It has been shown that a Bayesian approach may be used to improve the accuracy for the same amount of noise injected [16]. In addition, it has been shown that the expected level of privacy degrades significantly with differential privacy when the data exhibit correlation among them [13].

The addition of noise, either of Gaussian or Laplace distribution as in differential privacy, appears therefore to miss the goal of achieving individuals' data protection under correlation.

In this paper, we deal with the problem of guaranteeing data protection in statistical databases when the data are correlated, but at the same providing responses that exhibit the same statistical properties of the true data. In particular we wish to provide responses to queries that do not betray the presence of a specific individual, so that examining the response to the query does not allow us to understand whether that specific individual is actually present in the database. We proceed by proposing a novel approach that borrows methods from the field of statistical signal processing, namely the whitening and colouring transformation. We wish to stress that in this context we consider the data present in the database as an instance of a population described by a probability model, and provide a method that does not depend on the specific data contained in the database. A consequence of this approach is that the method works for any specific instance instead of needing to be reformulated for the specific database contents.

After describing a toy model, serving the purpose of demonstrating how the method works for a simple case, we provide the following results:

– we introduce a measure of practical indistinguishability (Sect. 3);

- we provide its mathematical expression (and its geometrical shape on the space of the individual's attributes) under uncorrelated noise addition when the data follow a multivariate Gaussian copula model (Sect. 3);
- we propose a recolouring (whitening plus colouring) transformation of the true data (Sect. 4);
- we provide the mathematical expression of the measure of indistinguishability under the proposed recolouring transformation.

2   The Single-Record Toy Model

In this section we define a toy model that allows us to represent the uncertainty associated to the value returned by from the database after a query.

The toy model is a database made of a single record.

Let's consider an individual (Alice) whose data are recorded on that database. For the time being we consider her data to be represented by the vector X_A, made of two attributes. For simplicity, we set those attributes equal to the value a, so that $X_A = (a, a)$. Actually, we imagine Alice being part of a population whose statistics related to the two attributes follow a Gaussian copula [9]. The generic variables X_1 and X_2 representing the two attributes are therefore described by the following relationships

$$X_1 = \rho M + \sqrt{1 - \rho^2} S_1$$
$$X_2 = \rho M + \sqrt{1 - \rho^2} S_2,$$

(1)

where M is the component common to the two attributes (representing correlation) and S_1 and S_2 are the idiosyncratic components of the two attributes. All the three variables introduced in Eq. (1) are supposed to be standardized Gaussian random variables. The correlation coefficient between the two attributes is therefore ρ.

Since the two values are set, the pertaining covariance matrix is fully zero.

If we adopt the typical action of adding noise to mask the exact values (e.g. i.i.d. Gaussian noise with variance σ^2), the attributes of Alice returned after a query are described by the vector X_A^*, whose components are

$$X_{A1}^* = a + n_1$$
$$X_{A2}^* = a + n_2$$

(2)

where n_1 and n_2 are i.i.d. random variables $\sim \mathcal{N}(0, \sigma^2)$. The covariance matrix is now

$$\Sigma_A = \begin{pmatrix} \sigma^2 & 0 \\ 0 & \sigma^2 \end{pmatrix}$$

(3)

If we replace Alice by a fictitious substitute, randomly drawn from the same population to which Alice belongs, i.e. whose attributes are described by Eq. (1), and adding noise as in the case of Alice, the attributes of the substitute that are returned after a query are

$$X_{R1} = \rho M + \sqrt{1 - \rho^2} S_1 + n_3$$
$$X_{R2} = \rho M + \sqrt{1 - \rho^2} S_2 + n_4, \tag{4}$$

where, again, n_3 and n_4 are i.i.d. random variables $\sim \mathcal{N}(0, \sigma^2)$. The covariance matrix is now

$$\Sigma_{R} = \begin{pmatrix} 1 + \sigma^2 & \rho \\ \rho & 1 + \sigma^2 \end{pmatrix}. \tag{5}$$

3   Measuring Practical Indistinguishability

In order to see if the attributes returned when Alice is present in the database and a substitute is present in her place, we compute the Impact Factor (IF) as the ratio of the probability density function of the attribute vector in the two cases. By indicating the two attributes as (x_1, x_2), we have

$$IF(x_1, x_2) = \frac{f_{X_R^*}}{f_{X_A^*}} = \frac{\frac{1}{2\pi\sqrt{[(1+\sigma^2)^2 - \rho^2]}} \exp\{-\frac{(1+\sigma^2)x_1^2 - 2\rho x_1 x_2 + (1+\sigma^2)x_2^2}{2[(1+\sigma^2)^2 - \rho^2]}\}}{\frac{1}{2\pi\sigma^2} \exp\{-\frac{(x_1-a)^2 + (x_2-a)^2}{2\sigma^2}\}}$$

$$= \frac{\sigma^2}{\sqrt{(1+\sigma^2)^2 - \rho^2}} \frac{\exp\{-\frac{(1+\sigma^2)x_1^2 - 2\rho x_1 x_2 + (1+\sigma^2)x_2^2}{2[(1+\sigma^2)^2 - \rho^2]}\}}{\exp\{-\frac{x_1^2 - 2a(x_1+x_2) + 2a^2 + x_2^2}{2\sigma^2}\}}$$

$$= \frac{\sigma^2}{\sqrt{(1+\sigma^2)^2 - \rho^2}} \times$$

$$\exp\left\{\frac{(x_1^2 + x_2^2)(\sigma^2 + 1 - \rho^2) + 2\rho\sigma^2 x_1 x_2 + 2a[(1+\sigma^2)^2 - \rho^2][a - (x_1 + x_2)]}{2\sigma^2[(1+\sigma^2)^2 - \rho^2]}\right\} \tag{6}$$

The closer the IF is to 1, the more difficult it is for the external observer to distinguish between the two cases (with and without Alice). We can therefore set two adequately close bounds to define a notion of practical indistinguishability:

$$e^{-\epsilon} < IF < e^{\epsilon}. \tag{7}$$

For any value of ϵ, the combination of Eq. (6) and the inequality (7) allows us to identify the couples of attribute values for which the two cases are practically indistinguishable. The larger that domain of (x_1, x_2) values, the more uncertainty surrounds the actual presence of Alice in the database.

The inequality (7) can be written in the following form,

$$e^{-\epsilon} \frac{\sqrt{(1+\sigma^2)^2 - \rho^2}}{\sigma^2}$$

$$< \exp\left\{ \frac{(x_1^2 + x_2^2)(\sigma^2 + 1 - \rho^2) + 2\rho\sigma^2 x_1 x_2 + 2a[(1+\sigma^2)^2 - \rho^2][1 - (x_1 + x_2)]}{2\sigma^2[(1+\sigma^2)^2 - \rho^2]} \right\}$$

$$< e^{\epsilon} \frac{\sqrt{(1+\sigma^2)^2 - \rho^2}}{\sigma^2} \iff$$

$$- \epsilon + \ln\left(\frac{\sqrt{(1+\sigma^2)^2 - \rho^2}}{\sigma^2} \right)$$

$$\leq \frac{(x_1^2 + x_2^2)(\sigma^2 + 1 - \rho^2) + 2\rho\sigma^2 x_1 x_2 + 2a[(1+\sigma^2)^2 - \rho^2][1 - (x_1 + x_2)]}{2\sigma^2[(1+\sigma^2)^2 - \rho^2]}$$

$$< \epsilon + \ln\left(\frac{\sqrt{(1+\sigma^2)^2 - \rho^2}}{\sigma^2} \right),$$

$$\tag{8}$$

whose bounds are represented by two conics. Namely, considering the general equation of a conic in the (x_1, x_2) plane

$$Ax_1^2 + Bx_1x_2 + Cx_2^2 + Dx_1 + Ex_2 + F = 0, \tag{9}$$

we have the following coefficients (two are indicated for F, since they differ for the two conics):

$$A = \frac{\sigma^2 + 1 - \rho^2}{2\sigma^2[(1+\sigma^2)^2 - \rho^2]}$$

$$B = \frac{2\rho\sigma^2}{2\sigma^2[(1+\sigma^2)^2 - \rho^2]} = \frac{\rho}{(1+\sigma^2)^2 - \rho^2}$$

$$C = A = \frac{\sigma^2 + 1 - \rho^2}{2\sigma^2[(1+\sigma^2)^2 - \rho^2]}$$

$$D = \frac{2a[(1+\sigma^2)^2 - \rho^2]}{2\sigma^2[(1+\sigma^2)^2 - \rho^2]} = \frac{a}{\sigma^2} \tag{10}$$

$$E = D = \frac{a}{\sigma^2}$$

$$F_1 = \frac{a^2}{\sigma^2} + \epsilon - \ln\left(\frac{\sqrt{(1+\sigma^2)^2 - \rho^2}}{\sigma^2} \right)$$

$$F_2 = \frac{a^2}{\sigma^2} - \epsilon - \ln\left(\frac{\sqrt{(1+\sigma^2)^2 - \rho^2}}{\sigma^2} \right)$$

In order to understand which type of conic they are, we can compute the discriminant

$$\Delta = \det \begin{pmatrix} A & B/2 \\ B/2 & C \end{pmatrix} = \det \begin{pmatrix} \frac{\sigma^2+1-\rho^2}{2\sigma^2[(1+\sigma^2)^2-\rho^2]} & \frac{\rho}{(1+\sigma^2)^2-\rho^2} \\ \frac{\rho}{(1+\sigma^2)^2-\rho^2} & \frac{\sigma^2+1-\rho^2}{2\sigma^2[(1+\sigma^2)^2-\rho^2]} \end{pmatrix}$$

$$= \frac{\sigma^4(1-\rho^2) + 2\sigma^2(1-\rho^2) + (1-\rho^2)^2}{4\sigma^4[(1+\sigma^2)^2 - \rho^2]^2} > 0. \tag{11}$$

The positivity of the discriminant tells us the nature of the two curves bounding the region in the (x_1, x_2) plane where we cannot practically distinguish between Alice and her substitute: they are ellipses.

In Fig. 1, we see two such ellipses for the parameter values reported in Table 1. We see that the shape of both ellipses is very close to a circle. Since they differ just for the value of the coefficient F, which does not impact on the ellipses' center, the two ellipses have the same center and differ just for the length of their axes.

Table 1. Parameter values for the sample cases

Parameter	Case 1	Case 2
a	1	1
ϵ	0.1	0.1
ρ	0.6	0.5
σ	0.3	0.5

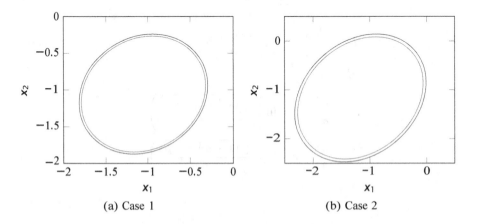

(a) Case 1   (b) Case 2

Fig. 1. Indistinguishability bounds in the absence of recolouring

Since the two ellipses are concentric, the differences between their areas can be taken as a measure of the region of indistinguishability: values of the two attributes x_1 and x_2 falling between the two ellipses lead to an IF close to 1 (how close it is depends on the choice of ϵ). Following the general form of Eq. (9), the area S of an ellipse is

$$S = \pi \frac{2CD^2 + 2AE^2 - 8ACF}{8(AC)^{3/2}} = \pi \frac{4AD^2 - 8A^2F}{8A^3}$$
$$= \pi \frac{D^2 - 2AF}{2A^2},$$

(12)

since $C = A$ and $E = D$ in our case, after Eq. (10). The size U of the region of indistinguishability is then

$$U \triangleq |S_2 - S_1| = \left| \pi \frac{D^2 - 2AF_2}{2A^2} - \pi \frac{D^2 - 2AF_1}{2A^2} \right|$$
$$= \pi \left| \frac{F_2 - F_1}{A} \right| = 2\pi\epsilon \frac{2\sigma^2 \left[(1 + \sigma^2)^2 \right) - \rho^2 \right]}{\sigma^2 + 1 - \rho}$$

(13)

The larger the value of U is, the more Alice is hidden, because we have a larger set of attribute values for which we cannot tell her presence from that of her substitute. For the parameter values of Table 1, we have $U = 0.1283$ for Case 1 and $U = 0.4123$ for Case 2.

4   Whitening and Colouring

As shown in Sect. 3, the addition of Gaussian noise allows us to obtain a set of values of attributes where Alice is practically indistinguishable from her substitute. However, the area of indistinguishability, embodied by the value U, may result too small. The area may be enlarged by increasing the amount of added noise (i.e. σ), but that unavoidably results in reducing the usefulness of the data output by the database. In this section, we propose a technique to process the attributes so that the output from the database is statistically equal to the population, which means that the presence of Alice is more difficult to detect.

The technique we propose consists in applying two subsequent processing stages, respectively implementing a whitening and a colouring transformation. For brevity, in the following we use the term recolouring to mean the sequential application of whitening and colouring (see Fig. 2). Such techniques are borrowed from statistical signal processing and will be employed here under the hypothesis that the population (of which the data present in the database is a sample) follows a multivariate Gaussian model. In our toy model, we actually have a bivariate Gaussian model, rather than a multivariate one, since we just consider two attributes, but we describe the procedure in rather general terms (i.e., with a set of n attributes).

The aim of the whole procedure is to obtain a set of data that follow the same distribution and have the same correlation properties as the population from

Fig. 2. Recolouring transformation

which the database is extracted. In response to a query the database therefore returns an output that is statistically identical to the population (preserving its usefulness), without providing a clue on the detailed actual contents of the database.

For convenience, such aim is pursued by performing first a whitening process, which returns a white noise process that destroys any correlation present between the attributes. That stage is followed by a colouring transformation that restores the first and second order statistical properties of the original population (i.e., the correlation among its attributes). In the following we adopt the description of the procedure reported, e.g., in [8].

Let $X \in \mathbb{R}^n$ be an n-dimensional Gaussian random vector with mean μ and covariance matrix Σ. This vector represents a record in our database. The probability density function of X is given by

$$f_X(x) = \frac{1}{(2\pi)^{\frac{n}{2}}|\Sigma|^{\frac{1}{2}}} \exp\left(-\frac{1}{2}x^T\Sigma^{-1}x\right) \tag{14}$$

We wish to transform it into a random vector whose covariance is the identity matrix, so that it possesses the statistical properties of white noise (total absence of correlation).

Assuming that the vector X has been reduced to zero mean by subtracting its mean value, the covariance matrix Σ is assumed to be positive definite (it can be easily verified for all the matrices involved in this paper that their eigenvalues are always positive), and can be expressed as follows:

$$\Sigma = \mathbb{E}[XX^T] = \Phi\Lambda\Phi^{-1} = \Phi\Lambda^{\frac{1}{2}}\Lambda^{\frac{1}{2}}\Phi^{-1}, \tag{15}$$

where Λ is the eigenvalues matrix of Σ with entries λ_i, its square root is the matrix $\Lambda^{\frac{1}{2}}$ such that $\Lambda = \Lambda^{\frac{1}{2}}\Lambda^{\frac{1}{2}}$, and Φ is the eigenvector matrix, $\Phi^{-1} = \Phi^T$. Let $Y = \Phi^T X$ and $W = \Lambda^{-\frac{1}{2}}Y = \Lambda^{-\frac{1}{2}}\Phi^T X$. The covariance of Y is

$$\mathbb{E}[YY^T] = \mathbb{E}[\Phi^T XX^T \Phi] = \Phi^T\mathbb{E}[XX^T]\Phi = \Phi^T\Sigma\Phi = \Lambda \tag{16}$$

The components of Y are therefore uncorrelated and the probability density function of Y is

$$f_Y(y) = \frac{1}{(2\pi)^{\frac{n}{2}}|\Lambda|^{\frac{1}{2}}} \exp\left(-\frac{1}{2}y\Lambda^{-1}y\right) = \prod_{i=1}^{n}\frac{1}{\sqrt{2\pi\lambda_i}}\exp\left(-\frac{y_i^2}{2\lambda_i}\right) \tag{17}$$

Since $\Lambda^{\frac{1}{2}}$ is symmetric, the covariance of W is

$$\mathbb{E}[WW^T] = \mathbb{E}[\Lambda^{-\frac{1}{2}T}YY^t\Lambda^{-\frac{1}{2}}] = \Lambda^{-\frac{1}{2}t}\mathbb{E}[YY^T]\Lambda^{-\frac{1}{2}} = \Lambda^{-\frac{1}{2}T}\Lambda\Lambda^{-\frac{1}{2}} = \mathbb{I}, \tag{18}$$

so that W has the same characteristics of white noise.

The linear transformation that whitens the input vector X is therefore $\Lambda^{-\frac{1}{2}}\Phi^T$ (the computation of the square root of a matrix can be always performed, at least numerically, e.g. as in [1]).

If we now wish to obtain the characteristics of the original population (i.e., a Gaussian random vector with covariance matrix Σ), we must perform a colouring transformation. Using the same notation as before, we can write

$$\Sigma = \Phi\Lambda\Phi^t = \Phi\Lambda^{\frac{1}{2}}\Lambda^{\frac{1}{2}}\Phi^t \tag{19}$$

We first apply the transformation

$$Y = \Lambda^{\frac{1}{2}}W \tag{20}$$

that scale the samples and then use

$$X = \Phi Y = \Phi\Lambda^{\frac{1}{2}}W \tag{21}$$

that rotates the data to obtain correlated data according to the desired covariance matrix. The colouring transformation is therefore $\Phi\Lambda^{\frac{1}{2}}$.

We can now apply those transformation to our toy model. If we recall the covariance matrix shown in Eq. (3) when Alice is present, its eigenvalues are $\lambda_{1,2} = \sigma^2$, and the corresponding eigenvectors are $v_1 = (1,0)$ and $v_2 = (0,1)$. The whitening transformation when Alice is present is then

$$W = \begin{pmatrix} \frac{1}{\sigma} & 0 \\ 0 & \frac{1}{\sigma} \end{pmatrix} \tag{22}$$

We can now turn to the colouring phase. Our aim is to obtain the covariance matrix $\Sigma^* = \begin{pmatrix} 1 & \rho \\ \rho & 1 \end{pmatrix}$. Since the eigenvalues of Σ^* are $\lambda^*_{1,2} = 1 \pm \rho$, and the corresponding eigenvectors are $v^*_1 = (\frac{1}{\sqrt{2}}, \frac{1}{\sqrt{2}})$ e $v^*_2 = (\frac{1}{\sqrt{2}}, -\frac{1}{\sqrt{2}})$, the colouring matrix is

$$C = \begin{pmatrix} \sqrt{\frac{1+\rho}{2}} & \sqrt{\frac{1-\rho}{2}} \\ \sqrt{\frac{1+\rho}{2}} & -\sqrt{\frac{1-\rho}{2}} \end{pmatrix} \tag{23}$$

The overall linear transformation that returns a vector following the original population distribution when Alice is present is

$$Z = CW = \begin{pmatrix} \sqrt{\frac{1+\rho}{2\sigma^2}} & \sqrt{\frac{1-\rho}{2\sigma^2}} \\ \sqrt{\frac{1+\rho}{2\sigma^2}} & -\sqrt{\frac{1-\rho}{2\sigma^2}} \end{pmatrix} \tag{24}$$

5 Indistinguishability Under Recolouring

After defining the procedure to transform the original data into a set of data that has the same first- and second-order statistical properties as the population, we wish to assess the goodness of the whitening+colouring procedure in hiding the presence of Alice. In this section, building on the measure of indistinguishability introduced in Sect. 3, we evaluate the improvement with respect to the simple addition of Gaussian noise.

The overall transformation (whitening plus colouring) defined by Eq. (24) provides an output whose covariance matrix is the following

$$\Sigma_Z = Z\Sigma_R^* Z^T = \begin{pmatrix} \frac{1+\sigma^2+\rho\sqrt{1-\rho^2}}{\sigma^2} & \frac{(1+\sigma^2)\rho}{\sigma^2} \\ \frac{(1+\sigma^2)\rho}{\sigma^2} & \frac{(1+\sigma^2)-\rho\sqrt{1-\rho^2}}{\sigma^2} \end{pmatrix} \qquad (25)$$

It is important to note that this is the end result irrespective of the actual input, i.e. whether Alice is present or not.

The discriminant of the matrix (25) is then

$$\det \Sigma_Z \frac{((1+\sigma^2)^2 - \rho^2)(1 - \rho^2)}{\sigma^4}. \qquad (26)$$

Similarly to what we have done in Sect. 3, we can now compute the Impact Factor under whitening+colouring (where $m = \rho\sigma^2\sqrt{1-\rho^2}$, $d = \sigma^2 - \rho^2$ and $s = 1 + \sigma^2$)

$$IF(x_1, x_2) = \frac{\frac{\sigma^2}{2\pi\sqrt{((1+\sigma^2)^2-\rho^2)(1-\rho^2)}}}{\frac{1}{2\pi\sqrt{1-\rho^2}} \exp\left(-\frac{x_1^2-2\rho x_1 x_2+x_2^2}{2(1-\rho^2)}\right)}$$

$$\times \exp\left(-\sigma^2 \frac{x_1^2(s - \rho\sqrt{1-\rho^2}) - 2s\rho x_1 x_2 + (s + \rho\sqrt{1-\rho^2})x_2^2}{2(s^2 - \rho^2)(1 - \rho^2)}\right)$$

$$= \frac{\sigma^2}{\sqrt{s^2 - \rho^2}}$$

$$\times \exp\left(\frac{x_1^2(d + m + 1) + x_2^2(d - m + 1) + x_1 x_2 2\rho(-d - 1)}{2(1 - \rho^2)((1 + \sigma^2)^2 - \rho^2)}\right) \qquad (27)$$

It is again a conic. In order to determine the type of conic, we compute its discriminant to evaluate its sign. By eliminating positive factors, and going through standard calculations, we end up with the following reduced form

$$\Delta \propto \det \begin{pmatrix} \sigma^2 - \rho^2 + \rho\sigma^2\sqrt{1-\rho^2} + 1 & \rho(-\sigma^2 - 1 + \rho^2) \\ \rho(-\sigma^2 - 1 + \rho^2) & \sigma^2 - \rho^2 - \rho\sigma^2\sqrt{1-\rho^2} + 1 \end{pmatrix}$$

$$= (1 - \rho^2)((1 + \sigma^2 - \rho^2)^2 - \rho^2\sigma^4) \qquad (28)$$

$$= \sigma^4 + (1 - \rho^2)^2 + 2\sigma^2(1 - \rho^2) - \rho^2\sigma^4$$

$$= \sigma^4(1 - \rho^2) + (1 - \rho^2)^2 + 2\sigma^2(1 - \rho^2) > 0$$

We have therefore an ellipse as in the case with simple noise addition.

We can now apply the condition of practical indistinguishability defined by the inequality (7) and obtain the following inequality (where $m = \rho\sigma^2\sqrt{1-\rho^2}$)

$$-\epsilon + \ln\left(\frac{\sqrt{(1+\sigma^2)^2 - \rho^2}}{\sigma^2}\right)$$

$$\leq \frac{x_1^2(\sigma^2 - \rho^2 + m + 1) + x_2^2(\sigma^2 - \rho^2 - m + 1) + x_1 x_2 2\rho(-\sigma^2 + \rho^2 - 1)}{2(1-\rho^2)((1+\sigma^2)^2 - \rho^2)} \quad (29)$$

$$\leq \epsilon + \ln\left(\frac{\sqrt{(1+\sigma^2)^2 - \rho^2}}{\sigma^2}\right)$$

whose bounds are again two concentric conics with the following coefficients as per the general form of Eq. (9):

$$A = \frac{\sigma^2\left(1 + \rho\sqrt{1-\rho^2}\right) + 1 - \rho^2}{2(1-\rho^2)[(1+\sigma^2)^2 - \rho^2]}$$

$$B = \rho\frac{\rho^2 - \sigma^2 - 1}{(1-\rho^2)[(1+\sigma^2)^2] - \rho^2]}$$

$$C = \frac{\sigma^2\left(1 - \rho\sqrt{1-\rho^2}\right) + 1 - \rho^2}{2(1-\rho^2)[(1+\sigma^2)^2 - \rho^2]}$$

$$D = 0 \quad (30)$$

$$E = 0$$

$$F_1 = \epsilon - \ln\left(\frac{\sqrt{(1+\sigma^2)^2 - \rho^2}}{\sigma^2}\right)$$

$$F_2 = -\epsilon - \ln\left(\frac{\sqrt{(1+\sigma^2)^2 - \rho^2}}{\sigma^2}\right)$$

In Fig. 3, we see the ellipses resulting for the cases of Table 1. For the sake of comparison, we have also reported the ellipses resulting in the absence of the whitening+colouring transformation (Noise addition). Though the ellipses appear very close to each other, the differences in their areas increase when we apply whitening and colouring.

We can check that that's the case through analytical means. Recalling the general expression of the area of an ellipse in Eq. (12), we have

$$S = \pi\frac{2CD^2 + 2AE^2 - 8ACF}{8(AC)^{3/2}} = -\pi\frac{F}{\sqrt{AC}}, \quad (31)$$

since $D = E = 0$.

Similarly to what we have done in Sect. 3, we can finally compute the difference between the areas of the two ellipses as a measure of the degree of uncertainty in assessing the actual presence of Alice in the database:

$$U = |S_1 - S_2| = \pi\frac{|F_1 - F_2|}{\sqrt{AC}}. \quad (32)$$

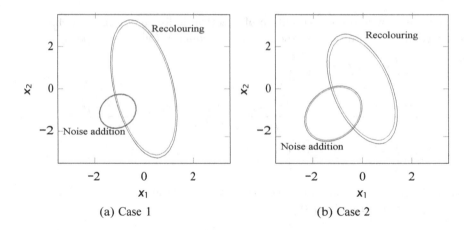

(a) Case 1   (b) Case 2

Fig. 3. Indistinguishability bounds after whitening+colouring

For the cases of Table 1, we obtain respectively $U = 0.9139$ for Case 1 and $U = 1.244$ for Case 2. If we compare these values with those obtained by simply adding noise, we see that the area of uncertainty has increased over sevenfold in Case 1 and threefold in Case 2. The whitening+colouring transformation proves to be very effective in hiding Alice over what the simple addition off Gaussian noise would do.

6   Conclusions

Both simple Gaussian noise addition and differential privacy under the form of Laplace noise addition have been demonstrated to be unable to actually protect the individual's data when the attributes of individuals are correlated.

The whitening+colouring transformation proposed in this paper has been shown instead to significantly increase the portion of the space of attributes where we cannot tell the presence of Alice (the individual we wish to protect) in the database.

At the same time, the response provided to the query is still useful, since it possess exactly the same first- and second-order statistical properties of the true population of which the database is a specific instance: the expected value and the correlation of the response are the same that we would obtain with the true data.

Though the effectiveness of the transformation has been proven for a toy model and Gaussian distribution for the data, it opens the way to devising privacy protection methods in statistical databases that are at the same time effective and true.

References

1. Björck, Å., Hammarling, S.: A schur method for the square root of a matrix. Linear Algebra Appl. **52**, 127–140 (1983)
2. Brand, R.: Microdata protection through noise addition. In: Domingo-Ferrer, J. (ed.) Inference Control in Statistical Databases. LNCS, vol. 2316, pp. 97–116. Springer, Heidelberg (2002). https://doi.org/10.1007/3-540-47804-3_8
3. Ciriani, V., De Capitani di Vimercati, S., Foresti, S., Samarati, P.: Microdata protection. In: Yu, T., Jajodia, S. (eds.) Secure Data Management in Decentralized Systems, pp. 291–321. Springer, Boston (2007). https://doi.org/10.1007/978-0-387-27696-0_9
4. Domingo-Ferrer, J., Sebé, F., Castellà-Roca, J.: On the security of noise addition for privacy in statistical databases. In: Domingo-Ferrer, J., Torra, V. (eds.) PSD 2004. LNCS, vol. 3050, pp. 149–161. Springer, Heidelberg (2004). https://doi.org/10.1007/978-3-540-25955-8_12
5. Dwork, C.: Differential privacy. In: Bugliesi, M., Preneel, B., Sassone, V., Wegener, I. (eds.) ICALP 2006. LNCS, vol. 4052, pp. 1–12. Springer, Heidelberg (2006). https://doi.org/10.1007/11787006_1
6. Dwork, C.: Differential privacy: a survey of results. In: Agrawal, M., Du, D., Duan, Z., Li, A. (eds.) TAMC 2008. LNCS, vol. 4978, pp. 1–19. Springer, Heidelberg (2008). https://doi.org/10.1007/978-3-540-79228-4_1
7. Dwork, C.: A firm foundation for private data analysis. Commun. ACM **54**(1), 86–95 (2011)
8. Galati, G. (ed.): Advanced Radar Techniques and Systems. Peter Peregrinus Ltd., London (1993)
9. Glasserman, P., Kang, W., Shahabuddin, P.: Large deviations in multifactor portfolio credit risk. Math. Financ. **17**(3), 345–379 (2007)
10. Heffetz, O., Ligett, K.: Privacy and data-based research. J. Econ. Perspect. **28**(2), 75–98 (2014)
11. Kim, J.J.: A method for limiting disclosure in microdata based on random noise and transformation, pp. 303–308. American Statistical Association (1986)
12. Li, C., Hay, M., Rastogi, V., Miklau, G., McGregor, A.: Optimizing linear counting queries under differential privacy. In: Proceedings of the Twenty-Ninth ACM SIGMOD-SIGACT-SIGART Symposium on Principles of Database Systems, PODS 2010, pp. 123–134. ACM, New York (2010)
13. Liu, C., Chakraborty, S., Mittal, P.: Dependence makes you vulnerable: differential privacy under dependent tuples. In: Proceedings of Network and Distributed System Security Symposium (NDSS 2016) (2016)
14. McClure, D., Reiter, J.P.: Differential privacy and statistical disclosure risk measures: an investigation with binary synthetic data. Trans. Data Privacy **5**(3), 535–552 (2012)
15. Mivule, K.: Utilizing noise addition for data privacy, an overview. arXiv preprint arXiv:1309.3958 (2013)
16. Naldi, M., D'Acquisto, G.: Differential privacy for counting queries: can Bayes estimation help uncover the true value? arXiv preprint arXiv:1407.0116 (2014)
17. Naldi, M., D'Acquisto, G.: Differential privacy: an estimation theory-based method for choosing epsilon. arXiv preprint arXiv:1510.00917 (2015)
18. Naldi, M., D'Acquisto, G.: Mr X vs. Mr Y: the emergence of externalities in differential privacy. In: Schweighofer, E., Leitold, H., Mitrakas, A., Rannenberg, K. (eds.) APF 2017. LNCS, vol. 10518, pp. 120–140. Springer, Cham (2017). https://doi.org/10.1007/978-3-319-67280-9_7

19. Sarathy, R., Muralidhar, K.: Evaluating laplace noise addition to satisfy differential privacy for numeric data. Trans. Data Priv. **4**(1), 1–17 (2011)
20. Spruill, N.L.: The confidentiality and analytic usefulness of masked business micro-data. Rev. Public Data Use **12**(4), 307–314 (1984)
21. Sullivan, G.R.: The use of added error to avoid disclosure in microdata releases. Ph.D. thesis, Iowa State University (1989)
22. Tendick, P.: Optimal noise addition for preserving confidentiality in multivariate data. J. Stat. Plan. Infer. **27**(3), 341–353 (1991)
23. Tendick, P., Matloff, N.: A modified random perturbation method for database security. ACM Trans. Database Syst. (TODS) **19**(1), 47–63 (1994)

A Democracy Called Facebook? Participation as a Privacy Strategy on Social Media

Severin Engelmann[1(✉)], Jens Grossklags[1],
and Orestis Papakyriakopoulos[2]

[1] Chair of Cyber Trust, Department of Informatics,
Technical University Munich, Munich, Germany
{engelmas, jens.grossklags}@in.tum.de
[2] Political Data Science, School of Governance,
Technical University Munich, Munich, Germany

Abstract. Despite its known inadequacies, *notice and consent* is still the most common privacy practice on social media platforms. Indeed, conceptualizing alternative privacy strategies for the social media context has proven to be difficult. In 2009, Facebook implemented a participatory governance system that enabled users to vote on its privacy policy. However, three years later, Facebook held a final vote that led to the termination of its participatory governance system. Here, we empirically assess this participatory privacy strategy designed to democratize social media policy-making. We describe the different components of Facebook's participatory governance system, show how users could influence privacy policy decision-making, and report the privacy policies users accepted and rejected by vote. Furthermore, we identify the common themes users discussed during the final electoral period by applying an unsupervised machine learning topic modeling algorithm to thousands of Facebook user comments. Our results demonstrate that users voiced concerns about being insufficiently informed about participation commitments and possibilities, attempted to orchestrate a transfer of the vote to a third-party platform, and engaged in spreading misconstrued data ownership claims. Based on our results, we analyze the key reasons behind Facebook's failure to implement a successful participation process. Finally, we highlight the significance of framing diversity for privacy decision-making in the context of a participatory privacy strategy on social media.

Keywords: Social media democracy · Social media governance
Privacy · Online participation · Topic modeling

1 Introduction

"So this was a major breach of trust and I'm really sorry that this happened. You know we have a basic responsibility to protect people's data and if we can't do that then we don't deserve to have the opportunity to serve people."

Mark Zuckerberg in an Interview with CNN following the Cambridge Analytica scandal, March 22, 2018 [1].

© Springer Nature Switzerland AG 2018
M. Medina et al. (Eds.): APF 2018, LNCS 11079, pp. 91–108, 2018.
https://doi.org/10.1007/978-3-030-02547-2_6

Today, social media platforms must solve a variety of different data-related problems such as fake news [2], election meddling [3], as well as numerous privacy challenges such as data breaches due to interdependent privacy violations [4, 5]. Even before the Cambridge Analytica data scandal became public, a study by Stieger [6] found that the majority of users ending their social media accounts had justified their virtual identity suicide due to privacy concerns.

To address privacy challenges, one can distinguish between two recognized approaches: first, the widely applied *notice and consent* strategy, commonly consisting of privacy disclaimers and privacy control interfaces, enabling users after registration to set their privacy preferences to various degrees [7]. Second, *privacy by design (PbD)*, essentially an architecture approach, requires data protection to be a built-in feature of information systems [8, 9]. Thus, PbD is not a matter of privacy policy design and communication, but an engineering solution with a focus on data minimization. For example, one goal of PbD is to minimize processing of personal data outside the scope of the data's original collection context, which is known as secondary use.

Both privacy methods come with specific drawbacks. For example, notice and consent has weaknesses related to the efficient informing of users and accounting for the complexity of data sharing contexts. It requires users to parse and understand lengthy and complex privacy disclaimers in order to evaluate whether the service's data practices are in line with their own privacy preferences [10]. Further, early digital privacy research has shown that individual privacy decision-making is subject to multiple biases and heuristics leading to deviations from preferred privacy behavior [11, 12]. The growing opaqueness of the current automated data collection practices including interoperable services, third-party data brokers, and ID-based cross-device tracking technologies (to name a few), have further amplified the incomprehensibility of privacy disclaimers and consequently the number of uninformed privacy choices – including those of some privacy experts [13]. Second, social media's notice and consent strategy usually comprises privacy control interfaces that have different degrees of data management capacities. The purpose of such controls is to allow users to manage their information disclosure. However, granular privacy controls can backfire: several studies found that more granular privacy control settings can lead merely to an increased data protection perception, a heightened sense of security, which, paradoxically, results in even more user information disclosure. Some authors have termed this phenomenon "privacy fatigue" [14, 15]. Notice interfaces may also be designed to subtly coax individuals to reveal more information than likely intended [16, 17].

PbD's focus on engineering privacy into information technology systems is even less suitable for the social media context: first, people-based marketing techniques are social media's economic lifelines and therefore hard to reconcile with PbD's minimization of data transfer, storage, and processing. Spiekermann and Cranor, for example, have pointed out that social media's business model requires linkage of identifiers across different databases creating data flows that render a PbD approach to privacy untenable [18]. Furthermore, as users have an incentive to engage in social interactions that necessarily produce vast data flows, social media user activity appears largely incompatible with PbD's strict data minimization principle.

Evidently, both notice and consent and PbD are inadequate privacy strategies for the social media context, which raises the question how alternative privacy strategies could be conceptualized and implemented. In this paper, we examine the feasibility of a participatory governance approach to privacy that relies on social media users to participate in data policy-making. For this purpose, we analyze the first, and to our best knowledge only, large-scale social media governance initiative with the objective to democratize data policy processes for a global online population. Between 2009 and 2012, Facebook implemented a participatory governance system that enabled users to vote on its privacy policy. The participatory governance process consisted of two main parts: First, in a blog post, Facebook published changes to its data policy documents and subsequently allowed thirty days for user comments [19]. A threshold of 7,000 user comments needed to be reached for the proposed changes be to subjected to a vote. This rule, however, was not applied to the initial proposal, the introduction of the participatory governance system itself. Generally, if a proposal did not reach the required 7000 user comments, Facebook implemented the changes without user voting. Second, if a vote was held, then 30% of the active user population needed to participate in order for the results to be binding. Within the three-year period, only two out of eleven proposed policy changes managed to reach the necessary number of comments to be subjected to a vote. Importantly, in late 2012, Facebook held a final vote, in which users lost their voting privileges since a pre-specified quorum of about 300 million users was decisively missed (i.e., only 668,872 Facebook users voted). Newspapers responded to this outcome with headlines such as "Facebook Democracy is Dead" [20] and "Whoever promised us Facebook 'rights'?" [21]. Despite such attention-grabbing press articles, however, no research has been conducted on Facebook's participatory privacy initiative.

To fill this gap, we first explain the different components of Facebook's participatory governance approach and show how it enabled users to exert influence over the data policy decision-making procedure. Second, we chronicle the events between 2009 and 2012, in particular, those that are relevant for the introduction and eventual elimination of the open governance initiative. Third, we apply an unsupervised machine learning topic modeling algorithm to 5269 Facebook posts surrounding the final vote in 2012. Thereby, we identify common themes based on the topics users engaged with most during the final electoral period. We then outline the main reasons why Facebook's effort to democratize its data policy design failed. Finally, we end by briefly discussing the significance of framing effects for participatory governance processes that rely on user judgment. Learning from Facebook's attempt to democratize data policy procedures, we argue that the success of future participatory privacy initiatives essentially depends on establishing competition among different data policy frames.

2 Background

In February 2009, Facebook received widespread protests from users and non-profit privacy organizations after it had changed its main data policy document called *The Statement of Rights and Responsibilities (SRR)* [22]. This change essentially granted Facebook the right to handle user information for advertising practices for indefinite time after users had left the platform [23]. In response to the public outcry, Facebook revised its decision and publicly announced to open up the policy design process to its users by launching a notice-and-comment rulemaking process [24]. Over a three-year period, Facebook drafted a total of twelve privacy proposals that were subject to this process. The first such policy proposal was published on April 26, 2009, which included the introduction of the novel participatory governance process (among others).

2.1 Facebook's Participatory Governance Process

The governance process was structured into three phases: during the initial phase, Facebook presented a new policy draft on a Facebook page called *Facebook Site Governance* [25]. This triggered a thirty-day period, the second phase, enabling Facebook users to provide comments on the proposal. Users were asked to place their comments on Facebook's blog page [26]. A rule specified a necessary threshold of 7000 user comments on a policy proposal for a vote to take place. However, for the first policy proposal in 2009, Facebook circumvented phase 2 and asked users to directly partake in a vote. Generally, once the number of comments exceeded 7000, in a final phase, users were given a seven-day time frame to cast their vote on the policy suggestions through a Facebook app. Importantly, a voting regulation required a minimum of 30% of active Facebook users to participate in the vote for the results to become binding (active users were defined as users who had logged on to Facebook at

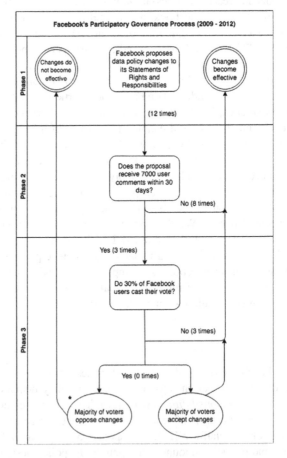

Fig. 1. The three phases of Facebook's participatory governance system (2009–2012). [* indicates user influence in the governance process. The first policy proposal did not include phase 2.]

least once in the last thirty days prior to the vote, see [19]). Figure 1 illustrates the three phases of the governance process.

A Facebook policy proposal could only be rejected by user vote once phase three of the process had been reached and 30% of active Facebook users had casted a vote with the majority opposing the proposal. Between 2009 and 2012, three out of a total of twelve policy drafts were subjected to a vote, however, as mentioned above, the initial policy proposal did not require user comments. No proposal reached the required participation percentage (see Fig. 2 for a detailed timeline of the relevant governance events).

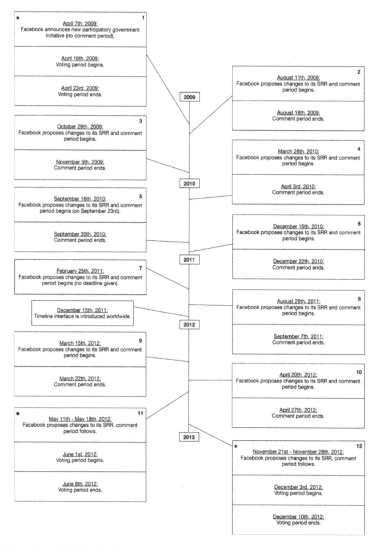

Fig. 2. Timeline of all Facebook policy proposals between 2009 and 2012. [* indicates proposal was subjected to a vote. No vote reached the required 30% voter turnout.]

A second policy change was subjected to a vote on June 8, 2012, that contained multiple modifications to the SRR. Among others, it explained in more detail how user information and information of users' friends is saved on users' phones, and provided more information on how advertisement is served on the platform [27]. Finally, on November 21, 2012, Facebook published its 12th and last policy draft that comprised three updates to the SRR: new filters to manage privacy controls of Facebook's messaging tool, the integration of users' Instagram data into their Facebook profile, and the termination of the voting component of Facebook's governance process [28].

The required 30% participation turnout was missed by large margins in all three votes. In fact, user participation did not exceed 0.4% of active Facebook users for any of the three votes (Fig. 3). The final vote in November 2012 mobilized the largest number of voters with 668.872 Facebook users voting out of a total of 1.060.000.000 active Facebook users at the time [29].

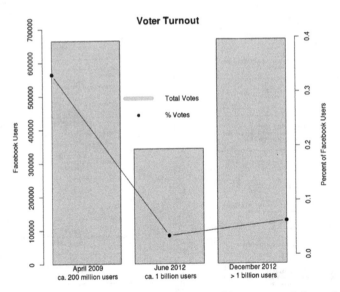

Fig. 3. Voter turnout. Bars represents the number of valid votes casted for each vote. Line represents the percentage of active Facebook users who voted.

All votes produced clear results. In April 2009, a large majority voted in favor (74.3%) of the introduction of the voting system itself [30]. In June 2012, a second vote produced a clear result with 86.9% of the voters rejecting Facebook's data policy proposal (see Fig. 4). Similarly, for the final vote in December, 88% of the voters opposed the data policy proposals to prevent Facebook to take away their voting rights [31]. As the final two elections failed to reach a voter turnout of 30%, Facebook went on to adopt the policy changes.

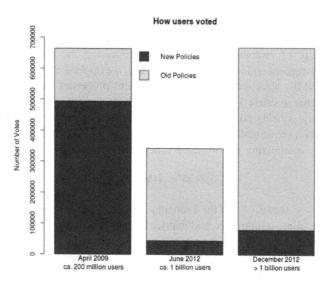

Fig. 4. How users voted. Voters accepted the first and rejected the second and third Facebook SRR data policy proposals by large margins.

3 Methods

For our empirical analysis, the Facebook Graph API was accessed to collect user comments associated with Facebook's participatory governance process. Specifically, Facebook comments on the following four dates surrounding the final vote were collected. On November 21, 2012, Facebook announced the end of the governance initiative in the context of a policy update. On December 3, 2012, Facebook announced the start of the voting period. Both posts were published on Facebook's blog [29]. On December 10 and December 11, 2012, Facebook published and commented on the voting results, respectively. These posts were published on the Facebook Site Governance page [25]. In total, 5269 user comments were collected on these four events on the corresponding pages in order to understand how users experienced and reacted to the voting process during the final vote.

We first employed a bag-of-words approach to analyze user comments. Thereby, we counted the weighted frequency of single words in every single comment by measuring their term frequency-inverse document frequency (TF-IDF) distribution on our sample [32]. A high frequency for a specific word in a mass of different comments does not mean that this word is very significant to a specific comment. On the contrary, single words that could be found very frequently in one specific comment are very often significant for this comment. TF-IDF copes with this issue and gives a more representative overview of the sample under investigation, which can be seen when reviewing the relevant word cloud (see Sect. 4.1, Fig. 6).

In the second step, we applied a topic modeling algorithm to find underlying discussion topics that exist in our sample and are not easily identifiable. Topic modeling is a family of probabilistic models for uncovering the underlying semantic structure of a document collection [33]. In our case, we applied a non-negative matrix factorization (NMF) algorithm to uncover immanent properties of our sample [34]. NMF assumes that a matrix V can be approximately factorized in two matrices H and W, with all matrices being non-negative: $V \simeq HW$. Given that someone knows matrix V, one can apply a sequentially coordinatewise algorithm [35] to acquire an estimation of H and W, by minimizing the objective function:

$$min||\mathbf{V} - \mathbf{HW}||_F$$

where V, H, W $\geq$ 0 and $||\cdot||_F$ is the Frobenius distance. In topic modeling, matrix V represents a document-term matrix, and matrices H and W a document-topic matrix and topic-word matrix, respectively. Given our sample, we created a document-term matrix by assuming that each user comment corresponds to one document. We removed all non-Latin characters in our sample, including punctuations. In order to derive the related document-topic and topic-word matrices from our document-term matrix, we needed to choose the number of topics a priori. We found the optimal number of topics by applying a density-based method proposed by Cao-Juan et al. [36]. The method calculates the document-topic and topic-word matrices for various models, assuming a different number of topics each time. Then, for each model, it calculates the mean cosine distance between the derived topics with the function:

$$D_k = \frac{\sum_{i=1}^{K} \sum_{i=i+1}^{K} c(T_i, T_j)}{K(K-1)/2}$$

where K represents the number of topics in a model, and $c(T_i, T_j)$ is the cosine distance between topics i and j, calculated by:

$$c(T_i, T_j) = \frac{\sum_{v=0}^{V} T_{iv}, T_{jv}}{\sqrt{\sum_{v=0}^{V} T_{iv}^2} \sqrt{\sum_{v=0}^{V} T_{jv}^2}}$$

where V is the number of words in the document-term matrix, and T_{iv}, T_{jv} the empirical distribution densities for word v in topics i and j, respectively, as derived from the topic-word matrix. The optimal model is the one that has the minimum mean cosine distance, in our case that was for K = 11 (Fig. 5).

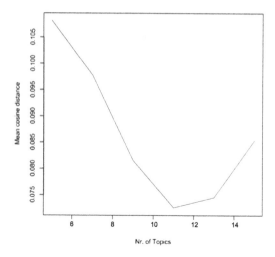

Fig. 5. Topic optimization process. The model with the minimum mean cosine distance consisted of 11 topics.

4 Results

4.1 Word Cloud Analysis

Our TF-IDF based word cloud analysis of the 5269 Facebook comments surrounding the final vote reflects users' dismissive stance towards Facebook's proposal to effectively end the voting component (Fig. 6). Users oppose the removal of their right to vote on future Facebook policies. The most prominent terms in the visual word cloud are: "opposed", "oppose", and "changes". Generally, the majority of terms in the word cloud address governance (e.g., "demands", "change", "policy", "voting"). Furthermore, users specifically refer to the concrete issues that are at stake in the final vote (e.g., "privacy", "control", "personal", "data"). The lack of unrelated terms in the word cloud illustrates users' serious interest in voicing their opinion towards the proposal at hand. Moreover, the word cloud contains English as well as German terms.

German-language user comments are also associated with general governance related terms (e.g., "abstimmen", "forderungen") as well as address their opposition to the proposal (e.g., "wiederspreche", "(¨a)nderungen", "daten", "weitergabe").

4.2 Topic Modeling Analysis

The NMF-based analysis produced eleven topic bags: five English topics, four German topics, one Spanish topic, and one German-English topic. An overview of the topic bags with their distribution across the relevant events of the final vote can be seen in Fig. 7. Topic 1 aggregates English comments of users that addressed the lack of notice provided by Facebook on the participation process. These user comments were

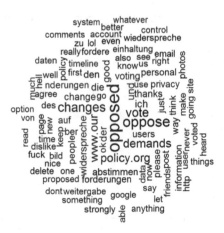

Fig. 6. Word cloud of user comments during the final electoral period in 2012 [November 21, December 3, December 10 & 11].

published on the day of the policy change announcement (24%), the voting period deadline (37%), and the day after the results had been published (31%). Also, on the day of the proposal announcement, users stated that their friends had not been informed about the governance process (Topic 2, 59%). Beginning with the announcement of the policy proposal and throughout the voting period, users voiced their general opposition to Facebook's data policy changes. These claims commonly included demands to move the vote to the platform www.our-policy.org (Topics 3 & 4). A URL to the archived version of the website mobilizing participants for the vote in June 2012 can be found in [37]. Topics 5 and 6 include German comments made almost exclusively on the voting period deadline day (97% and 100%, respectively). Topic 5 aggregates comments that are reposts of a prefabricated text stating the opposition to the commercial use of personal data. Topic 6 includes reposts of a text opposing the commercial use of personal photos with references to European data protection law. Similarly, Topic 7 consists of German posts with the same content but referring to German data protection law. These posts were all published on December 3, 2012, the first day of the voting period (100%). After the voting period had ended, comments in Spanish included personal data ownership statements (Topic 8, 100%). Topics 9, 10, and 11 collected similar comments in English, which were mostly prefabricated texts discernible by terms such as "hereby" and "declare" (Topic 10). Such comments were supposed to function as signed user statements, which had the intention to prohibit Facebook from using personal data for commercial purposes.

Based on the topics identified by the NMF algorithm, we can cluster them into three prominent emerging themes: (1) lack of notice provided by Facebook, (2) demands to move the vote to another platform, and (3) general opposition against Facebook's data practices by reference to various laws. We will discuss these themes below.

Emerging Theme 1: Lack of Notice Provided by Facebook

A common theme we discerned was users' dissatisfaction with Facebook's effort to adequately raise awareness about critical participatory events. As Topics 1 & 2 illustrate, users stated that they were not sufficiently informed of their right to vote. For example, users complained that none of their friends seemed to be aware of the vote on deadline day (see example comment 1).

Example comment (1), November 10, 2012 (end of voting period):

(1) *"...I personally went on a 6 day barrage of information to my limited number of friends over 99% of them had no idea the vote was going on much less how to access the proper page to vote..."*

Other users mentioned that they received the Facebook notification one day after the vote had ended either in their email spam folder or in their "other messages" inbox on Facebook; see example comment (2) & (3).

Example comments (2) & (3), December 11, 2012 (one day after voting period had ended):

(2) *"I'm just hearing about it today. Found this by accident. The only reason I'm even on this page today is because I found an email from you, dated 2 years ago that was hidden in my facebook spam inbox..."*
(3) *"...the notification I received about this was in my "other" messages folder. I just found out about this spam folder today, maybe that's not the best place to send these notifications..."*

Facebook had stated that it would first send out emails to all active Facebook users prior to a vote, second, inform about the vote on its Facebook Site Governance, and, third, its separate Facebook blog page. Nonetheless, our topic analysis indicates that users experienced timing and visibility problems for relevant governance-related notices. Moreover, the majority of user comments relating to notification problems were posted after the final vote had ended (Topic 1, December 11 & 12, 2012). Thus, many notification issues surfaced only when it was already too late.

Emerging Theme 2: Demands to Move the Vote to www.our-policy.org

Topics 3 & 4 cover German and English-speaking users' opposition against ("widerspreche", "oppose") the removal of voting rights. Additionally, groups from both language regions demanded to move the vote to the website www.our-policy.org ("moechte", "abstimmen", "demand", "vote"). This website was created by privacy activist Max Schrems in order to facilitate the mobilization of 7000 user comments to trigger a vote for the June 2012 proposals. Example comments (4) & (5) illustrate that these postings were copy-and-paste messages. The initiative was successful in breaking the voting threshold, but the eventual vote did not pass the required 30% turnout (see Sect. 2.1, Fig. 2).

Example comments (4) & (5) on November 21, 2012 (announcement of proposal):

(4) *"Ich widerspreche den Änderungen und will über die Forderungen auf* www.our-policy.org *abstimmen."*
(5) *"I oppose the changes and want a vote about the demands on* www.our-policy.org*"*

All user concerns calling for a move of the vote outside of Facebook occurred before and at the beginning of the voting period (Topics 3 & 4, 100% posted on November 21 & December 3). Since the website www.our-policy.org was available in English and German only, no such copy-and-paste messages can be found in Spanish (or any other language, see [37]).

Topic 1	Topic 2	Topic 3	Topic 4
didnt	dont	widerspreche	oppose
know	privacy	forderungen	changes
policy	change	moechte	demand
page	changes	ueber	vote
never	see	aenderungen	moechte
email	posts	wwwourpolicyorg	anderungen
voting	from	abstimmen	abstimmen
news	friends	abstimmung	wwwourpolicyorg
Theme 1: Lack of Notice		**Theme 2: Move vote to other website**	

Topic 5	Topic 6	Topic 7	Topic 8	Topic 9	Topic 10	Topic 11
lehne	widerspreche	widerspreche	datos	personal	hereby	companies
forderungen	weitergabe	weitergabe	personales	data	declare	share
ab	bild	daten	uso	photos	handwritten	users
verbiete	inhalte	inhalte	escrito	commercial	consent	information
daten	einhaltung	dritte	consentimiento	use	authorize	privacy
kommerziell	europäischen	erhaltung	totalmente	prohibited	personal	policy
anderweitig	datenschutz	urheberrecht	derechos	written	data	without
abstimmen	urheberrecht	deutschland	autorizo	control	use	permission
Theme 3: Opposition against Facebook's data practices by reference to copyright law						

Distribution across events	Topic 1	Topic 2	Topic 3	Topic 4	Topic 5	Topic 6	Topic 7	Topic 8	Topic 9	Topic 10	Topic 11
Announcement 21st Nov	0,24	0,59	0,02	0,78	0.02	0	0	0	0.53	0.17	0.55
Voting begins 3rd Dec	0,08	0,12	0,98	0,22	0.02	0	1	0	0.09	0.05	0.02
Voting ends 10th Dec	0,37	0,16	0	0	0.97	1	0	0.78	0.25	0.23	0.19
Day after vote 11th Dec	0,31	0,13	0	0	0.01	0	0	0.22	0.13	0.56	0.24

Fig. 7. Topic bags 1–11 (top) and their distribution (bottom) across the four significant events of the final vote.

Emerging Theme 3: Opposition Against Facebook's Data Practices by Reference to Copyright Law

Users from the different language regions expressed their discontent with Facebook's data practices in response to the final policy proposal. Yet, such user comments often did not address the specific content of the proposals. Rather, many of the posts were, again, copy-and-paste comments purported to have an effect on user data ownership rights on Facebook. Many users falsely believed that Facebook owns users' intellectual property, granting Facebook the right to publish and share user data without any constraints (independent of a user's privacy settings). In practice, signing up enables Facebook to share and redistribute user data as specified in users' privacy settings configuration. Similarly, German comments included statements prohibiting data use for commercial purposes (see Topic 5). German users stressed that their rights are under the jurisdiction of the law of the European Union (see topic 6) or German law (see Topic 7).

Example comment (6), December 3, 2012 (voting begins):

(6) *"Ich widerspreche den vorgeschlagenen Änderungen von Facebook und fordere die Einhaltung der Datenschutzund Urheberrechtsvorschriften der Bundesrepublik Deutschland und der europäischen Union."*

English and Spanish-speaking users also posted ownership-related messages. Commonly, users thereby announced that data controllers required handwritten authorization in order to use their personal data (see Topics 8–11).

Example comment (7), December 11, 2012 (one day after voting period had ended):

(7) *"I do not authorize use of my info posted or deleted before or after the changes made-by any third parties or any other group known or unknown to me. You must have my written consent or you do not have my permission."*

Example comment (8), November 10, 2012 (end of voting period):

(8) *"Les prohibo terminantemente usar cualquier tipo de información ma, es prohibida y/o solo con mi consentimiento puede ser usada. Cualquier uso sin mi consentimiento escrito es un hecho penal y será juzgado como tal Diego Bernal."*

Such declarations of data ownership were posted across all data collection dates. From the postings, it is unclear whether users were aware of the content of the policy draft, which may have contributed to a general fear of losing control over their personal data (see Topic 9, for example). Recently, a similar case occurred prior to the introduction of the General Data Protection Regulation (GDPR): a Facebook picture containing a satirical objection message was frequently reposted by German users to attempt shielding them from obligations associated with the GDPR. The message was shared more than 5000 times [38].

4.3 Analysis

The topics we identified are rooted in the weaknesses of Facebook's governance process and the role Facebook played as a governance organizer. First, the lack of notice (Theme 1) users complained about, was partly due to a complicated multiphase governance procedure: it required users to carry out different activities (read and understand the policy changes, write a comment on a separate page, download an app and hence cast a vote) under varying time constraints (comment and voting period). Contrary to its April 4, 2009, announcement, Facebook shortened the official thirty-day comment phase to seven and fourteen days for some of the policy proposals (see Sect. 2.1, Fig. 2). For the first vote in 2009, there was no comment phase at all. Such irregularities probably increased the confusion among users as to when and where their engagement was required. Furthermore, Facebook inconveniently scheduled the last vote for US users on November 21, 2012, exactly one week prior to Thanksgiving, when US users are more likely to travel or be occupied with other activities [39]. At the same time, rather than pinning relevant information on each user's individual timeline or newsfeed, Facebook sent out emails that ended up in some users' spam. Generally, social networks exhibit informational scalability that can dramatically mitigate the cost of reaching individuals – particularly for the platform operator. An experiment on 61 million Facebook users demonstrated that Facebook's mobilization messages for the 2010 congressional elections had a significant influence on voter turnout [40]. Thereby, experimenters showed that social mobilization on Facebook (automatically publishing "I voted" messages) is much more effective for political mobilization than for general information mobilization. For its own participatory policy process, however, Facebook did not apply such effective measures to increase voter turnout.

Second, the lack of effort to raise awareness undermined the legitimacy of Facebook as the organizer of the governance process among users. This is not only reflected by user calls to separate the electoral process from the Facebook platform (Theme 2) but also by the general passivity of Facebook as a mediator of user comments. Facebook did not react to user comments voicing concerns over insufficient information about the government process, it did not address the spreading of imprecise ownership claims, and did not respond to the orchestrated request to transfer the electoral procedure to a third-party platform.

Third, the imprecise statements regarding data ownership rights (Theme 3) expressed by English, German, and Spanish language groups reflect a wider disconnection between Facebook and its users. Evidently, both parties talked at cross purposes indicating the overall lack of informed user involvement in a governance process that did not provide users with the necessary resources to exert influence in the first place. This is perhaps best reflected in the regulatory requirements of the electoral procedure: only two out of eleven proposals that had required user comments managed to pass the 7000-comment threshold and triggered a vote, while voter turnouts remained below 0.4% of active users for all three votes. In the last election in December 2012, a clear majority decided against the SRR proposals, but the vote missed 317,331,128 votes to be effective (for comparison: the US population is about 325.7 million). Even when Facebook held the first vote in 2009, a vote would have required more than 66 million participants to be binding (population of France is 66.9 million).

Besides such electoral hurdles, users had little influence in co-designing, codirecting, or correcting SRR proposals. For example, users could not vote on specific sections of a proposal, but only accept or reject the entire policy document. Also, while the comment phase permitted users to express their views on the policy changes, user comments appeared to have little to no influence on the actual decision-making process. Facebook itself complained that user comments followed a "quantity over quality" [41] principle when justifying the termination of the voting component on November 21, 2012.

5 Discussion and Concluding Remarks

Facebook is not an elected government organization, it has no legal obligation to hold elections or enable user participation on data policy. Yet, the societal and political repercussions of the recent global privacy breaches put pressure on Facebook. The question is whether Facebook can continue operate solely as a for-profit company accountable first and foremost to its investors [42]. Its prime source of economic value is users' personal information. Thus, in protecting its economic advantages, Facebook should be accountable to its users, too. Sharing more responsibility over data policy governance with users could be a way to fulfill this role.

In this paper, we evaluated the first social media open governance initiative, which had the stated objective to democratize data policy processes for a global digital population. We described the different phases of Facebook's open governance initiative and chronicled the relevant events of its multi-year duration. We applied unsupervised machine learning to identify major themes Facebook users discussed during the final electoral period: first, users voiced their concerns about being insufficiently informed about their participation requirements; second, users expressed their discontent with Facebook's data practices and made uninformed references to data ownership; and third, users demanded moving the electoral process to another platform. Taken together, our analysis suggests that Facebook's participatory privacy strategy and its implementation did not provide a solution to the weaknesses of notice and consent implementations.

Given its micro-targeting advertising capabilities, Facebook could have used its own information infrastructure to target individual users about governance relevant information to better inform them about their participation opportunities. Moreover, the governance process provided too little meaningful participation possibilities leaving users with little influence. Finally, copy-and-paste messages manifested users' frustration: the process did not trigger sufficient exchange and debate between users and between users and Facebook.

Based on our analysis, we can identify a number of ways in which a better participatory governance process could be designed: among others, sharing decision-making on policy design so that users have more influence on policy outcomes, giving users more time to understand and vote on new policies, and implementing an electoral process without unrealistic voter turnout requirements. Discussing the implications of each of these insights for future participatory privacy strategies would go beyond the scope of this research. Yet, many of the issues participants expressed in the comments are a result of Facebook having a monopoly over controlling the framing of governance-relevant information.

Democratic theory provides a useful distinction between proceduralistic and non-minimalistic democratic systems. Facebook's governance system was fundamentally proceduralistic. Proceduralism denotes that the benefit of democratic governance, its core value, essentially lies in the characteristics of the governance process [43]. Such minimalist theories of democracy commonly make little demands on the epistemic quality of citizens' choices. Accordingly, Facebook's procedural strategy placed little value, and therefore relied only to a very small extent, on user's privacy decision-making competence. Thus, with a proceduralistic democratic policy process in place, user participation is unlikely to help overcome the shortcomings of notice and consent strategies.

Nonminimalistic democratic theories, on the other hand, emphasize democracy, allowing individuals to determine policy outcomes that reflect their preferences. Such theories and their implementations must necessarily rely on the quality of individual decision-making. Importantly, both privacy [44] and democratic theory research papers [45] have shown that controlling how choice-relevant information is presented, in so-called frames, represents a powerful position in shaping individuals' privacy and voting competence. Since individuals are known to be highly susceptible to framing effects, a governance system permitting only one framing channel can hardly produce informed decision-making. Multiple frames could help mitigate the inherent bias of each individual frame [46, 47].

As such, different frames could lead to more user deliberation of privacy preferences, more discussion about how to interpret choice-relevant information on the platform, and more exchange between voters on privacy policy. Note that such an approach likely necessitates the involvement of several third parties to produce competing policy frames. In summary, a participatory approach to privacy policy should follow a nonminimalistic conceptualization of participation by strengthening individual privacy decision-making through the provision of multiple competing frames.

Acknowledgments. We are grateful to Kathryn E. Lambert and Alan Nochenson for their contributions to data collection and preliminary analysis of the data. We also thank the anonymous reviewers for their comments. The research activities of Severin Engelmann and Jens Grossklags are supported by the German Institute for Trust and Safety on the Internet (DIVSI).

References

1. CNN: Mark Zuckerberg in his own words: The CNN interview. http://money.cnn.com/2018/03/21/technology/mark-zuckerberg-cnn-interview-transcript. Accessed 18 Apr 2018
2. Lazer, D., et al.: The science of fake news. Science **359**(6380), 1094–1096 (2018)
3. Allcott, H., Gentzkow, M.: Social media and fake news in the 2016 election. J. Econ. Perspect. **31**(2), 211–236 (2017)
4. The Atlantic: What took Facebook so long? https://www.theatlantic.com/technology/archive/2018/03/facebook-cambridge-analytica/555866/. Accessed 18 Apr 2018
5. Pu, Y., Grossklags, J.: Valuating friends' privacy: does anonymity of sharing personal data matter? In: Proceedings of the Symposium on Usable Privacy and Security, pp. 339–355 (2017)
6. Stieger, S., Burger, C., Bohn, M., Voracek, M.: Who commits virtual identity suicide? Differences in privacy concerns, internet addiction, and personality between Facebook users and quitters. Cyberpsychol. Behav. Soc. Netw. **16**(9), 629–634 (2013)
7. Cate, F., Mayer-Schönberger, V.: Notice and consent in a world of big data. Int. Data Priv. Law **3**(2), 67–73 (2013)
8. Langheinrich, M.: Privacy by design—Principles of privacy-aware ubiquitous systems. In: Abowd, G.D., Brumitt, B., Shafer, S. (eds.) UbiComp 2001. LNCS, vol. 2201, pp. 273–291. Springer, Heidelberg (2001). https://doi.org/10.1007/3-540-45427-6_23

9. Gürses, S., del Alamo, J.M.: Privacy engineering: shaping an emerging field of research and practice. IEEE Secur. Priv. **14**(2), 240–246 (2016)
10. Good, N., et al.: Stopping spyware at the gate: a user study of privacy, notice and spyware. In: Proceedings of the Symposium on Usable Privacy and Security, pp. 43–52 (2005)
11. Acquisti, A., Grossklags, J.: Privacy and rationality in individual decision making. IEEE Secur. Priv. **3**(1), 26–33 (2005)
12. Spiekermann, S., Grossklags, J., Berendt, B.: E-privacy in 2nd generation e-commerce: privacy preferences versus actual behavior. In: Proceedings of the ACM Conference on Electronic Commerce, pp. 38–47 (2001)
13. Gindin, S.: Nobody reads your privacy policy or online contract: lessons learned and questions raised by the FTC's action against Sears. Northwest. J. Technol. Intellect. Prop. **8** (1), 1–37 (2009)
14. Keith, M., Maynes, C., Lowry, P., Babb, J.: Privacy fatigue: the effect of privacy control complexity on consumer electronic information disclosure. In: Proceedings of the International Conference on Information Systems (2014)
15. Brandimarte, L., Acquisti, A., Loewenstein, G.: Misplaced confidences: privacy and the control paradox. Soc. Psychol. Pers. Sci. **4**(3), 340–347 (2013)
16. Bösch, C., Erb, B., Kargl, F., Kopp, H., Pfattheicher, S.: Tales from the dark side: privacy dark strategies and privacy dark patterns. Proc. Priv. Enhancing Technol. **4**, 237–254 (2016)
17. Nochenson, A., Grossklags, J.: An online experiment on consumers' susceptibility to fall for post-transaction marketing scams. In: Proceedings of the European Conference on Information Systems (2014)
18. Spiekermann, S., Cranor, L.F.: Engineering privacy. IEEE Trans. Softw. Eng. **35**(1), 67–82 (2009)
19. Facebook. https://www.facebook.com/notes/facebook/next-steps-on-facebook-governance/70896562130/. Accessed 18 Apr 2018
20. Buzzfeed: Facebook democracy is dead. https://www.buzzfeed.com/mattbuchanan/facebook-democracy-is-dead?. Accessed 18 Apr 2018
21. CNN: The end of digital democracy? Facebook wants to take away your right to vote. https://edition.cnn.com/2012/11/22/tech/social-media/facebook-democracy. Accessed 18 Apr 2018
22. Facebook: https://www.facebook.com/terms.php. Accessed 18 Apr 2018
23. The Guardian: Facebook privacy change angers campaigners. https://www.theguardian.com/technology/2009/dec/10/facebook-privacy. Accessed 18 Apr 2018
24. PCWorld: Facebook's Zuckerberg to Address User Privacy Concerns at Press Conference Thursday. https://www.pcworld.com/article/160304/facebook.html. Accessed 18 Apr 2018
25. Facebook. https://www.facebook.com/fbsitegovernance/. Accessed 18 Apr 2018
26. Facebook Newsroom. https://newsroom.fb.com/. Accessed 18 Apr 2018
27. Adweek: Facebook's proposed revisions to statement of rights and responsibilities, data use policy up for vote through June 8. http://www.adweek.com/digital/site-governance-vote/. Accessed 18 Apr 2018
28. Letter of the Electronic Privacy Information Center. https://epic.org/privacy/facebook/EPIC-CDD-Ltr-to-FB-Data-Use.pdf. Accessed 18 Apr 2018
29. Facebook Newsroom: Our Site Governance Vote. https://newsroom.fb.com/news/2012/12/our-site-governance-vote/. Accessed 18 Apr 2018
30. Facebook: Results of the Inaugural Facebook Site Governance Vote. https://www.facebook.com/notes/facebook/results-of-the-inaugural-facebook-site-governance-vote/79146552130/. Accessed 18 Apr 2018

31. CNN: Voting closes on Facebook policy changes, only 299 million votes short. https://edition.cnn.com/2012/12/10/tech/social-media/facebook-policy-vote/index.html. Accessed 18 Apr 2018

32. Aizawa, A.: An information-theoretic perspective of TFIDF measures. Inf. Process. Manag. **39**(1), 45–65 (2003)

33. Blei, D., Lafferty, J.: Topic models. In: Text Mining: Classification, Clustering, and Applications, pp. 71–93 (2009)

34. Lee, D., Seung, S.: Learning the parts of objects by non-negative matrix factorization. Nature **401**(6755), 788–791 (1999)

35. Franc, V., Hlaváč, V., Navara, M.: Sequential coordinate-wise algorithm for the non-negative least squares problem. In: Gagalowicz, A., Philips, W. (eds.) CAIP 2005. LNCS, vol. 3691, pp. 407–414. Springer, Heidelberg (2005). https://doi.org/10.1007/11556121_50

36. Cao, J., Xia, T., Li, J., Zhang, Y., Tang, S.: A density-based method for adaptive LDA model selection. Neurocomputing **72**(7–9), 1775–1778 (2009)

37. Our Policy, 7000 Comments for a better Privacy Policy. http://web.archive.org/web/20120617192456/, http://www.our-policy.org:80/html/en.html. Accessed 21 May 2018

38. Süddeutsche Zeitung: Nein, man kann den neuen Datenschutz-Regeln nicht per Facebook-Bild widersprechen. http://www.sueddeutsche.de/digital/eu-verordnung-nein-man-kann-den-neuen-datenschutz-regeln-nicht-per-facebook-bild-widersprechen-1.3984780. Accessed 18 May 2018

39. New York Times: A guide to (somewhat) painless thanksgiving travel. https://www.nytimes.com/2017/11/21/travel/thanksgiving-travel-tips.html. Accessed 18 Apr 2018

40. Bond, R., et al.: A 61-million-person experiment in social influence and political mobilization. Nature **489**(7415), 295–298 (2012)

41. Facebook newsroom: proposed updates to our governing documents. https://newsroom.fb.com/news/2012/11/proposed-updates-to-our-governing-documents/. Accessed 18 Apr 2018

42. Wired: The case for a Zuck-free Facebook. https://www.wired.com/story/the-case-for-a-zuck-free-facebook/. Accessed 21 May 2018

43. Estlund, D.: Democratic Authority: A Philosophical Framework. Princeton University Press, Princeton (2009)

44. Adjerid, I., Acquisti, A., Brandimarte, L., Loewenstein, G.: Sleights of privacy: framing, disclosures, and the limits of transparency. In: Proceedings of the Symposium on Usable Privacy and Security (2013)

45. Kelly, J.T.: Framing democracy: a behavioral approach to democratic theory. Princeton University Press, Princeton (2012)

46. Sniderman, P.M., Theriault, S.M.: The structure of political argument and the logic of issue framing. In: Studies in Public Opinion: Attitudes, Nonattitudes, Measurement Error, and Change, pp. 133–165 (2004)

47. Brewer, P., Gross, K.: Values, framing, and citizens' thoughts about policy issues: effects on content and quantity. Polit. Psychol. **26**(6), 929–948 (2005)

Compliance

The Right of Access Under the Police Directive: Small Steps Forward

Diana Dimitrova[1](✉) and Paul De Hert[2]

[1] FIZ Karlsruhe, Karlsruhe, Germany
Diana.dimitrova@fiz-Karlsruhe.de
[2] Vrije Universiteit Brussel, Brussels, Belgium
Paul.De.Hert@vub.be

Abstract. The present article sets out to examine the right of access under Directive 2016/680, which regulates the processing of personal data by EU Member States' law enforcement authorities. The article analyses in detail the provisions on the right of access. More precisely, it looks at whether the right provides for sufficient transparency towards the data subject and whether its scope allows for a harmonized data protection across the law enforcement sector in the EU. The article concludes that while the provisions on the right of access make a significant step towards more transparency, they also suffer from deficiencies. Also, the limited scope of the Directive takes away from the harmonization attempts.

Keywords: Right of access · Data protection · Law enforcement
Directive 2016/680

1 Introduction

The right of access to one's personal data plays an important role in allowing data subjects to exercise control over the processing of their data [1]. Its significance is evidenced by its explicit inclusion as a constitutive element of the fundamental right to data protection in Article 8 (2) Charter of Fundamental Rights of the European Union (CFREU) [2] and by its presence in every instrument on data protection in Europe, e.g. Article 12 (a) Directive 95/46/EC [3], Article 15 General Data Protection Regulation (GDPR) [4], as well as Council of Europe instruments [5].

Despite the lack of a comprehensive data protection framework in the law-enforcement sector in the EU until the entry into force of Directive 2016/680 [6], the right of access to one's own data has been provided for in different Area of Freedom Security and Justice (AFSJ) instruments, e.g. Article 17 2008 Framework Decision [7], which is about to be replaced by Directive 2016/680.[1] The said Directive is supposed to improve the protection of data subjects' personal data in the law enforcement sector,

---

[1] Article 59 Directive 2016/680.

© Springer Nature Switzerland AG 2018
M. Medina et al. (Eds.): APF 2018, LNCS 11079, pp. 111–130, 2018.
https://doi.org/10.1007/978-3-030-02547-2_7

not least because it expands the scope of application of the 2008 Framework Decision.[2] Thus, it will be applicable not only to the exchange of personal data between the competent Member State law-enforcement authorities but to the entire cycle of processing of personal data by them. As a result, data subjects may exercise their rights, e.g. the right of access, as regards all law enforcement data processing operations, subject to the limitations provided for in Directive 2016/680.

Further, by replacing the 2008 Framework Decision, Directive 2016/680 would be applicable to the already existing AFSJ instruments, to which the 2008 Framework Decision used to apply, such as SIS II Council Decision [8],[3] PNR [9],[4] and the instruments regulating the Member State law enforcement authorities' access to VIS [10][5] and to EURODAC [11].[6] These instruments themselves, except the EU PNR Directive, contain substantive and procedural rules on the rights of data subjects, e.g. the right of access. These more specific provisions leave Member States a certain margin of appreciation, e.g. as to the procedures for allowing data subjects to exercise their rights and as to the limitations to these rights.[7] Thus, at the time of the entry into force of Directive 2016/680 the patchwork of provisions on the right of access in the law-enforcement sector remains.

This situation gives rise, amongst others, to two questions. First, would the right of access in Directive 2016/680 allow data subjects to exercise their right of access in the law enforcement sector effectively? Second, does Directive 2016/680 bring about a harmonized and consistent application of the right of access in the law enforcement sector?

To answer these questions, the following Sect. 2 will examine the legal sources of the right of access in Europe, while Sect. 3 will examine the significance of that right. Section 4 will introduce the scope of the right of access under Directive 2016/680, followed by Sect. 5 on the information which the controller has to provide under that provision. Section 6 will examine the limitations of the right of access under Directive 2016/680. Next, Sect. 7 will focus on the procedural issues related to the exercise of the right of access. Last but not least, Sect. 8 will discuss in how far the right of access under Directive 2016/680 harmonizes the provisions on that right across the law-enforcement authorities in Europe.

2   Legal Sources of the Right of Access

In Europe, the right of access is one of the subjective rights granted to data subjects in several legal instruments. As mentioned above, the right is enshrined in Article 8 CFREU. It is further to be found in Article 8 (b) of Council of Europe Convention 108,

---

[2] Compare Article 2 Directive 2016/680 and Article 1 2008 Framework Decision.
[3] Recital 21 Council Decision SIS II.
[4] Article 13 (1) EU PNR Directive.
[5] Recital 9 VIS Council Decision.
[6] Recital 39 EURODAC Regulation.
[7] E.g. Article 58 Council Decision SIS II.

pursuant to which any person shall have the right to "obtain at reasonable intervals and without excessive delay or expense confirmation of whether personal data relating to him are stored in the automated data file as well as communication to him of such data in an intelligible form." [12][8] The provision on the right of access as enshrined in Article 12 (a) Directive 95/46/EC is similar. In addition to the requirements in Convention 108, it requires the controller to provide the requesting data subject a minimum set of detailed information about the processing of the data subject's personal data. Article 15 GDPR will replace Article 12 (a) Directive 95/46/EC and expand its scope. Article 15 GDPR applies in the framework of data processing by private and public actors which are not law enforcement or security authorities. It would require data controllers to confirm to the data subject whether they process personal data relating to him and provide him information concerning the processing of his data. The obligatory information pieces are more as compared to Directive 95/46/EC, e.g. as to the envisaged storage period, sources of the data and safeguards used for international transfers. In addition, the data subject has the right to one copy of his data free of charge.

As to the ECHR, Article 8 ECHR on the right to private and family life does not explicitly provide for a subjective right of access to one's data as such. However, in its case-law the ECtHR has tackled the topic of access to one's personal data as an essential part of one's enjoyment of his private and family life, e.g. obtaining details about one's past [13],[9] or as part of ensuring the legal processing of one's data, e.g. by the law enforcement authorities [14].[10] Also, it has assessed under Article 13 ECHR on effective remedies whether on a procedural level access to one's data or at least opportunities for independent supervision and review were provided for [15, 16].[11]

As to the police sector, the right of access to one's data has been enshrined since 1987 in Principle 6.2 of the Council of Europe Committee of Ministers Recommendation Nr. R (87) 15. It provides for the right of every data subject to have access to a police file, which is understood to mean a police file containing data concerning the particular data subject, at regular intervals and without excessive delay, in accordance with domestic law [5].

Following the recent legislative developments concerning data protection in the police sector, the right of access "at reasonable intervals, without constraint and without excessive delay or expense" in Article 17 2008 Framework Decision will be replaced by Article 14 Directive 2016/680. Its provisions and implications will be analyzed in Sect. 5.

---

[8] Article 8 (b) Council of Europe Convention 108 for the Protection of Individuals with regard to Automatic Processing of Personal Data, Strasbourg, 28.01.1981.

[9] ECtHR, *Gaskin v the United Kingdom*, Application no. 10454/83, 07. 07. 1989. *In casu*, obtaining information about claimed abuse while in foster care.

[10] ECtHR, *Khelili v Switzerland*, Application no 16188/07, 18 October 2011 (discussed below).

[11] ECtHR, *Segerstedt-Wiberg and Others v. Sweden*, Application no. 62332/00, 6.06.2006; ECtHR, *Amann v Switzerland*, Application no. 27798/95, 16 February 2000.

3   Four Main Purposes of the Right of Access

As mentioned in the introduction, the right of access is a tool which enables data subjects to exercise control over their data. This broad purpose could be broken down into four more concrete purposes. These are: (1) transparency, (2) supervision of legality of the personal data processing and an enabler of the exercise of the other data protection rights, (3) monitoring the execution of the corrective measures, and (4) raising awareness about practices that impact a large number of data subjects, thus triggering changes. The purposes were derived from case-law and academic literature and complied in the present section.

First, in *Rijkeboer*, the Advocate General (AG) argued that the purpose of the right of access is to give data subjects **transparency** by ensuring that they are aware of the information stored on them [17].[12] One could add that by enhancing transparency, the right of access contributes to the achievement of informational balance between the data subject and the controllers, which is especially important in the law-enforcement sector where the nature of the work involves more secrecy than other sectors.

Second, the knowledge of the personal information stored and the related details allows the data subject to "**supervise**" whether the processing of his data is **lawful and react to illegalities in the processing.** Thus, the right of access is "a means for a data subject to oversee and enforce observance of the law," especially the principles of data protection, *in casu* those enshrined in Article 6 Directive 95/46/EC such as fairness and lawfulness, purpose limitation, data accuracy, data minimization and limited storage period.[13]

In that respect it is argued that the right of access is a **pre-requisite and enabler for the exercise of the remaining informational rights**, "the gatekeeper enabling data subjects to take further action." [14, 18].[14] For the data subject to exercise the other rights – to rectification, erasure, restriction of processing, objection, the right not to be subject to automated individual decision-making such as profiling, and under the GDPR also data portability[15] – he first has to be aware that a certain controller is processing his data and obtain further information related to that processing. Although the data controller is obliged to provide the said information under his information obligations,[16] the two rights are not the same or mutually exclusive. The right of access

---

[12] CJEU, C-553/07, *College van burgemeester en wethouders van Rotterdam v M.E. E. Rijkeboer*, 7.05.2009 (Hereinafter "*Rijkeboer*"), Opinion of the Advocate General Ruiz-Jarabo Colomer, 22.12.2008, par. 33 and 34. In *Rijkeboer*, the applicant requested the College van burgemeester en wethouders van Rotterdam to inform him of the recipients to which it had transferred data relating to him, especially his address, in the two years preceding the request. The College provided the requested information only as regards the disclosure of the data one year prior to the request, the rest was automatically deleted.

[13] Ibid.

[14] See also Joined cases C 141/12 and C 372/12, *YS v Minister voor Immigratie, Inte- gratie en Asiel and Minister voor Immigratie, Integratie en Asiel v M* (Hereinafter "*YS*"), 17.07.2014, par. 44.

[15] Chapter III GDPR and Directive 2016/680.

[16] Art 10 and 11 Directive 95/46/EC, Articles 13 and 14 GDPR, Article 13 Directive 2016/680.

allows the data subject to inquire at any time the controller about the current and past stand of the processing of his data, i.e. the right of access *a fortiori* refers also to the past [17].[17]

Third, the right of access allows the supervision of the legality of the processing not only until the moment of the first access request. It further allows the data subject to **monitor whether a certain illegality has been effectively redressed and when.** A case in point is the ECtHR case of *Khelili.* The Geneva police had found business cards in the possession of the applicant, Khelili, whose content could suggest that she was a prostitute. Thus, she was entered in the police system as a "prostitute." She objected, claiming she was not a prostitute. She demanded the police to change her profession to "tailor." The police acknowledged that since they could not find evidence that the applicant was indeed a prostitute, the profession should be corrected. After subsequently requesting from the Geneva police information about her file several times, the applicant learned from police officials that "prostitute" seemed to have been corrected in the police information system, but not in the criminal record of the applicant, who had been later detained and sentenced on probation for small crimes. *Khelili* shows the importance of having a framework for (directly) accessing one's data in all files held by the police in order to detect illegalities and ensure their timely rectification. This is especially important in the police sector due to the potential consequences on the data subjects [14].[18]

Advocate General Kokott reminds in the *Nowak* case which concerns access to exam scripts, however, that exercising the rights of rectification, erasure or blocking is not the sole aim of the right of access. Rather data subjects in principle have a "legitimate interest in finding out what information about them is processed by the controller," when at all information is processed, i.e. it refers more broadly to transparency [20].[19] This confirms the plurality of the role of the right of access in protecting our private lives and right to data protection.

Fourth, the disclosure of different illegalities related to the processing of one's data could have a wider impact, i.e. **trigger political, judicial and policy-making action** by raising awareness about the processing operations which affect the public at large. An example is the case of Max Schrems's access to his Facebook data which lead to more Facebook users claiming access to their data and to judicial proceedings and legislative changes such as striking down the Safe Harbour and replacing it with the Privacy Shield [18].

---

[17] CJEU, C-533/07, *Rijkeboer,* par. 54.

[18] ECtHR, *Khelili v Switzerland*, Application no. 16188/07, 18 October 2011. The Court held in favour of the applicant, because "prostitute" was not deleted for a long time, the Swiss authorities gave contradictory statements as to whether the term "prostitute" was deleted, the police could not prove the accuracy of the data and that it had been rectified/deleted (a requirement under Swiss law), par. 68–71.

[19] CJEU, C-434/16, *Peter Nowak v Data Protection Commissioner*, Opinion of Advocate General Kokott, 20.07.2017, par. 38–39. The case concerns the request for access to one's exam scripts and the comments made by the examiners. The main question was whether exam scripts qualify as personal data.

4 Scope of the Right of Access in Directive 2016/680

The right of access is enshrined in Article 14 Directive 2016/680. Briefly said, it grants data subjects the right to be informed whether a controller processes data concerning them and receive certain details about the data and the data processing operations. Articles 12 and 17 regulate the modalities of the exercise, while Articles 15 regulates the limitations to the right, i.e. the cases in which the controller may restrict the right, the conditions that need to be fulfilled and the procedures which need to be followed in that case.

The right of access is to be exercised by the data subject against *the controller*. Only officials working in the field of law-enforcement when they carry out law-enforcement tasks on behalf of the competent EU Member State authorities may qualify as controllers under Directive 2016/680.[20] This means that theoretically if a data subject evokes his right of access against a controller from the private sector, e.g. Facebook Ireland, to check whether it disclosed his data such as exchange of messages to the Irish police authority, then the data subjects may not evoke Article 14 Directive 2016/680 against Facebook Ireland. In that scenario Facebook Ireland would still be acting within the scope of the GDPR since it is not a law enforcement authority itself [21], whereas the actions of the Irish police would fall within Directive 2016/680. Further, Directive 2016/680 does not apply to EU institutions, agencies and bodies which process personal data for law-enforcement purposes, e.g. EUROPOL,[21] or to processing which does not fall within the scope of EU law.[22]

5 The Controller Has to Provide Six Categories of Information to the Data Subject

When the data subject evokes the right of access under Directive 2016/680 and the controller decides to grant him that right, the controller shall first **confirm** to the data subject whether he is processing personal data concerning the data subject. If this is the case, he should further **grant him access to the said data** and **communicate** to the data subject **six categories of information** concerning the data processing.[23] By contrast, under Article 17 (1) (a) 2008 Framework Decision the data subject was entitled only to **three categories** (Table 1).[24]

---

[20] Article 2 (1) Directive 2016/680.

[21] Article 2 (3) (b) Directive 2016/680.

[22] Article 2 (3) (a) Directive 2016/680.

[23] Article 14 Directive 2016/680.

[24] Article 17 (1) (a) 2008 Framework Decision.

Table 1. Comparison between the 2008 Framework Decision and Directive 2016/680

Information to the data subject under the right of access	2008 Framework Decision	Directive 2016/680
Confirmation that data are being processed by the controller		√
Purposes of processing +		√
Legal basis for the processing		√
Categories of personal data		√
(Categories of) recipients	√	√
Envisaged storage period/criteria for the storage		√
Rights to rectification, erasure or restriction of processing		√
Right to lodge a complaint with the supervisory authority +		√
Contact details of the supervisory authority		√
Personal data undergoing processing +	√	√
Information about the origin of the data		√
Confirmation that data have been transmitted/disclosed	√	

Thus, one sees that the information concerning the processing which the controller needs to provide under Directive 2016/680 is broader than the details to which the data subject was entitled under the 2008 Framework Decision.

Below is a detailed discussion of the information to be provided to data subjects under Directive 2016/680.

5.1 The Purposes of and Legal Basis for the Processing (Art. 14 (a))

The provision of this information is essential for the data subject who needs to understand clearly why his data is being processed and most importantly - whether it has a legal basis. On that point Directive 2016/680 goes one step further from Article 15 GDPR which does not require the provision of information on the legal basis. The addition of this requirement in Directive 2016/680 could be due to the fact that Directive 2016/680, unlike the GDPR, does not contain a list of grounds for legitimacy of data processing, e.g. consent or contractual obligations.[25] Article 8 Directive 2016/680 only requires the data processing be *based on Union or Member State law*

---

[25] Article 6 GDPR.

and that it be *necessary for the performance of a task related to the prevention, investigation, detection or prosecution of criminal offences or execution of criminal penalties, carried out by the competent authority.*[26] Thus, pointing to the specific law underlying the processing is an indispensable piece of information for the monitoring of the legality of the processing.

The legal basis of the processing is not the same as the purpose of the processing, although the legal basis must specify the objective and purposes of the processing as well as the personal data to be processed.[27] Communicating the purposes of the processing in addition to the legal basis enables the examination of whether the purpose is legitimate and whether the other principles, namely data accuracy, minimization and storage, are complied with, as they are tested against the purpose. On that note, one should not forget that the original controller himself *or another controller* may conditionally process the data for another purpose, different from the one for which the data were collected.[28] This implies that also the change of purpose of and legal basis for the processing by the controller contacted should be communicated to the data subject. This is important, since change of purpose does not have to be communicated to the data subject under the controller's information obligations.[29] Thus, the only way for a data subject to stay aware of the (new) purposes of the processing of his data is by exercising his right of access "at reasonable intervals."[30]

However, the wording of Article 14 Directive 2016/680 suggests that the controller is obliged to communicate information only about the processing he is engaged in, not processing of the same data which is carried out by other controllers, e.g. for a different purpose. Thus, to have a clear overview of the full cycle of the processing of his data and the legality thereof, the data subject might need to file separate requests to the different controllers, of which he may gain knowledge through the information on the recipients of the data (see point 3 below).

5.2   The Categories of Personal Data, the Personal Data Which Is Processed and the Origin of the Data (Art.14 (b) and (g))

The essence of this provision is to allow the data subject to have an overview of the personal information which the controller processes, verify and possibly contest its accuracy and monitor other aspects of legality of the of the data, e.g. data minimization, and exercise his rights as a data subject.[31] While the GDPR grants data subjects the right to obtain a copy of their data,[32] this is not explicitly granted in Article 14 Directive 2016/680. Pursuant to the wording of Article 14 Directive 2016/680 and

---

[26] Article 8 (1) Directive 2016/680 j Article 1 (1) Directive 2016/680 (emphasis added).

[27] Article 8 (2) Directive 2016/680.

[28] Article 4 (2) Directive 2016/680. The provision is similar to the requirements in Article 8.

[29] Article 13 Directive 2016/680. See by contrast Article 13 (3) GDPR.

[30] Recital 43 Directive 2016/680. Note that the possibility to exercise the right "at reasonable intervals" is not mentioned in the text of Article 14 itself.

[31] Recital 43 Directive 2016/680.

[32] Article 15 (3) GDPR.

Recital 43 Directive 2016/680 it seems sufficient that the controller provide a "full summary … in an intelligible form" listing each piece of personal data. The summary could be provided also in the form of a copy of the data which are processed (see footnote 31). As the CJEU argued in the *YS* case, the form in which the personal data are provided to the data subject is immaterial as long as the data is presented in such a way as to allow the data subject to understand which personal data of his are being processed and monitor the legality of their processing.[33]

Where the data controller possesses information about the origin of the data, e.g. another law enforcement authority, this information could be precious to the data subject since it would reveal the details about the information held on them by other controllers. However, if the data originated from natural persons, their identity *should not* be disclosed, in particular if the sources are to remain confidential (see footnote 31). This could be attributed to the fact that the right of access should not cause harms to others, e.g. vulnerable witnesses. It is not surprising that the right of access may be restricted in order to "protect the rights and freedoms of others."[34] In addition, as Advocate General Sharpston argued in her *YS* Opinion, the right of access to one's personal data does not cover the right of access to the personal data of others.[35]

5.3 Recipients or Categories of Recipients, Especially in Third Countries (Art. 14 (c))

If the data controller further discloses the personal data to recipients, then he should include this in the response to the access request. This allows the data subject to control whether his data was treated with due confidentiality [22]. However, there are two caveats about this provision. In the first place, the controller may restrict the information only to "categories of recipients," thus not providing a full list of recipients. The article does not provide further guidance as to when the controller may choose to provide only the categories of recipients, e.g. does it depend on the effort involved in providing the complete information, or a conflict with a confidentiality requirement, etc.

In the second place, Directive 2016/680 excludes from the definition of recipients those public authorities which receive data in the framework of a particular inquiry in the general interest in accordance with Union or Member State law, e.g. tax and customs authorities.[36] This exception is quite broad and it is not clear why information

---

[33] Joined cases C 141/12 and C 372/12, *YS v Minister voor Immigratie, Integratie en Asiel and Minister voor Immigratie, Integratie en Asiel v M* (Hereinafter "*YS*"), 17.07.2014, par. 57–58. See also Advocate General Sharpston's Opinion of 12.12.2013, par. 77–78. The case concerned the application of Third Country Nationals to review the legal reasoning of the Dutch authorities' decision on their application for residence permits. The Court ruled that the analysis or the minutes are not personal data and do not fall within the scope of the right of access under Directive 95/46/EC and thus disclosing the whole legal analysis, i.e. providing a copy thereof, was not necessary, whereas a summary only of the personal data contained in the applicants' files was enough.

[34] Article 15 (1) (e) Directive 2016/680.

[35] Advocate General Sharpston's Opinion of 12.12.2013, par. 77, op. cit.

[36] Article 3 (10) and Recital 22 Directive 2016/680.

on the transmission of the data to any of these authorities shall be excluded from the information to be provided to the data subject.

Shortly put, Article 14 (c) Directive 2016/680 unfortunately does not oblige the data controller to provide complete information as to who has received the data of the data subject.

5.4 Envisaged Storage Period (Article 14 (d))

The controller should inform the data subject of the envisaged storage period. If this is not possible, the controller should at least indicate the criteria according to which the storage period will be determined. However, one should be aware that the purpose(s) of the processing might change. If at the time of the access request the future change of purpose is already certain and it is known that it would lead to a longer storage period, then for the sake of transparency the controller had better communicate the exact storage period or the criteria for determining it. However, if this is not the case but the purpose changes later, the data subject might not be aware of the new storage period and as explained above, the data controller is not obliged to inform the data subject of the purpose change.

5.5 Existence of Other Rights (Article 14 (e))

The controller should clearly indicate to the data subject that he may request the rectification, erasure or restriction of processing of his data. Such requests could follow after the data subject has examined the data undergoing processing and detected irregularities, e.g. the data is incorrect (such as wrong spelling of his name) or that data not concerning the applicant are wrongly attributed to him and have to be deleted.

Directive 2016/680, unlike the GDPR, does not grant data subjects the right to object to the processing of their data and it is questioned why data subjects are deprived of this right. Thus, also the data controller cannot inform the data subject of his non-existing right to object.

Another missing point is the obligation of the controller to disclose the existence of automated decision-making such as profiling, the algorithmic logic of the processing and the potential consequences for the data subject.[37] Nowadays the law-enforcement authorities are using more and more profiling techniques which could impact data subjects, even if this software does not itself take the final decision, e.g. PNR profiling which assesses the risk of each passenger.[38] While disclosing the exact logic of the algorithms might sometimes endanger the work of the law-enforcement authorities, it is not clear why the data subject may not be made aware of the mere existence of such automated decision-making. This might be needed in cases when even if the data is correct, the software might still wrongly process the data, e.g. a technical failure in the matching of biometric data when someone's fingerprints are matched against the

---

[37] Compare Article 15 (1) (h) GDPR.

[38] Article 6 EU PNR Directive.

database of available fingerprints, e.g. of convicts. Not being aware of such automated decisions could prevent the data subject from challenging the conclusions.

5.6   Lodging a Complaint with the Supervisory Authority (Article 14 (f))

This provision concerns the general right of data subjects to submit a complaint to the supervisory authority of their choice when they consider that the processing of their data infringes the provisions of Directive 2016/680.[39] Thus, the purpose of the provision is to inform the data subject of that right and provide them with the contact details of the supervisory authority, i.e. to facilitate the exercise of that right. This is compatible with the obligation of the controller in Article 17 (2) to inform the data subject that, in case the controller refuses to grant him access to his data, the data subject may exercise his right of access indirectly, via the supervisory authority.

6   The Right of Access Is Not Absolute

As already indicated above, the data subject's right of access to his data is not absolute. The data controller may wholly or partially restrict it if **four conditions** are met. First, the limitation must be based on a legislative measure adopted by the Member States. Second, the restriction may apply only for as long as it constitutes a necessary and proportionate measure. Third, due respect has to be taken of the fundamental rights and legitimate interests of the data subject.[40] In that regard, any limitation should be compatible with the CFREU and the ECHR.[41]

Fourth, the restriction should pursue at least one of the legitimate purposes provided in Article 15 (1) Directive 2016/680, namely:

(a) avoid obstructing official or legal inquiries, investigations or procedures;
(b) avoid prejudicing the prevention, detection, investigation or prosecution of criminal offences or the execution of criminal penalties;
(c) protect public security; (d) national security; (e) the rights and freedoms of others. However, as the AG in the *YS* case noted, the rights and freedoms of others do "not encompass the rights and freedoms of the authority processing personal data."[42]

These grounds for exemption are the same as the ones that applied under the 2008 Framework Decision [23].[43] Further, the Member States may adopt legislative

---

[39] Article 52 Directive 2016/680.

[40] Article 15 (1) Directive 2016/680.

[41] Recital 46 Directive 2016/680 and CJEU, C-465/00, 138/01, 139/01 *Öster- reichischer Rundfunk*, 20.05.2003. In that case the CJEU ruled that if a limitation on the data protection rights of individuals is not compatible with the fundamental rights, e.g. to privacy as enshrined in the ECHR and by extension nowadays in the CFREU, then the limitations cannot be deemed to be compatible with provisions of secondary law, e.g. Directive 2016/680.

[42] Opinion of Advocate General Sharpston in the *YS* case, op. cit., par. 93 (4).

[43] Art. 17 (2) 2008 Framework Decision.

measures about the categories of processing which may be subject to exemption.[44] The grounds are phrased quite broadly and thus the controller would have a wide margin of appreciation making use of these exceptions. As some have noted, the restrictions on the right of access might end up easily curtailing the effectiveness of the right of access of the concerned individuals [24].

It is still to be seen how broadly the Member States would phrase the exemptions when implementing Directive 2016/680. For example, the German implementing law requires that when the recipients of the data are intelligence, military counter intelligence, constitutional protection authorities and other authorities involved in national security, then information about these recipients could be given to the data subject only if the concerned recipient gives its agreement [25].[45] This restriction is beyond the control of the data controller and leaves the recipients a wide margin of appreciation.

Further, the German legislator allows the controller to restrict the right of access also when data are stored only due to legal requirements or they are used only for purposes of data security or data protection audits, when granting the right of access would pose disproportionate effort and all measures have been taken to prevent their processing for other purposes.[46] The right of access could be denied also if the data subject does not provide enough information which allows the controller to find his personal data without disproportionate effort.[47] Thus, new grounds for denial of access have been added by the German legislator. It is questionable whether they are in line with Directive 2016/680.

If the controller restricts wholly or partly the right of access of a certain data subject, he should inform the data subject of the complete refusal or the restriction of access, including the reasons for the decision. This information is to be communicated to the data subject "in writing" and "without undue delay." If disclosing such information would undermine one of the legitimate grounds for the restriction, then the controller may omit it. However, he has to inform the data subject of his right to lodge a complaint with a supervisory authority and to seek a judicial remedy.[48] While it is clear that the controller has to inform the data subject about the refusal to grant access in whole, the wording of the provision does not make it clear whether in case of a partial refusal the controller may inform the data subject at least about which part of his request has been refused or he should omit both this information and the reasons for the partial refusal. Reading this provision in light of the purpose of the right of access, as a matter of principle the controller should inform the data subject also if he partially restricts the right of access.

In any case, it is positive that the controller is to be accountable about his decision by documenting the factual or legal reasons for the refusal and making them available to the supervisory authorities.[49]

---

[44] Article 15 (2) Directive 2016/680.

[45] § 57 (5) German implementing law.

[46] Ibid, § 57 (2).

[47] Ibid, § 57 (3).

[48] Article 15 (3) Directive 2016/680.

[49] Article 15 (4) Directive 2016/680.

7 Directive 2016/680 Imposes Procedural Requirements

The controller, the supervisory authorities, as well as data subjects will have to follow the procedures established by Directive 2016/680, as discussed in the present Section.

7.1 Direct Access Becomes the Rule, Indirect - The Exception

Article 14 Directive 2016/680 is phrased in a way which suggests that the data subject may in all cases **directly** contact the data controller to request access to his own data [26]. The benefit of this direct contact is evident from the *Khelili* case discussed in Sect. 3. However, in the cases in which the controller decides not to grant him full or any access to his data, then the data subject may turn to the competent supervisory authority.[50] It is the controller who should make the data subject aware of this possibility.[51] When the data subject turns to the supervisory authority, the latter should carry out the necessary checks, e.g. check which data concerning the data subject are processed, whether the processing is lawful, whether the data are correct, etc. The supervisory authority should inform the data subject "at least" that the necessary verifications and/or review have been carried out and that the data subject may apply for a judicial remedy.[52] This means that further information may also be provided. Whether and which additional information may be further provided should be assessed on a case-by-case basis in accordance with the principles of proportionality and necessity. For example, an innocent person's name might be entered in a police database because of a spelling mistake. When the supervisory authority establishes and corrects this mistake, it seems unproblematic to communicate to the data subject the fact that there was a spelling mistake which was corrected. In that scenario the data subject still exercises his right of access, but only **indirectly**. Similarly, the ECtHR reached several times the conclusion that if direct access cannot be granted to the data subject, due to the need to balance different interests, then at least the decision of the controller should be reviewed by an independent authority.[53]

However, it is questionable whether indirect access fulfills the main purposes of the right of access, e.g. whether the supervisory authority is always in a position to detect irregularities, ensure they are rectified and if not, then the question arises how a data subject can pursue his case in court if he does not have access to his data and might not know whether the supervisory authority rectified the illegalities. Another problem is that the information which the supervisory authority may disclose will have to be "approved" by the law enforcement and possibly other authorities. This challenges the requirement that supervisory authorities be independent.[54] As the EDPS noted with regards to the Proposal for a EUROJUST Regulation, for an independent supervisory

---

[50] Article 17 (1) Directive 2016/680; also §57 (7) and §59 German Implementing Law.

[51] Article 17 (2) Directive 2016/680.

[52] Article 17 (3) Directive 2016/680.

[53] ECtHR, *Amann* and *Gaskin,* op. cit.

[54] Article 42 Directive 2016/680.

authority which is subject to court oversight, the decision should be taken independently, after consultation with the controller [36].

Granting data subjects the right of **direct** access, unless a restriction applies, represents a departure from current practice. For example, the right of access under the 2008 Framework Decision, SIS II and VIS may be exercised through the national supervisory authority which may decide what and how information is to be communicated to the data subject.[55] Other instruments, e.g. the EU PNR Directive and EURODAC Regulation simply refer the 2008 Framework Decision for the exercise of data subjects' rights, i.e. they allow for indirect access.[56] Now certain Member States might need to align their procedures with Directive 2016/680. As a result, access under the other instruments might also become direct, which might harmonize the access procedures under the different instruments. However, it is yet to be seen whether the procedures will be amended and whether instruments such as SIS II and VIS will be amended accordingly.

7.2 The Controller Should Communicate with the Data Subject Intelligibly and in a Timely Fashion

The controller should communicate in "clear and plain language," using "concise, intelligible and easily accessible form."[57] This is supposed to help data subjects actually comprehend the data processing and how they are affected by it. The controller should also facilitate the exercise of the rights, e.g. of access, and provide it free of charge if the request is not excessive or manifestly ill-founded. Otherwise he could charge a fee or even refuse the request, bearing the responsibility for proving that the request was excessive or ill-founded.[58]

Pursuant to Article 12 (5), the data controller may take measures to make sure that the applicant is the concerned data subject in case he has doubts about his identity.

Articles 12 and 14 Directive 2016/680 do not impose hard limits on the data controller to respond to a request by the data subject, unlike some AFSJ instruments.[59] He only has to inform the data subject of the follow-up to his request "without undue delay."[60] For example, in the case of *Haralambie* the ECtHR ruled that granting access to the requested data only six years after the request was submitted was not compatible with Article 8 ECHR [27].[61] Similarly, in the *Yonchev* case the ECtHR held that the

---

[55] Article 58 (1) and (2) Council Decision SIS II; 14 (1) and (2) VIS Council Decision; Article 17 (1) (a) 2008 Framework Decision.

[56] Article 13 (1) EU PNR Directive and 33 (1) EURODAC Regulation.

[57] Article 12 (1) Directive 2016/680.

[58] Article 12 (2) and (4) Directive 2016/680.

[59] E.g. Article 14 (6) VIS Council Decision and Article 58 (6) Council Decision SIS II. How are they different.

[60] Article 12 (3) Directive 2016/680.

[61] ECtHR, *Haralambie v Romania*, application no. 21737/03, 27.10.2009. The applicant wanted to know whether the security services had a file on him from the time during the Communist regime. A file indeed existed, but the applicant was allowed to see it only 6 years after he filed the request.

fact that the applicant was refused with finality access to his file only 5 years after the application for access was unduly long [28].[62]

8   Challenges Still Remain

The right of access under Directive 2016/680 is already a step forward towards more law enforcement accountability and transparency. Nevertheless, one should take into account the broader picture of law-enforcement use of personal data in the EU, including in the framework of EUROPOL, EUROJUST, SIS II, VIS and EURODAC, where different procedures on the right of access apply. This causes frictions, which take away from the effectiveness of the right of access.

8.1   Data Protection in the Law-Enforcement Sector in the EU Remains Fragmented

The first problem is the variety of law enforcement authorities processing personal data, the different information systems they operate with and thus the applicability of several legal instruments on data protection. Which authorities – national and European - process the personal data of a specific individual might not be known to the concerned data subject.

For example, a national authority may disclose the data which it holds on a data subject on one or several national information systems upon his request under Directive 2016/680. It is not clear whether the contacted authority also has an obligation to disclose information about data stored on the data subject on the EU-wide SIS II or whether the data subject has to file a separate request for access under the SIS II Council Decision. This is likely to depend on whether the contacted national authority is also a controller for SIS II or whether one will interpret the notion of "controller" broadly to mean that, e.g. any police authority if contacted has to provide access concerning all files held by the different police authorities in the particular Member State. Still in the case of SIS II, the decision on disclosure of SIS II data would be influenced by the Member State which entered the alert if the alert was not entered by the authority to which the data subject filed his request.[63] In case of denial of access in such cross-border cases effective cooperation between national supervisory authorities will be needed. It is also not clear whether in deciding if a restriction on the right of access applies in the case of SIS II only the grounds for exemption in Article 58 (4) Council Decision SIS II apply or also the ones in Article 15 Directive 2016/680.

EUROPOL and EUROJUST add another level of complexity. As EU agencies, they fall outside the scope of Directive 2016/680. Thus, if a national authority has

---

[62] ECtHR, *Yonchev v. Bulgaria*, application no. 12504/09, 7.12.2017, par. 61. The applicant requested access to the results of his psychological assessment as an applicant for a police mission abroad. It was refused on grounds of confidentiality. It turned out that the documents were not confidential, the decision was taken by a body which was not entitled to take such decisions and the procedure had taken too long.

[63] Article 58 (3) Council Decision SIS II.

forwarded data to EUROPOL, it is assumed that it will notify the data subject of this disclosure, pursuant to Article 14 (c) Directive 2016/680. However, EUROPOL might hold further data on the same data subject, obtained from other sources. To obtain access to all the data held on him by EUROPOL the data subject has to trigger the procedure prescribed by the EUROPOL Regulation, which provides for indirect access only via the national authority of the respective Member State, following a lengthy and complex procedure [29].[64]

Last but not least, the Commission has been promoting the concept of interoperability between the different AFSJ databases. This could lead to, amongst others, quicker and easier law enforcement access to data, e.g. on VIS and EURODAC, as well as new databases, e.g. the Multiple Identity Detector (MID) and the Common Identity Repository (CIR) [30, 31].[65]

The two interoperability proposals refer to the data subjects' rights as enshrined in the GDPR and Regulation 45/2001 on data protection by the EU institutions, bodies and agencies [32].[66] No references are made to Directive 2016/680.[67] This is peculiar since, for example, a law-enforcement authority such as SIRENE in the framework of SIS II, which could fall under Directive 2016/680, could qualify as a data controller in the context of MID.[68] However, for the definition of controllers the proposals refer only to the GDPR, although the processing of data in SIS II in the law enforcement context is subject to Directive 2016/680 [33].[69] It is not clear whether excluding the application of Directive 2016/680 is a mistake or not. The result is that if the proposal is not modified accordingly, then interoperability will lead to additional fragmentation and complication in the exercise of the right of access.

8.2 The Blurred Lines Between Law Enforcement and National Security Challenge the National Security Exemption in Directive 2016/680

Another problem are the blurred lines between law enforcement and national security authorities. The latter do not fall within the scope of Directive 2016/680.[70] For example, the PNR Directive, whose purpose is the fight against terrorism and serious crime,[71] poses challenges. The reason is that the PNR Directive leaves freedom to each Member State to establish or designate the authority which is responsible for fighting terrorism and serious crime and which will process PNR data, called Passenger Information Unit (PIU).[72] In some Member States the PIU is part of the national

---

[64] Article 36 EUROPOL Regulation.

[65] EU Interoperability Proposal 1 and 2, 2017.

[66] Regulation (EC) No 45/2001.

[67] Article 47 Proposals COM (2017) 794 final, Brussels 12.12.2017 and COM (2017) 793 final, 12.12.2017 op. cit.

[68] Article 29 (2) COM (2017) 794 final, Brussels, 12.12.2017, op. cit.

[69] See also Article 64 SIS II Proposal 2016.

[70] Recital 14 Directive 2016/680.

[71] Article 1 (2) EU PNR Directive.

[72] Article 4 (1) EU PNR Directive.

security agency [34, 35]. Normally national security falls outside the scope of Union law and by extension Directive 2016/680.[73] However, Directive 2016/680 and the procedures on the right of access in it are applicable to the PNR. Thus, when PIUs handle access requests, they have to follow the procedure established in Articles 12, 14, 15 and 17 Directive 2016/680.[74] The increasing role that security/intelligence authorities play in law-enforcement matters demonstrates that the separation between them in terms of the applicability of Directive 2016/680 is difficult to explain and may be detrimental for the consistent enforcement of the right of data subjects.

9 Conclusion

The discussion above demonstrates that the right of access to one's data under Directive 2016/680 is expected to improve the transparency and accountability of the law-enforcement sector and to trigger amendments to the currently existing procedures on right of access under the AFSJ instruments in force. In how far the new procedures for its exercise will be harmonized on national level and how broadly the exemptions of the right of access will be framed is still to be seen after the Member States adopt the necessary implementing laws. However, as the discussion evidenced, deficiencies can already be identified in terms of the transparency it seeks to ensure and consistency across the law enforcement authorities' data protection obligation on EU and Member State level. The problems can be summarized as follows:

1. The right does not include essential information such as on profiling measures and the recipients of the data;
2. The fact that the right is to be exercised against controller in a world of many interconnected controllers might make it difficult for the data subject to obtain a thorough overview of his data;
3. The different controllers are subject to different legal frameworks and procedures which causes fragmentation.

An ideal solution would be the harmonization of the substantive and procedural provisions on the right of access in all instruments. However, the fragmentation reflects the evolution of Member State police cooperation and EUROPOL as special areas, which might make harmonization politically challenging.

References

1. The Schengen Information System: A Guide for exercising the right of access. SIS II Supervision Coordination Group, p. 8, October 2015
2. Charter of Fundamental Rights of the European Union, O.J. C 364, 2000/C364/01, 18 December 2000

---

[73] Article 2 (3) Directive 2016/680.

[74] Article 13 EU PNR Directive j Article 59 Directive 2016/680.

3. Directive 95/46/EC of the European Parliament and of the Council of 24 October 1995 on the protection of individuals with regards to the processing of personal data and on the free movement of such data, O.J. L 251, 23 November 1995

4. Regulation (EU) 2016/679 of the European Parliament and of the Council of 27 April 2016 on the protection of natural persons with regard to the processing of personal data and on the free movement of such data, and repealing Directive 95/46/EC (General Data Protection Regulation), O.J. L 119, 4 May 2016

5. Principle 6 Recommendation No. R (87) 15, Council of Europe, Committees of Ministers to Member States regulating the use of personal data in the police sector, 17 September 1987

6. Directive (EU) 2016/680 of the European Parliament and of the Council of 27 April 2016 on the protection of natural persons with regard to the processing of personal data by competent authorities for the purposes of the prevention, investigation, detection or prosecution of criminal offences or the execution of criminal penalties, and on the free movement of such data, and repealing Council Framework Decision 2008/977/JHA, O.J. L 119/89-131

7. Council Framework Decision 2008/977/JHA of 27 November 2008 on the protection of personal data processed in the framework of police and judicial cooperation in criminal matters, O.J. L. 350/60-71, 30 December 2008

8. Council Decision 2007/533/JHA on the establishment, operation and use of the second generation Schengen Information System (SIS II), OJ L 205, ("Council Decision SIS II"), 7 August 2007

9. Directive (EU) 2016/681 of the European Parliament and of the Council of 27 April 2016 on the use of passenger name record (PNR) data for the prevention, detection, investigation and prosecution of terrorist offences and serious crime, OJ L 119, p. 132–149 ("EU PNR Directive"), 4 May 2016

10. Council Decision 2008/633/JHA of 23 June 2008 concerning access for consultation of the Visa Information System (VIS) by designated authorities of Member States and by Europol for the purposes of the prevention, detection and investigation of terrorist offences and of other serious criminal offences, OJ L 218, pp. 129–136 ("VIS Council Decision"), 13 August 2008

11. Regulation (EU) No 603/2013 of the European Parliament and of the Council of 26 June 2013 on the establishment of 'Eurodac' for the comparison of fingerprints for the effective application of Regulation (EU) No 604/2013 establishing the criteria and mechanisms for determining the Member State responsible for examining an application for international protection lodged in one of the Member States by a third-country national or a stateless person and on requests for the comparison with Eurodac data by Member States' law enforcement authorities and Europol for law enforcement purposes, and amending Regulation (EU) No 1077/2011 establishing a European Agency for the operational management of large-scale IT systems in the area of freedom, security and justice, O. J. L 180/1-30, ("EURODAC Regulation"), 29 June 2013

12. Council of Europe Convention 108 for the Protection of Individuals with regard to Automatic Processing of Personal Data, Strasbourg, 28 January 1981

13. ECtHR, Gaskin v the United Kingdom, Application no. 10454/83, 07 July 1989

14. ECtHR, Khelili v Switzerland, Application no. 16188/07, 18 October 2011

15. ECtHR, Segerstedt-Wiberg and Others v. Sweden, Application no. 62332/00, 6 June 2006

16. ECtHR, Amann v Switterland, Application no. 27798/95, 16 February 2000

17. CJEU, C-553/07, College van burgemeester en wethouders van Rotterdam v M.E. E. Rijkeboer, 7.05.2009, Opinion of the Advocate General Ruiz-Jarabo Colomer, par. 33 and 34, 22 December 2008

18. L'Hoiry, X., Norris, C.: Introduction – the right of access to personal data in a changing european legislative framework. In: Norris, C., de Hert, P., L'Hoiry, X., Galetta, A. (eds.) The Unaccountable State of Surveillance. LGTS, vol. 34, pp. 1–8. Springer, Cham (2017). https://doi.org/10.1007/978-3-319-47573-8_1

19. C 141/12 and C 372/12, YS v Minister voor Immigratie, Integratie en Asiel and Minister voor Immigratie, Integratie en Asiel v M, 17 July 2014

20. CJEU, C-434/16, Peter Nowak v Data Protection Commissioner, Opinion of Advocate General Kokott, 20 July 2017

21. Bäcker, M.: Art. 23 Beschränkungen. In: Jürgen Kühling, J., Buchner, B. (eds.) Datenschutz-Grundverordnung: Kommentar, p. 486, par. 14, C.H.Beck (2017)

22. Galetta, A., de Hert, P.: A European perspective on data protection and the right of access. In: Norris, C., de Hert, P., L'Hoiry, X., Galetta, A. (eds.) The Unaccountable State of Surveillance. LGTS, vol. 34, pp. 21–43. Springer, Cham (2017). https://doi.org/10.1007/978-3-319-47573-8_3

23. CJEU, C-465/00, 138/01, 139/01 Österreichischer Rundfunk, 20 May 2003

24. De Hert, P., Papakonstantinou, V.: The new police and criminal justice data protection directive: a first analysis. New J. Eur. Crim. Law 7(1), 12 (2016)

25. Gesetz zur Anpassung des Datenschutzrechts an die Verordnung (EU) 2016/679 und zur Umsetzung der Richtlinie (EU) 2016/680, Bundesgesetz- blatt Jahrgang 2017 Teil I Nr. 44, Bonn, ("German Implementing Law"), 05 July 2017

26. Computers, Privacy and Data Protection (CPDP) 2017 Conference. https://www.youtube.com/watch?v=g7YYlrxQe20

27. ECtHR, Haralambie v Romania, application no. 21737/03, 27 October 2009

28. ECtHR, Yonchev v. Bulgaria, application no. 12504/09, 7 December 2017

29. Regulation 2016/794 of the European Parliament and of the Council of 11 May 2016 on the European Union Agency for Law Enforcement Cooperation (Europol) and replacing and repealing Council Decisions 2009/371/JHA, 2009/934/JHA, 2009/935/JHA, 2009/936/JHA and 2009/968/JHA, O.J. L. 135/53-114, ("EUROPOL Regulation"), 25 May 2016

30. Proposal for a Regulation of the European Parliament and of the Council on establishing a framework for interoperability between EU information systems (police and judicial cooperation, asylum and migration), COM (2017) 794 final, Brussels ("EU Interoperability Proposal 1"), 12 December 2017

31. Proposal for a Regulation of the European Parliament and of the Council on establishing a framework for interoperability between EU information systems (borders and visa) and amending Council Decision 2004/512/EC, Regulation (EC) No 767/2008, Council Decision 2008/633/JHA, Regulation (EU) 2016/399 and Regulation (EU) 2017/2226, COM (2017) 793 final, ("EU Interoperability Proposal 2"), 12 December 2017

32. Regulation (EC) No 45/2001 of the European Parliament and of the Council of 18 December 2000 on the protection of individuals with regard to the processing of personal data by the Community institutions and bodies and on the free movement of such data, OJ.L. 8/1-22, ("Regulation 45/2001"), 12 January 2001

33. Proposal for a Regulation of the European Parliament and of the Council on the establishment, operation and use of the Schengen Information System (SIS) in the field of police cooperation and judicial cooperation in criminal matters, amending Regulation (EU) No 515/2014 and repealing Regulation (EC) No 1986/2006, Council Decision 2007/533/JHA and Commission Decision 2010/261/EUCOM (2016) 883 final, Brussels ("SIS II Proposal 2016"), 21 December 2016

34. The European Parliament adopted the Passenger Name Record (PNR) Directive for the Passengers with EU Air Carriers. The Republic of Bulgaria, Commission for Personal Data Protection, 19 April 2016. https://www.cpdp.bg/en/index.php?p=news_view&aid=954
35. Article 11 (a) Law on the State Agency "National Security" of the Republic of Bulgaria, Official Journal 109, 20 December 2007. Latest amendment: 19 January 2018
36. European Data Protection Supervisor: Opinion of the European Data Protection Supervisor on the package of legislative measures reforming Eurojust and setting up the European Public Prosecutor's Office ('EPPO'), Brussels, p. 18, par. 91, 5 March 2014

Legislative Compliance Assessment: Framework, Model and GDPR Instantiation

Sushant Agarwal[(⊠)], Simon Steyskal[(⊠)], Franjo Antunovic[(⊠)],
and Sabrina Kirrane[(⊠)]

Vienna University of Economics and Business, Vienna, Austria
{sushant.agarwal,simon.steyskal,franjo.antunovic,
sabrina.kirrane}@wu.ac.at

Abstract. Legislative compliance assessment tools are commonly used by companies to help them to understand their legal obligations. One of the primary limitations of existing tools is that they tend to consider each regulation in isolation. In this paper, we propose a flexible and modular compliance assessment framework that can support multiple legislations. Additionally, we describe our extension of the Open Digital Rights Language (ODRL) so that it can be used not only to represent digital rights but also legislative obligations, and discuss how the proposed model is used to develop a flexible compliance system, where changes to the obligations are automatically reflected in the compliance assessment tool. Finally, we demonstrate the effectiveness of the proposed approach through the development of a General Data Protection Regulatory model and compliance assessment tool.

Keywords: Compliance · GDPR · ODRL

1 Introduction

The interpretation of legal texts can be challenging, especially for people with non-legal backgrounds, as they often contain domain-specific definitions, cross-references and ambiguities [29]. Also, generally speaking legislations cannot be considered in isolation, for instance European Union (EU) regulations often contain opening clauses that permit Member States to introduce more restrictive local legislation. Additionally, depending on the legislative domain additional legislations may also need to be consulted. For example, when it comes to data protection in the EU, in addition to the General Data Protection Regulation (GDPR) [4], the upcoming e-privacy regulation (for e-communication sector) [5] or the Payment services (PSD 2) directive (for payments sector) [3] may also need to be consulted. As such, ensuring compliance with regulations can be a daunting task for many companies, who could potentially face hefty fines and reputation damage if not done properly. Consequently, companies often rely on legislative compliance assessment tools to provide guidance with respect to their legal obligations [8].

Over the years, several theoretical frameworks that support the modelling of legislation have been proposed [7, 10, 14, 22, 23, 25, 32], however only some of which were validated via the development of legal support systems [7, 10, 23, 25, 32]. One of

M. Medina et al. (Eds.): APF 2018, LNCS 11079, pp. 131–149, 2018.
https://doi.org/10.1007/978-3-030-02547-2_8

the major drawbacks of such approaches is the fact that some do not consider concepts like soft-obligations (i.e. obligations that serve as recommendations rather than being mandatory) [22, 25] or exceptions (i.e. scenarios where the obligations are not applicable) [10, 29]. Additionally generally speaking the models are only loosely coupled with the actual legislation text, making it difficult to verify the effectiveness of such systems. More recently, a number of compliance assessment tools have been developed [18, 26, 28]. However, these systems are either composed of a handful of questions that are used to evaluate legal obligations [18] or do not filter out questions that are not applicable for the company completing the assessment [26, 28]. One of the primary drawbacks of existing compliance assessment tools is the fact that they do not currently consider related regulations.

In order to address this gap, we propose a generic legislative compliance assessment framework, that has been designed to support multiple legislations. Additionally, we extend the Open Digital Rights Language (ODRL) [34] (which is primarily used for rights expression) so that it can be used to express legislative obligations. Both of which are necessary first steps towards a context dependent compliance system that can easily be adapted for different regulatory domains.

The contributions of the paper are as follows: (i) we devise a flexible and modular compliance assessment framework, which is designed to support multiple legislations; (ii) we propose a legislative ODRL profile that can be used to model obligations specified in different legislations; and (iii) we develop a dynamic compliance system that can easily be adapted to work with different legislations. The proposed framework is instantiated in the form of a GDPR compliance assessment tool, which is subsequently compared with alternative approaches.

The remainder of the paper is structured as follows: Sect. 2 presents different approaches that can be used to model data protection legislations, along with compliance assessment tools for the GDPR. Section 3 details our framework that decouples the legislative obligations from the compliance assessment tool. Section 4 introduces our legislative model and illustrates how it can be used to model the GDPR. Section 5 describes the compliance tool. In Sect. 6 we compare and contrast our proposal with alternative solutions. Finally, Sect. 7 concludes the paper and presents directions for future work.

2 Related Work

Although the modelling of legal text has been a field of study for many years, in this section we discuss those that focus on the modelling of data protection related legislations, and present three different tools that have been developed to help companies to comply with the GDPR.

Barth et al. [7] present a theoretical model for the representation of privacy expectations that is based on a contextual integrity framework [27]. The approach is validated via the modelling of the Health Insurance Portability and Accountability Act

(HIPAA)[1]. Broadly speaking, the modelling is based on two kinds of norms, positive (allowed) and negative (denied). Using their framework privacy provisions for the sharing of data with different actors can be represented. However, according to Otto et al. [29] actions and purposes are not well represented. For instance, it is possible to model if a company cannot share personal data with a third party, but it fails to include purposes such as statistical reasons whereby a company may be allowed to share data.

May et al. [25] also illustrate how their approach can be used to model the HIPAA. Conditions and obligations are represented as access control rules that allow/deny operations. Given that they use a formal modelling language called Promela [16], it is possible to leverage existing Promela tools, such as for query execution. However, their model can only represent specific access-control related obligations. Other obligations, which are not related to access-control such as providing information about the processing or ensuring appropriate security measures are difficult to model with their approach.

Apart from legislative texts, policies for privacy notice and data exchange have also modelled. The World Wide Web Consortium (W3C) has undertaken numerous standardisation initiatives which deal with the modelling of data related policies. The Privacy Preferences Project (P3P)[2] is one such initiative which deals with representing privacy preferences in a standard machine-readable format. Using P3P we can model different parts of a privacy notice such as what information is collected, how long is it stored and for what purposes it would be used [12]. Though use of P3P can improve transparency of data processing, it does not support representation of other data protection related obligations [15]. For instance, obligations such as for security, data portability and right to erasure are out of scope for the P3P. Open Digital Rights Language (ODRL) [34] is another W3C initiative which presents a standard language to represent permission and obligations for digital content. The ODRL has also been used for modelling data protection legislations, for example Korba et al. [22] have used it to model the older data protection directive of the EU [1]. They have, however, discussed a high level overview of the modelling process for the directive. As a result, it does not include specific details to model components of the legislation such as soft-obligations (i.e., obligations that serve as recommendations rather than being mandatory) and exceptions to legal obligations.

In terms of the GDPR, the Information Commissioner's Office (ICO) in the UK have developed an online self-assessment tool [18]. It provides two separate checklists, one for controllers[3] and one for processors[4]. The applicable assessment questions are shown for a set of obligations. For every question the users have an option to see additional information. After the questions are answered, a report can be generated which summarises the compliance levels and suggests actions to ensure full

---

[1] https://www.gpo.gov/fdsys/pkg/PLAW-104publ191/content-detail.html.

[2] https://www.w3.org/P3P/.

[3] https://ico.org.uk/for-organisations/resources-and-support/data-protection-self-assessment/controllers-checklist.

[4] https://ico.org.uk/for-organisations/resources-and-support/data-protection-self-assessment/processors-checklist.

compliance. The primary limitation of the tool is the fact that the questions do not assess the obligations in detail.

Microsoft has also developed a GDPR assessment tool [26]. Unlike the ICO tool, it is a spreadsheet based assessment i.e. users have to provide the input in the provided spreadsheet. The questions include references to the GDPR text for further reference. Questions are organised in a hierarchical way and categorised according to the associated concepts. After the input, a report can be generated.

Similar to the Microsoft's tool, Nymity has also developed a spreadsheet based assessment [28]. Obligations are referred to as *Privacy Management Activities*. Unlike Microsoft, the questions are not categorised but follow the order of the GDPR text, whereby each obligation is linked to the corresponding GDPR paragraph. The spreadsheet is designed to work with their commercial software, *Nymity Attestor*[5], through which a report can be generated.

Each of the aforementioned GDPR compliance assessment tools show a list of questions which do not have any contextual connections between them. For instance, even if consent is not the basis for processing, a user still needs to answer all questions for consent as the relations between the questions are missing. As a result, the user has to go through all the questions (162 questions for the Microsoft's tool), even questions which are not applicable, to finish the assessment. Also, surprisingly none of the tools currently consider related national or domain specific legislation.

3 Framework for a Compliance Assessment System

Due to the shift towards information and knowledge-driven economies, the use of software intensive information systems is increasing. When it comes to legislations such as the GDPR, companies need to ensure that the data processing and sharing carried out by such systems complies with relevant legal obligations. Ensuring compliance is important, otherwise non-compliance can lead to large penalties and reputation damage. As such, companies often rely on compliance assessment tools that can be used to help them to assess if their existing business processes and systems comply with relevant legal obligations.

From a requirements perspective, it is important that compliance tool vendors are able to demonstrate the exhaustiveness of their tool in terms of legal obligations, as wrong conclusions could potentially be drawn from incomplete assessments. Ensuring traceability i.e. providing references to the legislation text is considered to be important for such tools [9, 11, 29]. References, for instance, allow companies to consult the legislations in case of confusion or if they need to verify an assessment. Also, it is important that such tools are kept up-to-date and are capable of taking into account updated legal interpretation of the relevant regulations [9, 11, 20, 29]. For instance, the GDPR mentions *appropriate measures* for security (Article 32.1) where the measure of appropriateness can change over time.

---

[5] https://www.nymity.com/solutions/attestor/.

To address these requirements, we propose a framework for compliance assessment, as depicted in Fig. 1, which can be used to support multiple legislations as well as to manage changes in interpretation over time, by decoupling the data component from the compliance system.

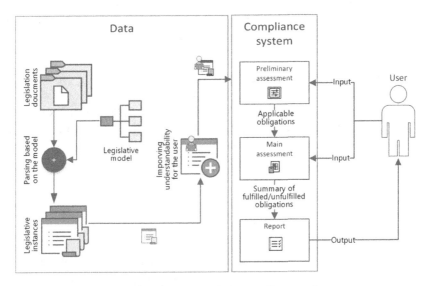

Fig. 1. Framework of the compliance tool

For the data component, a generic legislative model, ODRL, is used to represent legislative obligations and relations. For the *parsing process*, first the text defining obligations is extracted from the legislations. Next, the relations are identified between the extracted obligations and represented according to the legislative model. Following on from this, the modelled obligations are translated into a format that can be read by the compliance system, referred to as *Legislative instance*. Finally, the last step involves making the legislative instance more understandable for the user. Questions are prepared for the obligations such that the tool ask the user for the fulfilment of the obligations. Associated definitions are also added to ensure intelligibility of the questions.

The legislative instance is passed as input to the compliance system which assesses compliance based on the user-input and the legislative instance. As the modelled legislations could potentially govern multiple scenarios, it is possible that not all the defined obligations would be relevant for a compliance assessment. For instance, considering the GDPR, obligations related to processing outside the EU would not be applicable if a company does not transfer any personal information outside the EU. Therefore, to ensure that irrelevant obligations are not shown to the user, the assessment process is divided into two steps: (i) preliminary assessment; and (ii) main assessment. In the first step, the legislative instance is read and input from the user is taken. The input relates to the different scenarios which could affect the applicability of the obligations. For example, in case of the GDPR, whether the personal data is processed outside the EU. Based on the input, the system shortlists the applicable obligations and presents the assessment to the user. In the main assessment, the user provides input regarding the fulfilment of the obligations within their company. Once the required input is received, the system generates a report with a list of fulfilled and unfulfilled obligations.

Specific details on our implementation of the data component and the compliance system can be found in Sects. 4 and 5 respectively.

4   Data Modelling and the GDPR Instance

In this section, we provide an overview of the proposed Open Digital Rights Language (ODRL) profile that can be used to model legislative obligations. Following on from this we provide a sequence of steps that are required in order to represent existing legislative text using the proposed model.

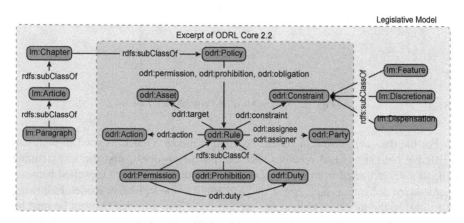

Fig. 2. The legislative model: based on an excerpt from ODRL Core 2.2 [34]

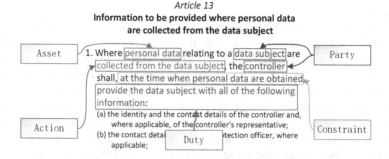

Fig. 3. Breaking down Article 13.1 of the GDPR according to the ODRL model

4.1   Legislative Model

Like Korba et al. [22] we chose ODRL [34], which was released as a W3C Recommendation in February 2018, for modelling the regulation. ODRL provides a standard means to define policy expressions and licenses for digital content. The primary motivation for choosing ODRL is the fact that it can easily be extended for other use-cases such as representation of legislations by defining additional profiles[6].

The central entity of the ODRL model, as depicted in Fig. 2, is a *Policy* which is used to specify *Rules* that are used to represent *Permissions*, *Prohibitions* and *Duties*. A *Permission* to perform an *Action* is granted if the associated *Duty* is fulfilled. While, an *Action* would not be allowed if any *Prohibition* is associated with it. Finally, a *Party* is an entity which participates in policy related transactions and an *Asset* is something which can be a subject to the policy under consideration.

Legal obligations are conceptually similar to ODRL duties. Consider Article 13 para 1 as depicted in Fig. 3. In this example, personal data can be considered as an *Asset*, the controller and the data subjects are the involved *Parties*. While, the collection of personal data from the data subjects would be the *Action* for which the *Duty* is defined. Also, for this *Duty*, a *Constraint* is defined, which indicates that the *Duty* should be fulfilled at the time when personal data is obtained.

Unfortunately, it is not possible to represent the following concepts using the core ODRL model and vocabulary:

Soft Obligations. The term soft-obligation refers to obligations which are non-mandatory. These are similar to recommendations in the sense that they represent best-practices. For instance, consider Example 1 where such a recommendation related to the use of icons is described. Here the text includes *"may be used"*, which indicates that the use of icons is optional. As a result, it should not be represented as a *Duty*.

Example 1: Example of an optional constraint from the GDPR
Article 12.7 : The information to be provided to data subjects pursuant to Articles 13 and 14 *may be provided* in combination with standardised icons....

Exceptions. Legislations also consist of exceptions, which if present take precedence over the *Duty*. Example 2 illustrates one such exception scenario where obligations defined in certain paragraphs are not applicable if the data subject already has the information.

Example 2: Example of an exception scenario from the GDPR
Article 13.4 : Paragraphs 1, 2 and 3 *shall not apply* where and insofar as the data subject already has the information.

---

[6] https://www.w3.org/TR/poe-ucr/.

Characteristics. There are additional constraints defined in the legislations which describe the features or characteristics of an obligation. Such features should also be fulfilled, along with the corresponding obligations. Example 3 shows constraints such as *conciseness* and *transparency* which should be ensured in order to comply with the *duty* defined in Article 13, depicted in Fig. 3.

> **Example 3:** GDPR text defining characteristics
> *Article 12.1:...provide any information referred to in Articles 13...in a concise, transparent, intelligible and easily accessible form...*

References to the Legislation Text. Additionally concepts are also required in order to represent relations with the corresponding legal text, such that it is possible to provide a link to the actual legislative text.

In order to represent these concepts, we define a legislative profile and extend the core ODRL model, as illustrated in Fig. 2. We use *Discretional* for the soft-obligations, *Dispensation* for representing exceptions and *Feature* for the characteristics. Also, in order to support referenceability, we define sub-components *Chapter*, *Article* and *Paragraph* under the *Policy* component.

4.2 Instantiation Process

Considering the proposed ODRL legislative model, we now discuss the instantiation process that can be used to represent existing legislations in a standard format. The created instance is used as input for the compliance system. The process, as shown in Fig. 4 is divided into 5 main steps -

(a) filtration of text that relates to obligations; (b) identification of interconnections in the text; (c) normalisation of the text; (d) representation of text in a machine-readable format; and (e) enhancing the readability for the user. In the following, we elaborate on these steps.

(a) **Filtration of text that relates to obligations.** Along with obligations, legislations usually discuss other topics such as the scope of the legislation, relevant definitions and fines for not adhering to the legislation. For a compliance assessment, we focus on the obligations for the stakeholder under consideration, like controllers and processors in the case of the GDPR. Thus, as the first step, the text which is not related to the obligations can be filtered out. For instance, in the GDPR, articles such as Articles 68–76 which define the working of the *European Data Protection Board* can be excluded as these do not introduce any obligations for the controllers or processors.

(b) **Identification of interconnections in the text.** To represent the filtered legal text as per the legislative model, we have to identify text related to the different components such as *Duty*, *Feature* and *Dispensation*. However, legislations consist of several references within the text to other paragraphs and articles [31]. Example 4 shows text stating connections with Article 13, 14, 15–22 and 34 defined in Article 12 para 1 of the GDPR.

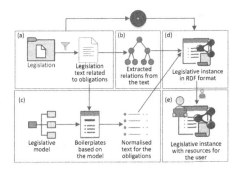

Fig. 4. Steps involved for the instantiation process

Example 4: Example of the interconnections defined in GDPR
Article 12.1: The controller shall take appropriate measures to provide any information referred to in *Articles 13 and 14* and any communication under *Articles 15 to 22 and 34* relating to processing to the data subject in a concise, transparent....

Thus, connected components are defined in different paragraphs and articles. In order to include all such references for the legislative instance, we extract and document all of the defined relations.

(c) **Normalisation of the text.** Next, we need to represent the legislation text according to the legislative model. To achieve this, it is necessary to manually identify and code parts of the text as components of the legislative model such as *Duty* and *Feature*. However, legislations often represent obligations in different legal styles, which increases the complexity of the coding process. Examples 5 and 6 illustrates two of the many different styles used in the GDPR.

Example 5: Example of the following style: *<processing> is lawful if...<condition>*
Article 8.1 :...*processing* shall be lawful only if and to the extent that *consent is given or authorised by the holder of parental responsibility over the child...*

Example 6: Example of the following style: *<processing> is prohibited unless...<condition>*
Article 9.1 : Processing of personal data revealing racial..origin...shall be prohibited.
Article 9.2 : Paragraph 1 shall not apply if...: (a) the data subject..explicit consent...

In the case of Example 5, if *<processing>* would be the *Action* then *<condition>* i.e. authorising consent by the holder of parental responsibility would represent the *Duty*. Similarly, considering Example 6, if *<processing>* would be the *Action* then corresponding *Duty* would be to not perform the *action* as described in Article 9.1. Based on Article 9.2, *<condition>* i.e. *explicit consent* would then be the dispensation scenario for the duty. However, this example can also be interpreted in a way similar to Example 5 where for the *Action* of *<processing>*, *<condition>* can also be considered as a *Duty*. Thus, different possibilities may exist for the representation of the text according to the components of the legislative model.

Table 1. Boilerplates used for expressing obligations in a standard style

Type	Boilerplate
Main	Party to perform Action on a given Asset should fulfil Duty in order to ensure compliance
Feature	Duty has additional requirement of Feature which must also be ensured
Dispensation	If Dispensation scenario for a Duty is true then that Duty is not applicable
Discretional	If Discretional for a Duty or Feature is true then that Duty or Feature is not compulsory

To overcome the confusion which arises due to different writing styles, in the field of requirements engineering, the use of boilerplates has been recommended which help in representing the text in a standard form [6, 17, 24]. A boilerplate is defined as a natural language pattern that restricts the syntax of the sentences to pre-defined linguistic structures [6]. Example 7 illustrates a boilerplate to represent the previous examples in a standard format.

Example 7: Illustration of a boilerplate to represent Example 5 and 6 in a standard form
Boilerplate: <Party> to perform <Action> on a given <Asset> should fulfil <Duty>
- *Controller* to perform *Processing* on *Minors' data* should *Obtain consent by their parents*
- *Controller* to perform *Processing* on *Sensitive data* should *Obtain explicit consent for it*

This way, based on a boilerplate, we first represent the text in a standardised format. As we are interested in identification of components like *Action*, *Duty* and *Feature*, the boilerplates are based on the components of the legislative model and are listed in Table 1.

(d) **Representation of text in a machine-readable format.** After the use of boilerplates, the obligations need to be expressed in a format which can be easily read by the compliance system and is standardised such that the data model can be reused for other systems as well. We chose, the Resource Description Framework (RDF) format [7] for the representation, which is also currently used for the exchange of legislation data in Europe [8]. To represent the obligations as RDF, Protege (an open-source ontology editor) [9] was used as it provides a simple GUI for accomplishing the task. Listing 1 shows a snippet of the text related to Article 13.1 of the GDPR in the RDF format. Using RDF, each triple, which is composed of a *subject-predicate-object* expression, asserts a binary relationship between two pieces of information. These triples are placed in common *namespaces*, referenced via *prefixes*. The prefix odrl represents the components from the ODRL

---

[7] https://www.w3.org/TR/rdf11-concepts/.

[8] http://www.eli.fr/en/.

[9] https://protege.stanford.edu/.

model <http://www.w3.org/ns/odrl/2/>. The prefix rdf is used for the RDF built-in vocabulary, lm to denote the legislative vocabulary <http://privacylab.at/vocabs/lm/>, and gdpr for the GDPR instantiation <http://privacylab.at/vocabs/gdpr/>.

Listing 1: Snippet of the GDPR instance based on the duty from Article 13.1

```
1  gdpr:P13_1 rdf:type lm:Paragraph .
2  gdpr:P13_1 odrl:duty gdpr:ProvideInfo .
3  gdpr:ProvideInfo rdf:type odrl:Duty .
4  gdpr:ProvideInfo odrl:action gdpr:DirectCollection .
5  gdpr:ProvideInfo lm:dispensation gdpr:DataSubjecthasInfo .
6  gdpr:ProvideInfo lm:feature gdpr:Transparency .
7  gdpr:ProvideInfo lm:feature gdpr:Conciseness .
8  gdpr:ProvideInfo lm:discretional gdpr:Icons .
```

In Example 4 we had illustrated an interconnection between Article 13 and 12. In Listing 1, along with representing the duty from Article 13.1, we also include connections to other articles and paragraphs. For instance, line 6 and 7 of the listing represent connections to *transparency* and *conciseness* from Article 12.1 as illustrated in Example 4. Similarly, line 5 of the listing represents the connection to the dispensation defined in Article 13.4 (see Example 2). Also, line 8 represents the discretional task of using privacy icons, illustrated in Example 1 from Article 12.7. Thus, the duty based on Article 13.1 is related to other parts of the text such as to Article 12.1, 12.7 and 13.4. These relations were established with the help of identified interconnections in step (b).

(e) **Enhancing readability for the users.** In the RDF model, additional information such as legal definitions can be added by defining new data fields for the components. For instance, in the GDPR, Article 4 is dedicated for such definitions which can be added to a GDPR instance. Along with the resources such as definitions, in order to take input from the user, questions need to be added to the instance. This way, the compliance system can present the data model in form of a questionnaire. Example 8 illustrates some templates used for creating such questions. Using, the template, the *Duty* for providing the required information to the data subject (Article 13.1) would correspond to a question: *"Does your organisation ensure that the required information is provided to the data subject?"*.

Example 8: Example for the structure of the questions
Action: Does your organisation (perform) <Action>?
Duty: Does your organisation (ensure) <Duty>?
Feature: Does your organisation (ensure) <Feature>?

Listing 2 illustrates how questions can be added to the instance. While, Listings 3 and 4 illustrate *Action* and *Feature* questions respectively.

Listing 2: Snippet of the GDPR instance from Listing 1 with the added question

```
1  gdpr:ProvideInfo rdf:type odrl:Duty .
2  gdpr:ProvideInfo odrl:action gdpr:DirectCollection .
3  gdpr:ProvideInfo lm:dispensation gdpr:DataSubjecthasInfo .
4  gdpr:ProvideInfo lm:feature gdpr:Transparency .
5  gdpr:ProvideInfo lm:feature gdpr:Conciseness .
6  gdpr:ProvideInfo lm:discretional gdpr:Icons .
7  gdpr:ProvideInfo lm:hasquestion "Does your organisation ensure that the
8                    required information is provided to the data subject?" .
```

Listing 3: Illustration of an *Action* with added question

```
1  gdpr:DirectCollection rdf:type odrl:Action .
2  gdpr:DirectCollection lm:hasquestion "Does your organisation collect
3                    personal information directly from the data subjects?" .
```

Listing 4: Illustration of a *Feature* related to the duty from Listing 2

```
1  gdpr:Transparency rdf:type lm:Feature .
2  gdpr:Transparency lm:hasquestion "Does your organisation ensure
3                    transparency for the provided information?" .
```

5   The Compliance System

After the definitions and questions are added to the legislative instance, it can be passed as input for the compliance system as shown in Fig. 5. We now elaborate on the compliance system and discuss how it can be used for GDPR compliance assessment. For the assessment, we split the process into three parts: (i) preliminary assessment; (ii) main assessment; and (iii) report.

5.1   Preliminary Assessment

The aim for the preliminary assessment is to find out the applicable obligations such that user does not have to identify and mark the non-applicable obligations similar to the existing tools [18, 26]. Based on the legislative model, as depicted in Fig. 2, in order to perform *Action*, the associated *Duty* must be fulfilled Hence, the component *Action* can be used for the preliminary analysis to filter the applicable obligations. For instance, consider the *Action* illustrated in Listing 3. The *Duty* shown in Listing 2, based on the connection with the considered *Action*, would only be applicable if that *Action* is performed. As shown in Fig. 6, a list of questions are presented to the user which can be answered as *Yes* or *No*. For every question, there exists a title to give some context for the question. In addition, on the top right corner of every question, "i" button has been provided to display the additional resources such as definitions or

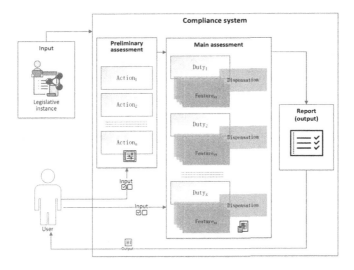

Fig. 5. Detailed process for the assessment of compliance

Fig. 6. A screenshot showing some questions from the preliminary analysis. The blue bubble shows additional information related to the question (Color figure online)

external links for further reference. Once the user submits all the answers, the system then uses this information to select the applicable parts which are associated with the actions where the user responds with a *Yes*.

5.2   Main Assessment

Based on the selected *Actions*, all the associated *duties* are extracted from the instance. These *duties* are the basis for the main assessment. Referring back to Fig. 2, the *Duty* component is connected to the constraints: *Feature*, *Dispensation* and *Discretional*. Thus, along with the *Duty*, other connected components are also presented to the user. Considering Listing 2, the assessment would also show the question for the *Duty* as well as for the connected components such as transparency, shown in Listing 4. Even

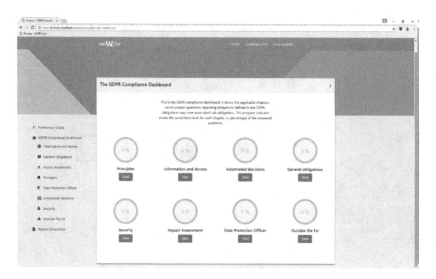

Fig. 7. Dashboard based on the GDPR chapters for the main assessment

after eliminating the non-applicable parts, the number of duties can be overwhelming to show as a flat list. Thus, in an attempt not to overwhelm the user with 100+ questions on a page, we group the questions, by clustering the questions according to the *chapters* as shown in Fig. 7. The user can start the assessment with any of the displayed chapters. Based on the preliminary assessment, the number of *chapters* shown may vary as the dashboard is dynamically created based on the applicable obligations. After the user selects a chapter, a list of questions is shown which is based on *duties* belonging to the selected *chapter*. Like the questions for the preliminary analysis, all questions for the main analysis have a short title and one "i" button on the top right corner. Initially, only the questions based on the *Duty* are shown. If the user selects *No* then nothing happens. However, if *Yes* is selected, a cascaded list of questions is displayed. These questions are based on the connected *Dispensation* and *Features*. By putting questions in a cascaded format, the user only sees the relevant parts. For instance, for duty illustrated in Listing 2, in case the user selects *No* for the question related to the *Duty* then the questions for the associated *features* like transparency, depicted in Listing 4 are not relevant and are not shown to the user. Only when the user selects *Yes* for the *Duty*, the related questions are shown. The user has the option to go back to the dashboard even when the all the questions have not been answered. The progress is saved and reflected as percentage complete on the dashboard.

5.3 Report

The last part for the compliance system is the report which provides a list of all the fulfilled and unfulfilled obligations. An obligation is considered to be fulfilled if a *Duty* is fulfilled along with all of the associated *Features*. *Duties* and *Features* represented as *Discretional* are also documented in the report. Along with the fulfilment status, references to the source (based on the *Articles* and *Paragraphs* which are defined in the legislative instance) are provided, such that users can refer to the legislation for additional information. Furthermore, fulfilled components (*Duty* and *Feature*) are shown in green boxes, *Discretional* components in orange and unfulfilled components are shown in red boxes.

6   Discussion

Our legislative model overcomes several of the challenges discussed in Sect. 2. It can represent both actions and purposes using the *Action* component of the model, which is one of the shortcoming for Bath et al's approach [7]. Also, as compared to May et al's approach [25] it can represent specifications for the obligations by using the *Feature* component. We have also considered soft-obligations and exceptions, which we refer to in our model as *Discretional* and *Dispensation* respectively.

To compare the capabilities of the compliance tools, we analyse 3 different capabilities: support for exceptions, management of evolving law and traceability. For the compliance tools, similar to legal modelling, **support for exceptions** is also important. For instance, in the GDPR, paragraphs like 17.3 define scenarios where obligation related to "right to be forgotten" is not applicable. Secondly, as law is considered to be dynamic where the interpretation involves based on amendments as well as on important judicial decisions [9, 11, 20, 29], the GDPR tools should support **management of evolving law** by ensuring provisions for updating the obligations accordingly. Lastly, **traceability** i.e. ensuring traceable references between the legal text and obligations is considered to be important [9, 11, 29]. References provide an overview of the articles and the paragraphs which a tool covers for the evaluation. With such traceable links, changes in the law can also be easily traced to the corresponding obligations defined for the tool.

Based on these criteria, in the following, we compare the GDPR compliance tools. The capabilities have been summarised in Table 2.

ICO   The checklist for data protection self assessment provided by ICO [18] does not consider the exceptions. However, the questions can be answered as *not applicable* for cases where a user is aware of the exceptions. Also, as the checklist is web-based the updation of obligations can only be managed by the ICO. In terms of traceability, references to the GDPR text are missing which makes it difficult to analyse how much of the GDPR is covered by their tool.

Microsoft   Microsoft's GDPR detailed assessment toolbox [26] also does not support exceptions but like ICO's tool provide an option to answer a question as *n/a*. As the tool is spreadsheet based, the users have an option to modify or update questions if any interpretation changes. The tool also provides references to the GDPR text. However, the references are not defined per obligation but rather for a group of obligations which makes it difficult to identify the reference of a single obligation.

Nymity   Nymity's GDPR readiness spreadsheet [28] also does not support exceptions but the questions are framed in a way to exclude the exception scenarios. For instance, for obligation related to "right to be forgotten" the question includes "*where required by law*". The references are then provided to the corresponding article and paragraph and a user can then refer to the GDPR text to check if that obligation is applicable or not. Also, as this tool is also based a spreadsheet the user has the option to modify or update obligations if required.

Table 2. Comparison of the compliance tools

Tool	Support for exceptions	Manage evolving law	Traceability
ICO	**No** manual selection as N/A	**Limited** controlled by ICO	**No** references are absent
Microsoft	**No** manual selection as N/A	**Yes** editing the spreadsheet	**Limited** not defined individually
Nymity	**Limited** has conditional questions	**Yes** editing the spreadsheet	**Yes** references to paragraphs
PriWUcy	**Yes** represented as dispensation	**Limited** requires self-hosting	**Yes** references to paragraphs

PriWUcy   In the data model as we defined a component *Dispensation* the exceptions are supported by the tool. For an obligation, if the dispensation is answered as *Yes* then that obligation would not be considered for the analysis. Like ICO's tool, PriWUcy is also web-based and users would not be able to change the obligations unless they self-host the tool. However, as the data component is decoupled from the user interface, updating the obligations based on the changes in the law would not be difficult. Also, by introducing *Chapter*, *Article* and *Paragraph* to the model, we were able to represent the references for all the obligations

Currently, for the questions used for PriWUcy, we have used the terms as defined in the GDPR. For instance, consider the term transparency defined in Article 12.1 where the corresponding question in the tool is "Does your organisation ensure transparency with respect to the processing of the information provided?" The use of the term *transparency* in the question introduces certain limitations regarding ambiguities. The question does not have a precise interpretation and for the user it is difficult to measure if transparency is ensured. Questions with such ambiguities can be confusing to answer. As a result, removing ambiguities is described as an important prerequisite for defining requirements for a system in the field of Requirements Engineering [2, 13, 33]. However, on the other hand, according to the legal literature, ambiguity in the legal texts can be intentional and should not be removed or resolved from the legal texts [29]. Moreover, resolving ambiguities can possibly result in wrong specification of the obligations [19]. So, in case if we do not resolve ambiguities then users may have different interpretations and might answer incorrectly. Also, if we resolve ambiguities, for instance describing transparency is some measurable form then we face of risk of misrepresentation of the GDPR text. This can lead to including a wrong question for the assessment which would lead to a wrong report. Either way, we risk ending up with a wrong assessment of compliance. Therefore, it is crucial to find a right balance for ambiguity in order to ensure correctness of the assessment.

7   Conclusions

In this paper, we described a flexible and modular compliance assessment framework, where changes to the legislative instances are automatically reflected in the compliance assessment tool. In addition we proposed a general legislative model and vocabulary based on the Open Digital Rights Language. In order to assess the effectiveness of the proposed framework and model we discuss how it can be used to model the General Data Protection Regulation. Additionally, we compare our compliance assessment tool with those provided by the Information Commissioner's Office (ICO) in the UK, Software vendor Microsoft, and a company called Nymity who provide tools and consultancy to privacy officers worldwide. Learning from one of the main shortcoming of the P3P [30] i.e. high complexity, we know that companies would also not adopt a compliance tool unless the complexity is kept to the minimum. Thus as a next step, we would work on the ambiguity issue such that the questions can be simplified without affecting the correctness of the questions from a legal perspective. Also, although in this paper we focus on modelling the GDPR, in future work we plan to demonstrate how our legislative model can be used to express related legislative obligations, such as those found in the e-Privacy regulation or the Payment Services Directive. Additionally, we plan to explore automation techniques such as those investigated by Kiyavitskaya et al. [21], which are designed to automatically extract obligations from legal texts. Such techniques could potentially help in reducing the manual efforts required for the modelling process.

Acknowledgments. Partially supported by the European Unions Horizon 2020 research and innovation programme under grant 731601 and the Austrian Federal Ministry of Transport, Innovation and Technology (BMVIT) DALICC. For Figs. 1, 4 and 6, icons have been taken from *icons8* (https://icons8.com/).

References

1. Directive 95/46/EC of the European Parliament and of the Council of 24 October 1995 on the protection of individuals with regard to the processing of personal data and on the free movement of such data. OJ L 281, 0031–0050 (1995). http://data.europa.eu/eli/dir/1995/46/oj
2. IEEE recommended practice for software requirements specifications: Approved 25 June 1998, IEEE Std, vol. 830–1998. IEEE, New York (1998)
3. Directive (EU) 2015/2366 of the European Parliament and of the Council of 25 November 2015 on payment services in the internal market, amending Directives 2002/65/EC, 2009/110/EC and 2013/36/EU and Regulation (EU) No 1093/2010, and repealing Directive 2007/64/EC. OJ L 337, 35–127 (2015). http://data.europa.eu/eli/dir/2015/2366/oj

4. Regulation (EU) 2016/679 of the European Parliament and of the Council of 27 April 2016 on the protection of natural persons with regard to the processing of personal data and on the free movement of such data, and repealing Directive 95/46/EC (General Data Protection Regulation). OJ L 119, 1–88 (2016). http://data.europa.eu/eli/reg/2016/679/oj

5. Proposal for a Regulation of the European Parliament and of the Council concerning the respect for private life and the protection of personal data in electronic communications and repealing Directive 2002/58/EC (Regulation on Privacy and Electronic Communications). COM (2017) 2017/03 (COD) (2017)

6. Arora, C., Sabetzadeh, M., Briand, L.C., Zimmer, F.: Requirement boilerplates: transition from manually-enforced to automatically-verifiable natural language patterns. In: 2014 IEEE 4th International Workshop on Requirements Patterns (RePa), pp. 1–8. IEEE (2014)

7. Barth, A., Datta, A., Mitchell, J.C., Nissenbaum, H.: Privacy and contextual integrity: framework and applications. In: 2006 IEEE Symposium on Security and Privacy, p. 15. IEEE (2006)

8. Biasiotti, M., Francesconi, E., Palmirani, M., Sartor, G., Vitali, F.: Legal informatics and management of legislative documents. In: Global Center for ICT in Parliament Working Paper **2** (2008)

9. Boella, G., Humphreys, L., Muthuri, R., Rossi, P., van der Torre, L.: A critical analysis of legal requirements engineering from the perspective of legal practice. In: 2014 IEEE 7th International Workshop on Requirements Engineering and Law (RELAW), pp. 14–21. IEEE (2014)

10. Breaux, T.D., Vail, M.W., Anton, A.I.: Towards regulatory compliance: extracting rights and obligations to align requirements with regulations. In: 14th IEEE International Requirements Engineering Conference (RE 2006), pp. 49–58 (2006)

11. Breaux, T.D.: Legal requirements acquisition for the specification of legally compliant information systems. North Carolina State University (2009). http://www.lib.ncsu.edu/resolver/1840.16/3376

12. Cranor, L.F.: P3P: making privacy policies more useful. IEEE Secur. Priv. **99**(6), 50–55 (2003)

13. Génova, G., Fuentes, J.M., Llorens, J., Hurtado, O., Moreno, V.: A framework to measure and improve the quality of textual requirements. Requir. Eng. **18**(1), 25–41 (2013)

14. Ghanavati, S., Amyot, D., Peyton, L.: Towards a framework for tracking legal compliance in healthcare. In: Krogstie, J., Opdahl, A., Sindre, G. (eds.) CAiSE 2007. LNCS, vol. 4495, pp. 218–232. Springer, Heidelberg (2007). https://doi.org/10.1007/978-3-540-72988-4_16

15. Grimm, R., Rossnagel, A.: P3P and the privacy legislation in Germany: can P3P help to protect privacy worldwide? In: Proceedings of the ACM Multimedia, November 2000

16. Holzmann, G.J.: Design and validation of protocols: a tutorial. Comput. Netw. ISDN Syst. **25**(9), 981–1017 (1993)

17. Hull, E., Jackson, K., Dick, J.: Requirements Engineering. Practitioner Series, 2nd edn. Springer, London (2005). https://doi.org/10.1007/b138335

18. Information Commissioner's Office (ICO) UK: Getting ready for the GDPR (2017). https://ico.org.uk/for-organisations/resources-and-support/data-protection-self-assessment/getting-ready-for-the-gdpr/

19. Kamsties, E., Berry, D.M., Paech, B.: Detecting ambiguities in requirements documents using inspections. In: Proceedings of the First Workshop on Inspection in Software Engineering (WISE01), pp. 68–80. Citeseer (2001)

20. Kiyavitskaya, N., Krausová, A., Zannone, N.: Why eliciting and managing legal requirements is hard. In: 2008 Requirements Engineering and Law, RELAW 2008, pp. 26–30. IEEE (2008)

21. Kiyavitskaya, N., et al.: Automating the extraction of rights and obligations for regulatory compliance. In: Li, Q., Spaccapietra, S., Yu, E., Olivé, A. (eds.) ER 2008. LNCS, vol. 5231, pp. 154–168. Springer, Heidelberg (2008). https://doi.org/10.1007/978-3-540-87877-3_13

22. Korba, L., Kenny, S.: Towards meeting the privacy challenge: adapting DRM. In: Feigenbaum, J. (ed.) DRM 2002. LNCS, vol. 2696, pp. 118–136. Springer, Heidelberg (2003). https://doi.org/10.1007/978-3-540-44993-5_8

23. Massacci, F., Prest, M., Zannone, N.: Using a security requirements engineering methodology in practice: the compliance with the Italian data protection legislation. Comput. Stand. Interfaces **27**(5), 445–455 (2005)

24. Mavin, A., Wilkinson, P., Harwood, A., Novak, M.: Easy approach to requirements syntax (EARS). In: 17th IEEE International Requirements Engineering Conference, pp. 317–322. IEEE (2009)

25. May, M.J., Gunter, C.A., Lee, I.: Privacy APIs: access control techniques to analyze and verify legal privacy policies. In: 19th IEEE Computer Security Foundations Workshop, p. 13. IEEE (2006)

26. Microsoft Trust Center: Detailed GDPR Assessment (2017). http://aka.ms/gdprdetailed assessment

27. Nissenbaum, H.: Privacy as contextual integrity symposium - technology, values, and the justice system. Wash. Law Rev. **79**, 119 (2004)

28. Nymity: GDPR Compliance Toolkit. https://www.nymity.com/gdpr-toolkit.aspx

29. Otto, P.N., Anton, A.I.: Addressing legal requirements in requirements engineering. In: 15th IEEE International Requirements Engineering Conference (RE 2007), pp. 5–14. IEEE (2007)

30. Schwartz, A.: Looking back at P3P: lessons for the future. Center for Democracy & Technology (2009). https://www.cdt.org/files/pdfs/P3P_Retro_Final_0.pdf

31. Agarwal, S., Kirrane, S., Scharf, J.: Modelling the general data protection regulation. In: 20. Internationales Rechtsinformatik Symposion (IRIS) 2017, 23–25 Feb 2017, Salzburg (2017)

32. Toval, A., Olmos, A., Piattini, M.: Legal requirements reuse: a critical success factor for requirements quality and personal data protection. In: Proceedings IEEE Joint International Conference on Requirements Engineering, pp. 95–103. IEEE (2002)

33. van Lamsweerde, A.: Requirements Engineering: From System Goals to UML Models to Software Specifications, vol. 10. Wiley, Chichester and Hoboken (2009)

34. W3C ODRL Community Group: ODRL Information Model 2.2 (2018). https://www.w3.org/TR/odrl-model/

Legal Aspects

Compatibility as a Mechanism for Responsible Further Processing of Personal Data

Wouter Seinen, Andre Walter[(✉)], and Sari van Grondelle

Baker McKenzie Amsterdam N.V., Claude Debussylaan 54,
1082 MD Amsterdam, Netherlands
Andre.Walter@bakermckenzie.com

Abstract. Further processing is probably one of the lesser researched features of the General Data Protection Regulation ("GDPR"). This is remarkable since much of the data to be processed involves data that was collected at an earlier stage and further processing is highly relevant for data controllers.

"Further processing" in this article refers to the processing of personal data for a purpose other than that for which it was initially collected. Article 6(4) of the GDPR provides the legal basis for such further processing. The key mechanisms are *consent* and a *compatibility assessment*.

Many privacy advocates consider consent to be the gold standard for further processing and pay little attention to the compatibility option. Consent, however, puts a significant cognitive load on individuals (the "data subjects"), while it confronts data controllers with serious challenges in obtaining consent and recording its validity. On the other hand, the compatibility assessment allows data controllers to justify the further processing based on the criteria given in Article 6(4), but it might leave individuals powerless.

In this article, we compare the two key mechanisms for further processing, consent and compatibility, and we discuss various compensating measures controllers can take to ensure that compatibility-based processing is a real alternative to consent.

Keywords: GDPR · Personal data · Data subjects · Data controllers
Consent · Compatibility · Privacy impact assessment

1 Introduction

"Further processing" of personal data gets little attention in legal literature. The General Data Protection Regulation (EU) 2016/679 (hereinafter the GDPR) provides legal grounds for processing and privacy principles that are at the foundation of the protection of personal data. Its principles define restrictions to the lawful use of personal data. For example, on the basis of the *principle of purpose limitation*, use of personal data shall generally be limited to the purpose for which the data was originally collected. In practice, further processing is highly relevant for most data controllers: they often have valid reasons to reuse data for further processing purposes. The GDPR provides the legal basis for such further processing in Article 6(4).

M. Medina et al. (Eds.): APF 2018, LNCS 11079, pp. 153–171, 2018.
https://doi.org/10.1007/978-3-030-02547-2_9

The key mechanisms to legitimate further processing under the GDPR require demonstrating (i) that such further processing takes place on the basis of *consent* or (ii) that a *compatibility assessment* demonstrates the compatibility of such further processing with the initial purpose [1].

In this article we will assess whether the compatibility is an alternative to consent in guaranteeing a balance between the rights and freedoms of the individuals concerned and the interests of the data controller. We will analyze the privacy protection of the data subject in the situation of further processing by systematically comparing the two key mechanisms for further processing: consent and compatibility. We will address where the two mechanisms reveal deficiencies and discuss possible compensating measures that data controllers can take to ensure effective protection of personal data when processing data on a compatibility-basis.

We will look into (1) the general privacy principles, (2) the lawfulness of the initial processing of personal data, (3) the further processing of personal data, (4) consent as a mechanism for further processing, (5) compatibility as a mechanism for further processing, and we will provide (6) a comparison of the two key mechanisms of further processing. When discussing shortcomings of the data protection principles and data subjects' rights, we will also discuss potential compensating measures a controller might take to mitigate these shortcomings. In the conclusion (7) we will establish whether and when compatibility-based processing can be a real alternative to consent as a mechanism.

2   General Privacy Principles

Data protection is usually associated with the principles of proper data management, which include a number of requirements that must be imposed on the processing of personal data [2]. The importance of these requirements has been internationally accepted since the 1970s, and they are reflected in the general privacy provisions and principles in the GDPR: lawfulness of processing principle, transparency principle, fairness principle, purpose limitation principle, data minimization principle and storage principle [3, 4].

As not all principles will be equally relevant for our comparison, we will only concentrate in this article on those principles that are directly related to the further processing of personal data.

3   Lawful Initial Processing of Personal Data

Article 5(1)(a) GDPR prescribes that the processing of personal data must always be lawful, fair, and transparent, where lawfulness requires one of the following processing grounds to apply [5]:

a. the data subject has given consent to the processing of his or her personal data,
b. processing is necessary for the performance of a contract,
c. processing is necessary for compliance with a legal obligation,

d. processing is necessary to protect the vital interests of an individual,

e. processing is necessary for the performance of a task carried out in the public interest, or

f. processing is necessary for legitimate interests pursued by the controller or by a third party.

In the case of processing on the basis of consent (ground (a)), the data subject is responsible for determining whether he or she believes that the processing activity envisaged is appropriate in the context of their interests (i.e., rights and freedoms). In case of the other legal grounds (grounds (b) through (f)), the data controller is the actor who needs to determine whether the processing activity envisaged is necessary and possibly outweighs the interests of the data subject.

From a business perspective, a controller should rely on consent only in cases where none of the other grounds apply. Consent is a very fragile concept; it can be withdrawn at any time by the data subject, and the validity of consent might be challenged by data subjects as well as by supervisory authorities. Moreover, consent-based processing comes with additional burdens for the controller such as extended data subject rights and the requirement to create an audit trail to prove that consent was obtained or withdrawn in a valid manner.

4 Further Processing of Personal Data

Despite the purpose limitation mentioned above, the GDPR provides an opening for further processing of data for purposes other than that for which the personal data have been initially collected [6]. This requires that the further processing is based on (i) the data subject's consent, (ii) Union or Member State law, which constitutes a necessary and proportionate measure in a democratic society to safeguard the objectives referred to in Article 23(1), or that (iii) the controller ascertains that the further processing is compatible with the initial purpose.

In the remainder of this paper, we will focus on the two key mechanisms of further processing: consent and compatibility. The aim of the paper is to understand the dynamics between controllers and data subjects and to assess their ability to take responsibility in the further processing in order to materialize a high standard of privacy and data protection.

We assume here that personal data initially collected on the basis of consent will have to be further processed based on consent. In its guidance on consent, the Working Party 29 (hereinafter: WP29) is of the opinion that if a controller wishes to continue processing the personal data on another lawful basis, it cannot silently migrate from consent to that other lawful basis [7]. Although the GDPR does not specifically mention ascertaining of compatibility as a lawful ground of processing in Article 6(1), expert opinions vary on this matter [8].

5 Consent as a Mechanism for Further Processing

The first mechanism of further processing of personal data that we consider is consent. To obtain consent for further processing, the same requirements apply as in the case of consent for the initial collection. The GDPR requires obtaining consent by way of a clear affirmative act, establishing a freely given, specific, informed, and unambiguous indication of the data subject's agreement to the processing of personal data relating to him or her, such as by a written statement (including by electronic means) or an oral statement [9].

Such information must ensure that the data subject is aware of the fact that consent is given and the extent to which it is given. For consent to be informed, the data subject should be aware, *inter alia*, of the identity of the controller and the purposes of the processing for which the personal data are intended [10]. Furthermore, consent may be given by the data subject for the processing of his or her personal data for one or more specific purposes. It shall cover all processing activities carried out, and when the processing has multiple purposes, consent shall be given for all of them.

Under the GDPR, whenever processing is based on consent, the controller is obligated to demonstrate that the data subject has consented to the processing of his or her personal data. Consent shall therefore be recorded in such a way as to provide evidence that, and show how, consent was given. This means that a controller shall implement an effective audit trail of the process deployed for obtaining consent and keep it up to date.

For the data subject, processing on the legal basis of consent means that he or she is in control and is responsible for determining whether the processing activity envisaged is appropriate and desirable with regard to their interests, rights, and freedoms. The data controller may ask consent for a processing activity and then leave the assessment of the appropriateness thereof to the data subject.

Finally, where the data subject has given consent for a specific further processing, the controller should be allowed to further process the personal data irrespective of the compatibility of the purposes [11].

6 Compatibility as a Mechanism for Further Processing

The purpose limitation principle of the GDPR does not impose a requirement of compatibility; rather it prohibits *incompatibility* [12]. The European legislator intended to provide some flexibility regarding further processing. In a fast-moving world, this flexibility may be needed to allow for a change of scope or focus in situations where the business environment changes or expectations of the data subject and/or of the society at large change on the notion of what further processing may be appropriate and compatible.

Compatibility is not a straightforward concept. Compatibility of further processing purposes needs to be assessed on a case-by-case basis, and the data controller cannot legitimize incompatible processing by simply constructing a new lawful processing ground. Moreover, the GDPR states that, in such a case of further processing, no legal basis separate from that which allowed the initial collection of the personal data is required [11].

After having met all the requirements for the lawfulness of the original processing, a controller should perform a compatibility assessment for further processing of personal data, considering, *inter alia,* the following factors:

a. any link between the purposes for which the personal data have been collected and the purposes of the further processing intended;
b. the context in which the personal data have been collected, in particular the reasonable expectations of data subjects, based on their relationship with a data controller, as to their further processing;
c. the nature of the personal data, in particular whether special categories of personal data or personal data related to criminal convictions and offenses are processed;
d. the possible consequences of the intended further processing for data subjects; and
e. the existence of appropriate safeguards, which may include encryption or pseudonymization.

The compatibility assessment considers the five factors described above in order to establish whether the further processing may be considered compatible. An inherent characteristic of such a multifactor assessment is that shortcomings of certain factors may in some cases be compensated by better performance in other areas [13]. The performance of the five factors can therefore balance each other.

In practice, such an assessment cannot be regarded as an entirely quantitative assessment or a purely mathematical exercise, such as by simply averaging the scores assessed in the five categories. A qualitative judgment of the situation by a qualified legal or data protection expert is always recommended and often a necessity. Such an assessment should be documented and kept available for internal and external review by the privacy officer, an auditor, supervisory authorities, or even the data subjects concerned.

Besides this, the GDPR explicitly privileges further processing of personal data for historical, statistical, or scientific purposes, provided that Member States implement appropriate technical and organizational measures [14]. When there is compliance with the safety measures required, processing for these purposes is explicitly considered to be compatible [15]. The privileging rule covers a broad range of processing activities, such as purposes of public interests (e.g. medical research), as well as commercial purposes (e.g. analytical tools of websites or big data applications aimed at market research) [16]. Member State laws may provide for additional situations that justify the further processing of personal data that was obtained for other purposes and specify the tasks and purposes for which the further processing should be regarded as compatible and lawful.

7   Comparison of the Key Mechanisms of Further Processing

Many privacy advocates consider consent to be the gold standard for further processing and pay little attention to the compatibility option. Consent, however, puts a significant cognitive load on data subjects while it confronts data controllers with serious challenges in obtaining consent and recording its validity. Alternatively, the compatibility assessment allows data controllers to justify the further processing based on the criteria given in Article 6(4), but it might leave the individual powerless.

The two key mechanisms of enabling further processing of personal data – consent and compatibility – will be discussed below, and a complete overview of the comparison will be provided in Appendix 1. The comparison covers the three most important areas of materializing privacy protection: (i) the principles of personal data processing, [17] (ii) data subject rights and freedoms, and (iii) controller obligations and interests. We aimed for an objective comparison of how the two mechanisms of consent and compatibility perform in terms of privacy protection based on the legal requirements of the GDPR and the feasibility of implementation.

Initially, consent seems to be the better choice for living up to the principles of personal data processing and guaranteeing data subjects' rights and freedoms. In terms of feasibility of implementation, though, compatibility appears preferable. Table 1 in Appendix 1 gives more insight into our considerations for this baseline assessment. In the section Summary of Compensating Measures, we will review possible improvement areas where compatibility falls short compared to the consent mechanism. Additional measures will be discussed that could improve performance to make it comparable with consent.

7.1   Data Protection Principles

The GDPR privacy principles and their importance for the protection of human rights and fundamental freedoms for data subjects have been mentioned in Sect. 2 above. For some of the data protection principles, we identified no differences or only very limited differences (see Appendix 1): accuracy, integrity/confidentiality, and accountability.

Lawfulness of Processing Principles. As described in Sect. 4 above, data initially collected by consent should not be further processed based on other lawful grounds. Although the GDPR language does not give clear guidance on this, we respect the view of the supervisory authorities on this point, and in further discussion below we exclude data that is initially collected on the basis of consent [18]. Further research will be needed to examine the current position taken by the supervisory authorities.

Transparency Principle. To live up to the transparency principle, the controller will have to provide a publicly available privacy notice that explains the purpose and modalities of the further processing. Using compatibility as a mechanism, the controller should also disclose the compatibility assessment methodology that has been applied in order to justify the further processing of the data.

As much of this information will appear complex to the data subject and to the broader public, the controller should strive for increasing transparency and reducing the cognitive load on the data subject. Information should be made easily accessible, using clear and plain language, and should be supported by visual means of presentation where possible and appropriate.

Further processing through consent requires presenting the data subject a just-in-time notice specifically focusing on the processing purpose envisioned. As this is generally not required for further processing based on compatibility, the controller should therefore consider providing additional transparency controls voluntarily. The WP29 coins the term *pull notices* for these transparency controls that provide data subjects access to additional information, and it specifically mentions methods such as privacy dashboards and "learn more" tutorials. [19]

Fairness Principle. Appendix 1 indicates a weakness of compatibility related to the fairness principle, because the controller makes the decision whether the purpose of the further processing is compatible with the initial purpose, while consent leaves this decision to the data subject. To become comparable with consent, the controller should provide additional features to compensate for this shortcoming, allowing data subjects to opt out of the further processing that has been deemed compatible by the controller. The options should be offered in a user-friendly and intuitive manner in order to get on an equal footing with consent. Withdrawal of consent has to be as easy as giving consent, and the WP29 adds that it must be possible to give and withdraw consent via the same interface [20]. Permission management systems would be a workable way to provide the additional choice and options features [21].

Purpose Limitation Principle. Purpose limitation is relevant with regard to one specific element of the compatibility assessment, namely the link and distance between the purpose for which the personal data have been collected and the purposes of the intended further processing. The controller should be very transparent about the differences between these purposes and the distance between them, and should disclose the compatibility assessment methodology and policy decisions that apply to the operation at hand. Consent leaves this decision about the gap between the purposes to the data subject. Therefore, the controller making this decision based on compatibility should not leave the individual powerless and should provide the data subject with tools allowing unconditional opt-out possibilities. To become comparable with consent, this should go further than just providing the "right to object." In the "right to object" scenario, the controller can take his or her time to evaluate the objection and come up with compelling reasons to reject the request, weakening the data subject's position [22].

Data Minimization Principle. Data minimization is an important aspect in the pursuance of guaranty proportionality and necessity of the data processing. In applying the compatibility assessment, the controller is the actor who will determine proportionality and necessity. Based on the assumption that the compatibility assessment assures compatibility with the initial purpose but does not define a new lawful ground of processing, the GDPR provides the data subject the right to object to this decision only if the initial processing has taken place in the context of public interest or the controller's legitimate interest. Moreover, as explained under the purpose limitation principle, the controller can reject the objection request under certain circumstances, risking leaving the individual powerless. Again, permission management features would be appropriate to reach comparability with consent.

Storage Limitation Principle. To live up to the storage limitation principle, compatibility needs additional measures to be comparable with consent. Although the principle that personal data shall be erased if no longer needed applies to all processing grounds, withdrawal of consent triggers the erasure process explicitly [23]. For processing grounds other than consent, the controller's retention policy has to be applied. To become comparable with consent in this respect, here too a voluntary opt-out feature could be the solution to triggering the same erasure process as a consent withdrawal.

7.2 Data Subjects – Rights and Freedoms

The GDPR grants data subjects a range of specific data subject rights that they can exercise under certain conditions, with a few exceptions. Given the focus of supervisory authorities on these rights, GDPR compliance should specifically enable the exercise of these rights. Some data subject rights are independent of the lawful processing ground, including *data subject access* requests, the *right to restriction of processing*, and the *right to rectification*. For exercising these two rights, it makes no difference whether consent or compatibility is used as a mechanism for further processing of data. However, the exercise of some data subject rights depends on the lawful ground of the initial processing. This applies to the *right to erasure*, the *right to portability*, and the *right to object* to the processing of personal data concerning the data subject. We will now discuss how to come on an equal footing with consent for these rights.

Right to Erasure. The *right to erasure* (Article 17 GDPR) is triggered by consent withdrawal. For processing grounds other than consent, the controller's retention policy has to be applied. To become comparable with consent in this respect, further processing via compatibility should provide a voluntary opt-out feature triggering the same erasure process as consent withdrawal.

Right to Portability. The *right to portability* (Article 20 GDPR) is only applicable for personal data that is provided by the data subject himself or herself, including data collected under consent and for the performance of contract. The right to portability is not applicable for other lawful grounds of the initial purpose. Therefore, the right to data portability applies to all personal data further processed based on consent, but it does not necessarily have to be provided for further processing based on compatibility. To compensate this shortcoming of compatibility, controllers could consider granting a voluntary data portability right for *all* data used for secondary purposes, when relying on compatibility.

Right to Object. The *right to object* (Article 21 GDPR) is generally only provided for processing that takes place in the context of the controller's legitimate interest, direct marketing, or for processing in the public interest. However, in practice, the consent withdrawal mechanism too gives unconditional objection power. Moreover, the GDPR requires this unconditional objection power *a priori* when data are used for direct marketing purposes 24]. It also raises the bar for processing purposes based on legitimate grounds, by obliging the controller to demonstrate *compelling* legitimate grounds to reject such an objection request [25]. To become comparable with consent, an effective mitigation measure would provide an unconditional opt-out feature for all processing purposes based on compatibility.

Choice and Options. Giving choice and options to data subjects to control their data is promoted by the GDPR as an objective [26]. The ICO, for example, is promoting consent as a "higher ideal," stating: "Consent means giving people genuine choice and control over how you use their data" [27]. Conceptually this is right: giving and withdrawal of consent should provide the means for genuine choice, but the challenge lies in the practical implementation. Thoroughly implemented permission management systems providing user-friendly features for data subjects to exercise control over their data can realize this "higher ideal." These systems could equally facilitate choice and options for both mechanisms: opt-in (consent) or opt-out (compatibility).

7.3   Controller Obligations and Interests

Generally, controller obligations and the provisions for transfers of personal data to third countries are independent from lawful grounds of processing [28, 29]. There are small nuances of data transfer derogations for specific situations, which will not be discussed in this article in further detail [30].

Implementation and Continuity. Unlike for the data subject, the compatibility mechanism has many upsides for controllers compared to consent. The implementation and impacts are different. The compatibility approach works better for further processing activities with regard to continuing the processing operations. For example, although a data subject has the right to object to the processing, he or she cannot stop a processing immediately and unconditionally, with a few exceptions. With consent, the data subject can withdraw the consent at any time, unconditionally.

Profiling. Profiling is another purpose many controllers pursue. Collecting consent for profiling can be challenging for controllers because in such an early stage of analysis, data subjects do not see "what's in it for them." Further processing for profiling operations that pass the compatibility assessment could be performed without the consent of the data subject.

Special Categories of Data. Processing of this category of data is generally prohibited under the GDPR unless a number of specific exemptions apply [31, 32]. One of the exception grounds is *explicit consent*, which makes consent the preferred mechanism for secondary use of special categories of personal data, as referred to in Article 9(1). There are only limited exception grounds that lift the prohibition on further processing of special categories of personal data based on compatibility. Examples of this are, *inter alia*, processing in the employment context, for vital or substantial public (health/research) interests, and certain processing in the context of foundations, associations, or any other not-for-profit bodies.

7.4   Summary of Compensating Measures

Measures that can be used to compensate for the shortcomings of compatibility compared to consent are summarized and further elaborated below.

Pull Notices. Pull notices are suitable for providing additional transparency controls. They provide an additional layer of communication to the data subject over push notices which usually cover the information requirements laid down in the GDPR, typically referred to as privacy notices or just-in-time information notices [33]. Typical implementation examples in practice are dedicated privacy portals, permission management that facilitates direct communication channels with the data subject, privacy dashboards, and "learn more" tutorials. Pull notices allow for a more user-centric transparency experience for the data subject.

Voluntary Opt-Out. Data subjects have the right to object to the processing of their personal data when it is based on legitimate grounds of the controller. The objection should reflect grounds relating to the data subject's particular situation, and the processing should be stopped until the controller has demonstrated "compelling legitimate grounds" to continue. The WP29 has clarified that for legitimate interests to be considered compelling, a higher threshold is required than the lawful ground of legitimate interest as found in Article 6(1)(f) GDPR [34].

The above highlights two important points. First, it should be possible to provide an opt-out from certain personal data processing based on the data subject's particular situation. Second, there might be compelling reasons for the controller to pursue its legitimate interests despite the data subject's objection. Thus there must be a range of *non-compelling* processing purposes where the controller should offer the data subject unconditional opt-out possibilities.

Current guidance and earlier investigations by supervisory authorities support the idea of providing voluntary opt-out possibilities to mitigate negative consequences for the data subject. The ICO, for example, states in the context of the legitimate interests assessment that it might be helpful to consider offering an opt-out to balance the interest of the controller with that of the data subject [35]. The Dutch DPA indicated the same in an earlier Wi-Fi tracking investigation [36].

Permission Management. Permission management systems are typically personalized applications and are designed to assist their users to manage their permission settings in a transparent and user-friendly manner. These permission management systems should at least cover all further processing purposes in order to be an effective compensating measure. In the privacy context, these systems are sometimes referred to as "consent managers," [37] focusing primarily on consent-based processing. These systems can typically manage the granting and withdrawal of consent, including the registration of it. Besides this, there are other concepts entering the privacy arena, for example *Customer Identity Access Management* (CIAM) [38, 39] These systems are mainly driven from the marketing and logical access management side. *Personal information management systems* (PIMS) originated in a movement in society to give data subjects more ownership and control over their data [40]. These tools could offer effective mechanisms for objecting, such as a user-controlled opt-out feature.

Erasure Trigger. Erasure will have to be triggered at consent withdrawal. In practice this requires triggering the data retention process within the controller's organization. For other processing grounds, the controller could implement a similar erasure trigger that activates the retention process in the same way as consent withdrawal would. A straightforward practical solution could be to initiate that trigger by the opt-out feature as explained above.

Extended Data Portability Scope. A controller needs to have a system for "privacy bookkeeping" in place to identify the lawful ground of processing at the point at which a portability request is received. This could, for example, be implemented in the Record of Processing [41]. As personal data that are processed based on consent are in the scope of the right to portability – and therefore the further processing of the personal data concerned is as well – controllers might want to consider granting a voluntary portability right for *all* personal data used for further processing based on compatibility too. Practically, the Record of Processing should then be extended to give insight into further processing based on compatibility. This would bring consent and compatibility to the same level for portability.

7.5 Relationship Between Compensating Measures and the Compatibility Assessment

In Sect. 6 above we explained that it is an inherent characteristic of compatibility that shortcomings of certain factors may in some cases be compensated by better performance on other factors. Hence, the performance of the five factors can to a certain extent compensate each other. Therefore it is valuable to understand the relationship between the five capability factors (a) through (e) and the compensating measures described above.

a. link between the purposes: ***Pull notices*** can be provided to increase transparency about the distance between the original and intended further purposes and about the compatibility methodology, including related policy decisions, to clarify the controller's view of the differences between the purposes. Furthermore, the controller should not leave the individual powerless and could provide ***permission management*** features, including ***voluntary opt-out*** possibilities to the individual to object to the controller's decision about the relationship between the purposes.
b. context of data collection: ***Pull notices*** are a suitable means to explain the context of the intended further processing of personal data and to manage the expectations of the data subjects concerned. Another aspect is the relationship between the data subjects and the controller: in certain situations there might be a power imbalance in that relationship, for example in the employment context or where the controller has a dominant market position. The GDPR introduces a new right of data portability that empowers data subjects to get more access and control over their personal data in that it facilitates copying or transmitting personal data easily from one data controller to another. This reduces the switching barriers between controllers. Voluntary ***scope extension for data portability*** would enable individuals to exercise this right for all personal data used for further processing purposes.
c. nature of data: ***Pull notices*** can be used to give insight into the nature of the personal data involved in the further processing, in particular whether special categories of personal data are concerned. The risk to the rights and freedoms of data subjects will differ, depending on the nature of the personal data categories involved in the processing; these might include pseudonyms or other indirect identifiers, metadata, contact details or other direct identifiers, and/or special categories of data. The controller should be transparent about the different personal data categories

involved in the further processing and about its view on the potential consequences this might have for the rights and freedoms of the data subjects.

d. possible consequences for the data subject: **Permission management** systems can enable the data subjects to manage the possible consequences for them of the intended further processing. Although the controller might do their utmost to assess these consequences for their entire data subject base, the conclusions might differ significantly from individual to individual. In practice a better approach might be to enable the data subject to make his or her own choice effectively by offering a **voluntary opt-out** option.

e. appropriate safeguards: **Erasure trigger** connected to a **voluntary opt-out** mechanism can serve as an additional measure to ensure a level of security appropriate to the risk. Case law and the interpretation of the laws of the European data protection authorities show that controllers may be asked to observe strict – and therefore very limited – retention periods unless the controller can make a plausible case that the data has to be retained for the purposes to be achieved [42]. Moreover, additional safeguards, such as encryption or pseudonymization, might be applied to reduce the risk to the rights and freedoms of data subjects inherent to the data processed.

8 Conclusion

We have focused here on further processing of personal data that was initially collected for another purpose. The GDPR provides for further processing based on three concepts. Two of them – consent and compatibility of the future purpose with the one for which the personal data was initially collected – are the key mechanisms we researched in this article. We assessed *whether compatibility is a useful and realistic alternative to consent in enabling further use of personal data in compliance with the GDPR* with the objective of guaranteeing a proper balance between the rights and freedoms of the data subjects concerned and the interests of the data controller, which we consider the fundamental goal of article 6(4) GDPR.

To compare these two key mechanisms, we evaluated the three most important areas of realizing privacy protection, namely (i) the privacy principles, (ii) the data subjects' rights and freedoms, and (iii) the controllers' obligations and interests.

Initially we made this comparison based on the legal bottom line of the GDPR requirements, without including any voluntary measures to improve the performance of one of the key mechanisms. We found that consent seems to be the better choice for adhering to the principles of personal data processing and to guarantee data subject rights and freedoms. In terms of feasibility of implementation, however, the compatibility mechanism appears to be the preferred solution.

By addressing shortcomings, we discussed additional measures that could achieve performance improvements that would allow compatibility to reach an equal footing with consent. All privacy principles, data subject rights, and controller obligations in which compatibility shows weaknesses have been reviewed in this respect.

Our review showed (see full overview in Appendix 1) that all shortcomings of compatibility versus consent, in almost any of the relevant factors, can be compensated for by additional measures in order to bring the compatibility mechanism to the same level as consent. The only area where compatibility cannot be elevated to an equivalent of consent is the further processing of special categories of data. Here we may continue to face limitations to finding exception grounds to lift the prohibition of further processing, as described in Appendix 1 in more detail.

Finally, we have found that the compensating measures we identified are limited in number and that permission management and active communication with the data subject are the strongest features. As many permission management systems currently available have user-centric architectures – for example, web portals, consent managers, or Customer Identity Access Management (CIAM) systems – these solutions naturally provide ideal channels for direct communication with the user. This means that these systems should potentially also be capable of providing pull notices to the data subject, thereby enabling more proactive and effective communication with the data subject, beyond the minimum required by law.

Compatibility-based processing of personal data compels the data controller to make a thorough assessment of the processing activities involved and of both the interests of the data subject and the controller, and it forces the data controller to be transparent about the processing activities that are employed.

Controllers who are prepared to implement advanced permission management systems, including features for direct communication with the data subject, may have a great potential to base many of their further processing activities on the concept of compatibility. For these advanced players in the market, consent-based further processing of personal data may become the exception rather than the rule.

Appendix 1 – Table Overview Including All Compensating Measures

The table below shows an overview of the two key mechanisms that can be applied to enable further processing of personal data. The two mechanisms of consent and compatibility are compared on the three most important aspects of realizing privacy protection: (i) the principles of personal data processing, (ii) the data subject's rights and freedoms, and (iii) the controller's obligations and interests.

Initially, the comparison was done with no compensating measures in place to improve the performance of one or the other of the mechanisms. In a second consideration, the compensating measures discussed above were added to improve the performance of the compatibility assessment, possibly bringing it to the same level as consent.

Table 1. Comparison of compatibility and consent as mechanisms for further processing of personal data

Principles of personal data processing				
Privacy aspects	*Compatibility*			*Consent*
Lawfulness of processing	All lawful grounds of processing, except "Consent," Article 6(4) jo. 6(1)(b)-(f)	☒	☑	All lawful grounds of processing Article 6(4) jo. 6(1)(a)-(f)
	Out of scope: see assumption in section 3: Further Processing of Personal Data[43]	☒		
Transparency	Privacy notice & disclosure of standardized compatibility assessment.	☒	☑	Privacy notice & specific just-in-time notice per specific processing purpose.
	Compensation measures: • *pull notices*		☑	
Fairness	Controller makes the decision whether new purpose is compatible with the original purpose.	☒	☑	Freely given consent of data subject to new purpose, while having genuine and free choice to refuse or withdraw consent without detriment.
	Compensation measures: • *pull notices* • *permission management* • *voluntary opt-out*		☑	
Purpose limitation	Controller determines the remoteness of the new purpose vs. the original purpose.	☒	☑	Consent given by the data subject to a specific further processing purpose.
	Compensation measures: • *transparency on compatibility policy* • *permission management* • *voluntary opt-out*		☑	
Data minimization in pursuance of proportionality and necessity principles.	Controller to determine proportionality and necessity of new purpose, while data subject has right to object if processing takes place in the context of direct marketing, public interest, or controller's legitimate interest.[22]	☒	☑	Data subject has the opportunity to decide if new purpose is proportional and necessary before processing starts.
	Compensation measures: • *permission management* • *voluntary opt-out*		☑	

Accuracy	Data subject can be educated in privacy notice on the possibilities to verify the accuracy of and rectify the personal data.	☑	☑	Data subject can be educated in privacy notice on the possibilities to verify the accuracy of and rectify the personal data.
Storage limitation	Controller's retention policy applies.	☒	☑	Controller's retention policy applies. Additionally, data subject can withdrawal consent and with it trigger the erasure obligation.[23]
	Compensation measures: • *additional erasure trigger*	☑		
Integrity and confidentiality	Apply controller's information security baseline, including the appropriate technical or organizational measures	☑	☑	Apply controller's information security baseline, including the appropriate technical or organizational measures
Accountability, i.e. demonstrate compliance with the principles above	Document compatibility assessment.	☑	☑	Collecting and recording of valid consent.

Data Subjects – Rights and Freedoms

Subject assess request	Data subject right to get insight in personal data processed by controller is independent from lawful ground of processing.	☑	☑	Data subject right to get insight in personal data processed by controller is independent from lawful ground of processing.
Right to erasure	Triggered by objection to legitimate interest, but possibility to be overruled by controller.	☒	☑	Right to erasure triggered by withdrawal of consent.
	Compensation measures: • *additional erasure trigger*	☑		
Right to portability	Applicable for all processing based on contract, or data provided by data subject, not otherwise.	☒	☑	Right to portability of consent-based processing.
	Compensation measures: • *extended data portability*	☑		
Right to restriction	Right to restriction of processing is independent from lawful ground of processing.	☑	☑	Right to restriction of processing is independent from lawful ground of processing.

Right to object	Right to object if processing takes place in the context of direct marketing, public interest or controller's legitimate interest, not for other lawful grounds.[22]	☒	☑	Right to object triggered by withdrawal of consent in practice.
	Compensation measures: • *unconditional opt-out option*	☑		
Choice & options	Giving choice and options to data subjects to control their data is more an objective than a legal requirement of the GDPR.	☒	☑	Consent giving and withdrawal mechanism is legally mandatory.
	Compensation measures: • *permission management*	☑		
Cognitive load on the data subject	Disclosure of standardized compatibility assessment policy. Controller manages and discloses the proportionality and necessity decisions.	☑	☒	Risk of information fatigue of having to read multiple just-in-time notice (per specific processing purpose). Decision making is not always easy and some case not in the ability of the data subject
Controller – Obligations and Interests				
Controller obligations	The controller obligations (pursuant to chapter 4 of the GDPR) are independent from lawful ground of processing.	☑	☑	The controller obligations (pursuant to chapter 4 of the GDPR) are independent from lawful ground of processing.
International data transfer	In the presence of an adequacy decision,[44] or appropriate safeguards,[45] including binding corporate rules, the obligations for international data transfer are independent from the processing ground.	☑	☑	In the presence of an adequacy decision[44] or appropriate safeguards,[45]including binding corporate rules, the obligations for international data transfer are independent from the processing ground.
Special categories of data	Limited exception grounds can be found that lift the prohibition of processing, incl. processing in the employment context, for vital or substantial public (health/research) interests, as well as for certain foundations, associations, or any	☒	☑	Explicit consent is one of the exception grounds that lift the prohibition of processing. However, <u>explicit</u> consent requires a higher compliance standard than "ordinary" consent.

	other not-for-profit bodies.			
	Compensation measures: *n/a*	☒		
Profiling, i.e. evaluating personal aspects, without making (solely automated) decision based on significance of legal effect on data subject	Under the terms of compatibility, no further approval of data subject required	☑	☒	Risk of low conversion rates of consent requests, as the added value of profiling might be difficult to explain to the data subject.
Implementation feasibility	Appropriate compensating measures to protect the data subject's rights and freedoms and legitimate interests, including transparency measures might be reasonably feasible to implement.	☑	☒	Reaching out to the data subject might bear the risk of unsolicited communication. Collecting and recording of valid consent is challenging in practice. Providing transparent information might prove impossible or could involve a disproportionate effort.
Implementation impact	Characteristic of multifactor compatibility assessment is that shortcomings on certain factors may be compensated by a better controls on other factors.[46] This also provides the possibility to level out implementation challenges to come to a feasible mix of technical and organizational measures and controls to balance the data subject's rights and freedoms with legitimate interests of the controller.	☑	☒	High implementation effort of technical and organizational measures and controls of collecting and recording valid consent.
Processing continuity	Data subject has the right to object, while controller has the final say in many cases.	☑	☒	Withdrawal of consent is easy as giving it and lifts the legal ground for the processing.
Direct marketing	Unconditional right to object to direct marketing processing activities.	☑	☑	Withdrawal of consent has to be as easy as giving it.

References

1. For completeness, further processing is also possible on the basis of Union or Member State law, which constitutes a necessary and proportionate measure in a democratic society to safeguard the objectives referred to in Article 23(1) GDPR. Given the specific nature and limited scope of this feature, we will not elaborate further on this in this article
2. Report of the State Commission on the Protection of Privacy 1976, pp. 26–27
3. Blok, P.H.: Het recht op privacy (The Right to Privacy). The Hague: Boom Juridische Uitgevers, p. 135 (2002)
4. Article 5 GDPR
5. Article 6 GDPR
6. This is not a new concept: earlier, in the context of the Directive 95/46/EC, the Working Party 29 (hereinafter: WP29) published an opinion on further processing of personal data and the assessment of compatibility thereof in its working paper on purpose limitation. The GDPR codified this approach in Article 6(4)
7. WP29 Guidelines on Consent under Regulation 2016/679, WP259 rev. 01, (hereinafter: WP29, WP259), adopted on 10 April 2018, p. 23
8. Feiler, Lukas, Forgó, Nikolaus, Weigl, Michaela: The EU General Data Protection Regulation (GDPR): A Commentary, p. 83. UK, Global Law and Business Ltd (2018)
9. Article 4(11) GDPR and Recital 32 GDPR
10. Recital 42 GDPR
11. Recital 50 GDPR
12. Article 5(1)(b) on the principle of purpose limitation
13. WP29, WP203, III.2.2.d, p. 26
14. Article 5(1)(b) and (e) GDPR
15. See final sentence of Article 5(1)(b) GDPR
16. WP29, WP203, p. 29
17. Pursuant to Article 5 GDPR and based on Article 8 of the European Convention on Human Rights (ECHR)
18. WP29, WP259, p. 23
19. WP29 Guidelines on transparency under Regulation 2016/679, WP260 rev. 01, (hereinafter: WP29, WP260), adopted on 11 April 2018, p. 20
20. WP29, WP259, p. 21
21. WP29 recognizes permission management systems as meaningful measures for "pull notices" in WP29, WP260, p. 20
22. Article 21 GDPR
23. Article 17(1)(b) GDPR
24. Article 21(3) Where the data subject objects to processing for direct marketing purposes, the personal data shall no longer be processed for such purposes
25. It is clear from the wording of Article 21 GDPR that the balancing test is different from that found in Article 6(1)(f) GDPR. In other words, it is not sufficient for a controller to just demonstrate that an earlier legitimate interest analysis was correct. This balancing test requires the legitimate interest to be *compelling*, implying a higher threshold for overriding objections. (WP29 Guidelines on the Automated Individual Decision-Making and Profiling, WP251 rev. 01, adopted on 6 February 2018)
26. Recital 7 GDPR: Natural persons should have control of their own personal data
27. Information Commissioner's Office (ICO). Consultation on GDPR consent guidance, March 2017
28. Chapter 4 of the GDPR

29. Chapter 5 of the GDPR
30. Article 49 GDPR and WP29 Guidelines on Article 49 of Regulation 2016/679, WP262, February 6, 2018
31. Article 9(1) GDPR
32. Article 9(2) GDPR
33. Articles 12, 13, and 14 GDPR
34. WP29 Guidelines on the Automated Individual Decision-Making and Profiling, WP251 rev. 01, adopted on 6 February 2018, p. 19
35. ICO. 2018. Guide to the General Data Protection Regulation (GDPR), version 1.0.34, p. 44, 22 March 2018
36. Dutch DPA. 2015. Wifi-tracking van mobiele apparaten in en rond winkels door Bluetrace (Wifi-tracking of mobile devices in and around stores by means of Bluetrace), (hereinafter: Dutch DPA 2015), 13 October 2015
37. International Association of Privacy Professionals (IAPP). Privacy Tech Vendor Report (2018). www.iapp.org
38. KuppingerCole: Leadership Compass: CIAM-Platforms (2016)
39. Gartner: Critical Capabilities for Identity and Access Management as a Service, Worldwide (2016)
40. Ctrl-Shift. Is the EC waking up to PIMS?" (2015). (https://www.ctrl-shift.co.uk/news/2015/11/30/is-the-ec-waking-up-to-pims/)
41. Article 30 GDPR
42. Dutch DPA 2015
43. See working assumption in Section 3 that personal data initially collected based on consent will also have to be further processed based on the data subject's consent
44. Article 45(3) GDPR
45. Article 46 GDPR
46. WP29, WP203, p. 22

DPIA: How to Carry Out One of the Key Principles of Accountability

Jules Sarrat$^{(\boxtimes)}$ ⓘ and Raphael Brun ⓘ

Wavestone, Tour Franklin: 100 - 101 terrasse Boieldieu,
92042 Paris La Défense, France
{jules.sarrat, raphael.brun}@wavestone.com

Abstract. New projects and initiatives are continuously and increasingly taking place in large organizations. Therefore, privacy teams are legitimately wondering if all these projects need a Data Protection Impact Assessment, and which one need to be supported in priority. And what about other projects? Generally speaking, can these GDPR compliant projects rely on the existing ecosystem? And what to do with processing activities already implemented? Many questions to which we will try to answer in this paper.

Keywords: Data protection impact assessment · Privacy by design
WP29 criteria · Processing operation sensitivity

1 Most of Processing Operations Don't Require a DPIA

DPIA is a fundamental measure of GDPR compliance for organizations' personal data processing activities.

But setting up associated processes must follow a few key principles to be fully operational and to avoid creating reluctance and tension among business and IT stakeholders.

1.1 GDPR Does not Require Systematic Implementation of DPIA

DPIA, which stands for Data Protection Impact Assessment, is a new exercise for companies. **DPIA is not mandatory** for all personal data processing activities of a company. The regulation stipulates that a DPIA is necessary when the processing operation is "likely to result in a high risk to the rights and freedoms of natural persons".[1] Therefore, we generally find that in the flow of new projects generated by companies, **a majority does not present a high risk to privacy. Thus, less than one-third** of the personal data processing operations are concerned in organizations with the most sensitive processing activities (BtoC, medical world …). Even **less than 10 %** of the processing are concerned in organizations with least sensitive processing activities (generally BtoB).

In addition, a project related to an existing processing operation (because it has the same purposes and the same legal ground) and on which a DPIA has already been

---

[1] GDPR, article 35: Data Protection Impact Assessment.

© Springer Nature Switzerland AG 2018
M. Medina et al. (Eds.): APF 2018, LNCS 11079, pp. 172–182, 2018.
https://doi.org/10.1007/978-3-030-02547-2_10

carried out, will not require a specific DPIA. The project may rely on the existing DPIA (and associated risk assessment). However, to avoid performing a new DPIA, it will be essential to comply with the target compliance level previously defined and to implement all protection measures of personal data defined in the previous DPIA.

1.2 Rare Expertise Requiring Companies to Focus Their Efforts on the Most Sensitive Projects

Beyond this regulatory analysis, the DPIA is a complex exercise that requires resources with **specific knowledge and skills on a wide range of topics**: risk management, business expertise, IT security expertise, legal knowledge… This **knowledge is rare and often shared between different people in the organization**. This observation confirms (for obvious workload reasons) the idea that companies must focus on most sensitive projects. The objective is to focus on the few available experts on perimeters that require it. This prioritization will allow organizations to avoid business and IT teams overload who will have to answer multiple questions and requests for clarification regarding DPIA.

1.3 Prioritize New Projects Rather Than Old Processing Operations that Have Been Subject to a First Level of Analysis

DPIA's approach concerns both existing processing activities and future projects. However, processing operations that have already been declared to a supervisory authority or to the privacy officer of the company are presumed to be compliant and therefore do not immediately require a DPIA. If no change has occurred in data processing conditions of implementation (purposes, collected data, risks, new technology etc.), DPIAs must be regularly reviewed. Therefore, for DPIAs to be carried out on the first months/years of compliance, companies must focus on new projects that have never been subject to a declaration or a request for authorization to the regulator.

Nevertheless, in many cases, prior formalities correspond to administrative formalities filled by project managers. Most of the time, privacy issues within their projects are partially addressed or not addressed at all. Moreover, by definition, these declarations are incomplete since they do not fully consider GDPR new requirements. Due to the absence of prior advanced reflection or retrospective controls, the controller and the DPO must therefore keep in mind that some of their processing operations may have major non-compliance issues. They will have to ensure, within the next few years after May 25th, 2018, that these sensitive processing operations are well-analyzed through a DPIA.

This prioritization strategy will allow companies to **focus their efforts on new projects** and thus to prioritize the workload of available experts, without neglecting a global compliance by 2021.

1.4 Post May 25, 2018, Be Part of a Continuous Improvement Process

As seen above, several perimeters were deprioritized at first to allow privacy teams to focus on new sensitive projects. In a second step, legacy (projects or processing activities declared and implemented before May 25th) identified as sensitive should be subject to a DPIA within a defined period following the application of the GDPR.

Beyond this first analysis, all these new DPIAs will have to be part of **a continuous improvement cycle which aims at reviewing each DPIA** – for example, every three years as initially proposed by the WP29 in its previous guideline on DPIA. This period should allow privacy teams not to continuously review DPIA but at the same time to ensure compliance over time. These regular reviews must guarantee DPIA to be relevant and aligned with potential changes (new scope, changes in purpose, new data or recipients, increased risk, etc.).

To summarize, the first step of a DPIA approach in an organization will be to identify **among projects** those **requiring a DPIA** and considered as the **most sensitive** to be assessed as soon as possible. From our experience, only a small proportion of projects is concerned. The challenge is therefore to better **identify and prioritize** them rather than massively deploying privacy impact analysis.

2 Adapt the WP29 Criteria and Know How to Go Beyond

2.1 Each Company Must Interpret and Specify the WP29 Criteria in Its Context

To qualify the sensitivity of a project, the WP29 proposes a list of criteria[2] (Fig. 1).

The WP29 recommends carrying out a DPIA if two of these criteria are met (or in some case if only one is met). These criteria are a valuable help in identifying the most sensitive processing operations.

But this **logic has its limits**. A strict application of those criteria does not allow to simply decide when to trigger a DPIA.

Every company, every individual can have his own interpretation. Every criterion **must be specified and contextualized** to simplify and standardize the qualification of processing sensitivity by non-expert persons such as a marketing or product project manager. The aim is to prevent some people from considering that a processing on 10,000 people represents a large-scale processing while others estimate that 1,000,000 is not (for example, 1 million clients could represent only a small percentage of the customer database). This specification allows some companies which customer databases contains tens of millions of people (former companies in monopoly position such as energy or transport sectors) not to consider all their processing operations as mass processing. The question may also arise for employees who, according to WP29, may be considered vulnerable because of their relationship of subordination with their employer (see footnote 2).

---

[2] Guidelines on data protection impact analysis (DPIA) and how to determine whether the processing is 'likely to cause a high risk' for the purposes of Regulation (EU) 2016/679 - WP 248 rev. 01.

/ Evaluation or scoring (including profiling and predicting)

/ Automated-decision making with legal or similar significant effect

/ Systematic monitoring of data subject

/ Sensitive data or data of a highly personal nature

/ Data processed on a large scale

/ Matching or combining datasets

/ Data concerning vulnerable data subjects

/ Innovative use or applying new technological or organizational solutions

/ Processing preventing data subject from exercising a right or using a service or a contract

Fig. 1. DPIA triggering criteria defined by WP29

2.2 Performing a DPIA Based on WP29 Criteria Is Necessary but not Sufficient

A **strict application of the WP29 criteria is not enough to qualify the sensitivity of a processing operation**. In other words, triggering a DPIA based on two criteria (or less) should not be systematic. Just like the GDPR requirements for automated decisions, **the decision to trigger a DPIA should not be fully automated** and a human intervention should be systematic, or nearly so.

First, if several criteria are met, it does not necessarily mean that a DPIA must be performed. This is the case for a company which systematically meets one or more criteria for all or part of its processing operations (see example above). A project, such as a mobile application, can effectively target all the customers of a company (several millions) but be effectively downloaded by tens of thousands of users. The criterion "data processed on a large scale" could possibly be fulfilled at the same time another criterion is met (innovative use). However, given the actual total number of customers, and the purposes of the service it may not require a DPIA.

Then, it is not necessary to meet two criteria to trigger a DPIA. As proposed by the WP29, a single criterion can be considered when the stakes require it. This is particularly the case for sensitive personal data processing operations. These data are defined in Articles 9 and 10, special categories and infraction data, but also considered as a possible way to increase the risk for the rights and freedoms of individuals (financial data, geolocation, etc.). By default, a DPIA should be performed on a project handling such data – for instance, in France when using the NIR (social security number) which is well regulated from a privacy point of view.

Moreover, the purposes or the context of a project are not considered if an automated use of the WP29 logic is followed. See for example a database used to create badges for law enforcement officers. If this processing is simply qualified using the WP29 criteria, *a priori*, it does not require a DPIA: no sensitive data (surname and first name), a small population, no innovative technology, etc. Nevertheless, considering the current context of terrorist threat in which police forces are one of the main targets, this processing must logically be considered as sensitive. Disclosure of an exhaustive list of these individuals could have serious consequences.

It is therefore necessary to provide during the qualification phase, in addition to the application of the WP29 criteria, an **intervention of an expert (DPO, privacy team, etc.)** who will be able to determine the actual level of sensitivity of the processing and validate whether a DPIA is needed.

2.3   Know How to Split a Processing to Perform a DPIA on the Relevant Perimeter

To avoid carrying out a DPIA over a too large perimeter, **a processing could be split in two**: a processing grouping together all non-sensitive purposes and, another one, purposes requiring a DPIA. Indeed, in some projects, most of purposes could prove to be non-sensitive but a specific purpose, a type of data or a particular population could lead to carry out a DPIA.

For example, when setting up a market place, it may be necessary to carry out a DPIA on the distribution and sale of children's products (games, clothing, etc.) to supervise potential use of children's personal data, and to consider that the rest of the processing should not be subject to a DPIA.

3   A Project Without DPIA Is not a Non-supported Project

3.1   A Privacy by Design Process to Identify All Initiatives and Ensure Projects Compliance

As we have seen, most projects will not perform a DPIA. However, they must all comply with GDPR requirements.

A **Privacy by Design process must therefore be set up to intercept as many projects as possible as soon as possible.** In this way, privacy teams can support them in their compliance process even in the absence of a DPIA: answer to questions of business or IT teams, provision of guidelines, registration in the records of processing activities... but above all to ensure that by default, all projects incorporate the basic requirements of the regulation and include them in their specifications:

- Purposes must be **legitimate** and based **on a pre-defined legal ground (purpose limitation)**;
- Collection of personal data is **proportionate to the purposes** for which they are processed (**minimization**);
- Collected personal data is **accurate and kept up to date (accuracy)**;
- Personal data are **retained for a defined period** consistent with the purposes of the processing (based on legal requirements, business requirements, etc.);
- Security measures are **implemented to guarantee the protection** (availability, integrity and confidentiality) of personal data during their processing;
- Information **about the processing** (characteristics, rights of persons, contacts within the company, etc.) are communicated to natural persons (**transparency**);
- If the data subject's consent is needed, it must be **explicitly collected through a positive act** (for example: opt-in) and must be logged and stored;

- The data controller must enable individuals to **exercise their rights**: access and data portability, rectification and data erasure (right to be forgotten), restriction and objection;
- When personal data are transferred to data processors or outside the EU, measures must be taken to regulate such transfers (standard clauses, Binding Corporate Rules, etc.).

All these steps are essential for projects to be GDPR compliant even if a DPIA is not required. Above all, it is important for the DPO to be kept informed of project devel- opment. He must be able to assist projects with these matters, help them to identify appropriate solutions (realistic and GDPR compliant) and ensure that they are properly implemented.

3.2 A Regular Awareness of Project Stakeholders Is Essential to the Privacy by Design Approach

In addition, project stakeholders (IT and business project managers, security experts, architects...) **must be trained** to ensure that **they assimilate and integrate the Privacy by Design methodology**.

For example, marketing project managers must be specifically trained on profiling and on customer scoring to raise awareness on potential impacts on individual rights and freedoms; or teams managing artificial intelligence projects on decisions based solely on automated processing. Equally, IT teams must be trained, for example, on minimization that directly affects them: flow management, sending flat-files between applications, etc. which often contain a lot of personal data that is not needed for the implemented processing.

4   At a Process Level, Nothing New

4.1   Integrate Privacy by Design into Existing Project Processes

The arrival of the Privacy by Design principle **should not completely disrupt existing project processes**. An effective way of ensuring that protection of personal data in projects is considered is to fit into existing processes.

Privacy by Design consists in supporting projects at several levels: business project managers, IT project managers, developers, etc. It must therefore be included in existing project processes such as the **integration of security into projects (ISP)** process.

"Privacy sensors" can be integrated in business committees, where projects are undertaken. These sensors aim at identifying projects processing personal data as soon as possible and allow privacy teams to support them. For example, a "privacy sensor" can be a paragraph on personal data management in business requirements definition deliverable, a recurring question in management committees or steering committees (for launching projects) or a privacy criterion to check when unlocking budgets.

If these processes are well-established, the result is a minor evolution of project methodologies. Then **Privacy by Design process only becomes a specific focus** in a proven project methodology, and the **DPIA an analysis like any other** (Fig. 2).

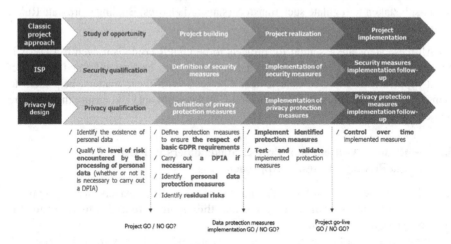

Fig. 2. Integration of Privacy by Design process into existing project processes

For DPIAs and security risk analysis, privacy issues and privacy risks must be integrated to the ISP methodology and security risk analysis tools must be merged with the DPIA tool.

Note, however, **merging those tools is not done without some adaptations**. New GDPR aspects and particularities are to be considered.

4.2   Impacts Must not Only Be Considered for the Company but also for the Rights and Freedoms of Individuals

For the DPIA, qualification of the risks is logically done by orienting the reflection from a data subject point of view. Nevertheless, this approach which may seem simple at first, may be more complex than it seems. Indeed, cybersecurity teams today have well-established reflexes. Their reflection may be biased by years of information system security practices focused on impacts from a business point of view. For example, nowadays, a data leak is not analyzed regarding the consequences for person privacy, but rather in terms of client churn or a corporate image degradation. Therefore, **cybersecurity experts and privacy teams must work together** to make analysis as objective as possible and to gradually change their practices.

4.3   A Historical Approach by Information System that Must Evolve to Include Processing Operations

So far, information system security has been applied from an application point of view. Risks and security measures were considered at an application or information system level. The approach for the DPIA must **be based on the processing of personal data** (approach more oriented on business process).

Indeed, an application supports in most cases only a part of a processing. It is therefore necessary to consider all the information system taking part in a processing operation to ensure overall consistency (legal basis, retention periods, information of individuals). This approach should also provide a holistic view of privacy risks faced by data subjects and, therefore, apply a consistent level of protection to all information system.

It therefore ensures **an end-to-end GDPR compliance** of the processing operation, from the collection of personal data to their possible transfers.

4.4   A Compliance Layer to Add to the Information System Security Base

The major innovation of the DPIA in comparison to the information system security risk analysis is the compliance aspect which is added to cybersecurity risks. Indeed, a **GDPR compliance gap analysis** (see GDPR requirements base for the Privacy by Design) must be carried out to have a complete DPIA (Fig. 3).

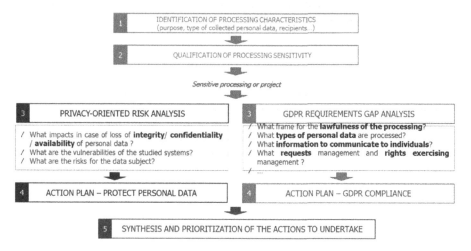

Fig. 3. Adding a GDPR gap analysis step to the security risk analysis (with impacts on privacy of individuals) for a full DPIA

To this end, the CNIL proposes a software[3] featuring all the key steps of the expected approach to help companies achieve their DPIA step by step.

This tool, simple to use and user-friendly, provides a solid basis of knowledge. It is particularly useful for companies still relatively immature regarding GDPR especially on GDPR compliance and legal part.

---

[3] https://www.cnil.fr/en/open-source-pia-software-helps-carry-out-data-protection-impact-assesment.

Security risk analysis approach concepts are present in this tool. The simplified approach chosen (only three macro-risks: illegitimate access to data, unwanted modification of data, data disappearance) allows a quick appropriation of the tool and issues by people with little experience on GDPR. Nevertheless, it does not guarantee an appropriate level of protection measures, particularly from a cybersecurity point of view. For example: information system vulnerabilities that could be exploited (and associated risks) such as hacking, possible phishing attempts, fire in a datacenter, etc. are not considered in detail.

The CNIL software is constantly improving and is frequently updated. New features could be added such as, for instance, access management or a quick and easy way to review DPIAs. Access management could be a real plus regarding the DPIA level of sensitivity. A review functionality could help privacy teams to easily update DPIAs and facilitate the continuous improvement process. For this purpose, the CNIL provides an open-source software allowing organizations to adapt this DPIA tool to suit their specificities or specific needs (integration to an existing tool for example).

This tool can be very useful for small and medium sized enterprises (SMEs) wishing to carry out DPIAs and which do not possess their own tool. However, for larger or more mature companies, this analysis should be supplemented by a more comprehensive security risk analysis to cover all cyber risks. Often, this methodology already exists and is carried by the CISOs (Fig. 4).

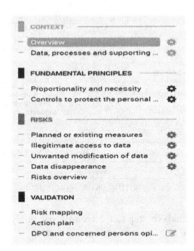

Fig. 4. DPIA tool proposed by the CNIL, French supervisory authority

5   Compliance of a Project Does not Mean Compliance of the Legacy

95% of new projects are evolutions (business process evolution, a new service, a new brick of an information system) that integrate the legacy: application, information system or existing processing operations.

It may be tempting to take advantage of the project dynamics to make the legacy and new elements GDPR compliant. Nevertheless, it is not a pragmatic and realistic solution: the compliance of the whole system is an **expensive and heavy process (in time and money) that most projects cannot afford**.

One of the major risks of adopting such a strategy is that, eventually, project teams will override the privacy teams, which could be viewed as a huge constraint. Project managers must focus on the compliance of project new aspects: new kind of collected data, new subcontractors, new features, new use cases (including innovative use cases). GDPR compliance of the legacy must therefore be carried out by a dedicated stream within a GDPR program. It is this same program that sets up the new processes, defines the privacy governance, formalizes guidelines, creates new tools. This program will have its own budget, independent from the Privacy by Design process, to achieve these compliances. Many of them can certainly be mutualized.

For example: as part of customer claims and claims management, client advisor support applications have typically been in place for many years: claims collection systems, processing optimization, responses, comment management… With new technologies and new use cases they allow, new features are created to improve customer experience or the efficiency of the request processing: chatbots, reconciliation of the different channels (telephone, digital, etc.), automation and artificial intelligence. Without any doubt, these projects must be subject to a DPIA. However, those projects will not drive the compliance of existing processing operations such as the "cleaning" of comment areas. Indeed, such a project does not have the overview of the underlying processing operations and applications. Project managers do not have enough knowledge or legitimacy to bring the entire ecosystem into compliance. In addition, these projects can cost tens of thousands of euros while full GDPR compliance can cost up to ten times more.

6   In Conclusion

Carrying out a DPIA **is not mandatory** for all existing or future processing operations or projects. A **prioritization of new projects** according to their **level of risk** and efforts regarding privacy teams' ability to support projects is essential. As a first step, a focus on new projects should be preferred rather than trying to bring all processing operations into compliance.

Identification of the most sensitive projects contributes to this prioritization. Criteria defined by the WP29 can be **helpful to qualify the sensitivity** of processing operations or new projects. Nevertheless, the suggested logic is not sufficient. It is often necessary to **specify these criteria** and to **involve an expert** to qualify sensitivity and take the final decision to carry out a DPIA.

Following the identification of projects with highest risks, **most new projects will not go through a DPIA**. However, it does not imply that these projects should not be supported by privacy teams. They must **go through a Privacy by Design process** that guarantees the project compliance with the basic requirements of the regulation.

Privacy by Design is a new concept of the regulation. Nevertheless, its implementation should not question the existing processes. On the contrary, it is strongly recommended to **capitalize on set-up processes and to incorporate privacy issues**. This is particularly true with the process of integrating security into projects that can serve as a solid and proven foundation for a Privacy by Design process and a functional DPIA method.

Finally, in order to better manage privacy risks, teams in charge of DPIAs and more generally Privacy by Design must be **pragmatic**. It would be better to support a small proportion of projects with a suitable compliance and guarantee an adequate protection rather than to look for an absolutist position, theoretically ideal, but keeping away project sponsors and processors. The risk is that project teams **override the compliance phase** regarding consequences on their constraints (costs, time, customer experience) and that projects or information systems **go live with major non-compliances**.

References

1. Regulation (EU) 2016/679 of the European Parliament and of the Council of 27 April 2016
2. Guidelines on Data Protection Impact Assessment (DPIA) and determining whether processing is 'likely to result in a high risk' for the purposes of Regulation 2016/679 - WP 248 rev. 01
3. CNIL Guidelines on DPIA. https://www.cnil.fr/fr/PIA-privacy-impact-assessment
4. Documentation on CNIL DPIA tool. https://www.cnil.fr/en/open-source-pia-software-helps-carry-out-data-protection-impact-assesment

'Privacy by Design' in EU Law

Matching Privacy Protection Goals with the Essence of the Rights to Private Life and Data Protection

Maria Grazia Porcedda[(✉)]

Centre for Criminal Justice Studies, School of Law,
University of Leeds, Leeds, UK
m.g.porcedda@leeds.ac.uk

Abstract. In this paper I tackle the question, currently unaddressed in the literature, of how to reconcile the technical understanding of 'privacy by design' with the nature of 'privacy' in EU law. There, 'privacy' splits into two constitutionally protected rights– respect for private and family life, and protection of personal data– whose essence cannot be violated. After illustrating the technical notion of privacy protection goals and design strategies, developed in the privacy threat modelling literature, I propose a method to identify the essence of the two rights, which rests on identifying first the rights' 'attributes'. I answer the research question by linking the technical notion of privacy protection goals and strategies with the attributes and related 'essence' of the rights to private life and to the protection of personal data. The analysis unveils the need to adjust and further develop privacy protection goals. It also unveils that establishing equivalences between technical and legal approaches to the two rights bears positive effects beyond PbD.

Keywords: Data protection by design · Privacy by design
Information security canons · Protection goals · Essence · Privacy
Data protection · Charter of Fundamental Rights

1 Introduction

Privacy by design (hereafter PbD), which stems from PETs but has almost supplanted them [1], aims to embed 'privacy' in information technologies, network and information systems and business practice (Cavoukian as in [2]), and possibly also processes and physical design [3].

The PbD challenge launched by Cavoukian [4] has been keenly taken by computer scientists, legal scholars, or a combination of both. Computer scientists have focused on developing technical 'protection goals' that embed legal requirements into software and hardware development. This was the case of the authors of the LINDDUN project [5], and of the ENISA Paper on engineering PbD [6].

Legal scholars have highlighted the limitations of PbD requirements stemming from the applicable law. Pagallo [7], Leenes and Koops [1], as well as Schartum [2], argue that it is not possible to hard–wire legal rules in computer systems, notably

© Springer Nature Switzerland AG 2018
M. Medina et al. (Eds.): APF 2018, LNCS 11079, pp. 183–204, 2018.
https://doi.org/10.1007/978-3-030-02547-2_11

because legal rules require flexible application [1, 7]. Furthermore, PbD approaches would need to be harmonized with the principle of technology neutrality inherent in the applicable law [1]. Importantly, PbD, whether in its form of a legal provision [1], or a standard [8], should not be seen like a shortcut to ensure automated compliance with data protection principles. Rather, the enforcement of those principles always require the active intervention of individuals [7–10]. Another inherent constraint in the implementation of PbD principles, rightly observed by Bieker et al. [10], Kamara [8] and Rachovitsa [9], lies in the fact that 'privacy' is a qualified right subject to permissible limitations.

All authors studying PbD call for a multi/interdisciplinary approach taking into account substantive legal understandings of privacy as well as technology and software development [1, 2, 9, 11] to 'operationalise PbD'. Multidisciplinary approaches see computer scientists joining forces with social scientists. Bieker et al. [10] combine PbD and legal approaches to develop a methodology for impact assessments. As for interdisciplinary approaches, Schartum proposes starting from substantive legal rules to develop a method transforming "privacy rules into computer routines and functions" [2] leading to legally compliant software.[1] Unfortunately, this is easier said than done. Legally, 'privacy' is not just a matter of statutory law, but, as noted above, also a right [9, 10, 12]. Yet, international law, which represents the universal framework to respect, protect and fulfil human rights, including privacy, is not immediately translatable into workable concepts for PbD [9]. In the end of the day, the applicable law addressing 'privacy' is specific to each jurisdiction.

In the European Union (hereafter EU), which I focus on in this paper, 'privacy' splits into two constitutionally protected rights: respect for private and family life, home and communications, and protection of personal data, enshrined respectively in Articles 7 and 8 of the Charter of Fundamental Rights [13]. These rights can be limited, yet, limitations cannot violate the essence of the rights. Just like PbD, there is an ongoing debate about the meaning of the essence of fundamental rights [14–16, 31]. While this adds further variables to the search for a workable implementation of PbD, at the same time it can also make the identification of clear rules for PbD in EU law easier.

To my knowledge however, scholarship has not linked PbD to the nature of private life and data protection in EU law, that is, two rights whose essence cannot be violated. This paper fills the gap in the literature by asking how to reconcile the technical understanding of PbD with the nature of the two rights in EU law. My proposition is to map the equivalences between the legal concept of the essence of the fundamental rights to private life and data protection with the technical notion of privacy/data protection goals.

The paper develops as follows. In section two, I illustrate existing technical approaches to PbD. In section three, I expound the nature of privacy in EU law and seek to operationalize the two corresponding rights by introducing the concept of the 'attributes'. I propose how to reconcile legal and technological approaches in section four. The analysis

---

[1] Schartum's method crosses four legally inspired 'design techniques' with four software 'design elements'. The resulting matrix informs nine-stepped iterations (which he sketches, without unfortunately developing them).

shows the need for adjusting and further developing privacy protection goals. In the conclusions I summarize my findings, and advance the idea that establishing equivalences between technical and legal approaches can be applied beyond PbD.

2 Technological Approaches: Protection Goals and Threats to Privacy

Privacy by Design consists of devising technical and operational rules to protect privacy – a.k.a. protection goals. PbD can be seen from an alternative perspective, which consists in implementing rules to avert threats[2] embodied by technology that could damage data and communications, thereby affecting the rights of individuals. In other words, Pbd represents for rules compliance what threat modelling is for rules violation.

Protection goals and threats are studied and defined within the field of information security. In information security, threats to information, and the corresponding rules or canons of protection, are the two sides of threat modelling for information security, which is performed by analyzing the system to be protected through the lenses of a potential attacker. Threat modelling is part of risk assessment, in turn a part of risk management [17], which belongs with information security management.

There exist several models of threat modelling [18–21], but a reference point in the field is Microsoft's STRIDE model [22, 23]. The name is the acronym of the threats that a network and information system could suffer from: spoofing, tampering, repudiation, information disclosure, denial of service and elevation of privilege. These threats are the negation of information security canons, chiefly the triad of confidentiality, integrity and availability, a.k.a. CIA [5, 6], and also authentication, non-repudiation, authorization and utility,[3] which are canons that have been acknowledged over time [17, 24, 25]. Spoofing means that the attacker replaces the verified user of a system and is the opposite of authentication. Tampering means corrupting the data and is the opposite of integrity. Repudiation, which is the negation of non-repudiation, means that an action cannot be correctly associated with its origin. Information disclosure consists in making confidential information available to illegitimate recipients, and negates confidentiality. Denial of service means making a service unavailable as otherwise expected, thus negating availability. Finally, elevation of privileges consists in gaining access to a system without having the necessary privileges, which challenges authorization (a.k.a. control).

Threats to personal data protection and confidentiality of communications, and the corresponding rules of protection, can be identified by means of threat modelling. However, unlike information security, there is little work on threat modelling in the field of privacy [6]. The LINDDUN project [5] and the ENISA study on engineering PbD [6] fill the gap by defining protection goals. LINDDUN [5] also contains a fully-fledged privacy threat modelling.

---

[2] Defined by ENISA in [17].

[3] Note that the canon 'utility' is defined by the International Telecommunications Union [24], but not by ENISA.

2.1 Privacy Protection Goals

The protection goals proposed by the authors of LINDDUN [5] are built on the assumption, borrowed from Danezis, that privacy is either soft or hard. Hard privacy consists in the minimization of disclosure of information; consequently, the individual does not need to rely on the data controller for protection. It is identified with the protection goal of data minimization: the data, which is not disclosed, is secure. Soft privacy consists in the knowledge that information has been disclosed, and thus the data subject has to trust the data controller(s). Then, taking inspiration from the data protection goals identified by Pfitzman, LINDDUN identifies the relevant privacy canons by dividing them into the two categories of hard and soft privacy canons. Hard privacy canons are: 'unlinkability', 'anonymity and pseudonimity', 'undetectability and unobservability', with the addition of 'plausible deniability' and 'confidentiality'. Soft privacy canons are extracted from applicable law and are 'content awareness' and 'policy and consent compliance'. While acknowledging the importance of availability and integrity to privacy, LINDDUN does not explicitly list them.

Differently, in the ENISA study [6], Danezis, Domingo-Ferrer, Hansen [26], Hoepman [27], Métayer, Tirtea, and Schiffner list protection goals starting from the classic information security CIA triad and then add unlinkability, transparency and intervenability. In the absence of a standard [8], I experimentally attempt to merge the two sets of canons. The so-merged protection goals produce: unlinkability (including anonymity & pseudonymity, and undetectability & unobservability), plausible deniability, availability, integrity, confidentiality, transparency (including content awareness and policy consent & compliance) and intervenability, as illustrated and described in Table 1.

Table 1. Privacy protection goals for LINDDUN and ENISA

Privacy canons	LINDDUN	ENISA
Unlinkability	**Unlinkability**: hiding the link between two or more actions, identities, and pieces of information	Privacy-relevant data cannot be linked across domains that are constituted by a common purpose and context, and that means that processes have to be operated in such a way that the privacy-relevant data are unlinkable to any other set of privacy relevant data outside of the domain. Mechanisms to achieve or support unlinkability comprise data avoidance, separation of contexts (physical separation, encryption, usage of different identifiers, access control), anonymisation and pseudonymisation, and early erasure or data
	Anonymity: hiding the link between an identity and an action or a piece of information. **Pseudonymity**: to build a reputation on a pseudonym and the possibility to use multiple pseudonyms for different purposes	
	Undetectability and unobservability: hiding the user's activities (e.g. impossibility of knowing whether an entry in a database corresponds to a real person)	

(continued)

Table 1. (*continued*)

Privacy canons	LINDDUN	ENISA
Plausible deniability	The ability to deny having performed an action that other parties can neither confirm nor contradict (e.g. a whistleblower can deny his actions) [opposite of non-repudiation]	
Integrity	/	The fact that data is accessible and services are operational. (ENISA Glossary)
Confidentiality	Hiding the data content or controlled release of data content (e.g. encrypted email)	The protection of communications or stored data against interception and reading by unauthorized persons. (ENISA Glossary)
Availability	/	The confirmation that data which has been sent, received, or stored are complete and unchanged. (ENISA Glossary)
Transparency	**Content Awareness**: users are aware of their personal data and that only the minimum necessary information should be sought and used for the performance of the function to which it relates **Policy and consent compliance**: the whole system – including data flows, data stores, and processes – has to inform the data subject about the system's privacy policy, or allow the data subject to specify consent in compliance with legislation, before users access the system	All privacy-relevant data processing including the legal, technical and organisational setting can be understood and reconstructed at any time. The information has to be available before, during and after the processing takes place. Mechanisms for achieving or supporting transparency comprise logging and reporting
Intervenability	/	Intervention is possible concerning all ongoing or planned privacy-relevant data processing, in particular by those persons whose data are processed The objective is the application of corrective measures and counterbalances where necessary Mechanisms for intervenability comprise established processes for influencing or stopping the data processing fully or partially, manually overturning an automated decision, data portability precautions to prevent lock-in at a data processor, breaking glass policies, single points of contact for individuals' intervention requests, switches for users to change a setting

2.2   Threat Modelling: LINDDUN and ENISA

In LINDDUN [5], each identified privacy protection goal or canon corresponds to a technology threat from which, similarly to Microsoft's STRIDE, comes the acronym LINDDUN: **L**inkability, **I**ndentifiability, **N**on-repudiation, **D**etectability **D**isclosure of information, content Unawareness, policy and consent Non-compliance, (see Table 2). Each threat to an item of interest (hereafter IoI), understood variably as a user, action, content etc., is defined from the perspective of the attacker. Thus, 'linkability' means being able to establish whether two IoIs are related. 'Identifiability' means connecting a user to an IoI. 'Non-repudiation' allows proving that a user has performed a given action. 'Detectability' means that an IoI exists. 'Information disclosure' refers to loss of confidentiality. 'Content unawareness' means that either too much, or the wrong information has been disclosed, leading to the identification of wrong decisions. Finally, 'policy and consent non-compliance' refers to the case in which a system disregards the privacy policy it purports to respect.

Table 2. LINDDUN privacy threat modelling

Privacy canons (LINDDUN)	Threats to canons
Hard privacy	
Unlinkability	Linkability
Anonymity and Pseudonimity	Identifiability
Plausible deniability	Non-repudiation
Undetectability and unobservability	Detectability
Confidentiality	Disclosure of information
Soft privacy	
Content awareness	Content unawareness
Policy and consent compliance	Policy and consent non-compliance

LINDDUN follows the same steps as STRIDE (but does not reach the stage of risk analysis). Therefore, the most fundamental step is the identification of data flow diagrams, i.e. the essential sub-units to which the threats are applied [5]. Based on such associations, it becomes easier to study mitigation strategies, e.g. in the form of PETs applying PbD.

Danezis et al. [6] do not explicitly propose a privacy threat model. Yet, the only protection goal identified in the study conducted by Danezis et al. under the aegis of the ENISA [6] that was not considered by LINDDUN is intervenability, the threat to which can be identified, with a good degree of confidence, in non-intervenability, understood as the inability or impossibility to intervene at any level of the system to prevent or mitigate a threat.

Instead of threat modelling, Danezis et al. [6] propose design strategies safeguarding the protection goals which either apply directly to the data (data-oriented strategies) or apply to procedures (process-oriented strategies), following the work of Hoepman. In detail, a system of data processing should first of all (following Gürses, Troncoso and Diaz [45]) *minimize* the amount of data, *hide* it from view, *store* data in separate batches, and *aggregate* data whenever possible. A system of data processing should enable its controllers to *inform* individuals whose data are being collected, *enforce* the rules, and *demonstrate* their enforcement; moreover, it should enable both controllers and individuals to *control* how the system works and to question the data.

Some of these practices correspond directly to protection goals: 'inform' corresponds to transparency, 'hide' to confidentiality, and 'control' to intervenability. As a result, they can be easily linked to threats. Yet, the other actions can also be linked to a protection goal, and therefore a threat. 'Separate', whereby data should be processed in compartments, can be connected to the goal of unlinkability. Similarly, 'minimize', whereby only the necessary categories of data are collected, enables pseudonimity (and anonymity). 'Aggregate', which encourages to process data at the highest level of aggregation and hence the minimum degree of detail, also pursues unlinkability. Intervenability is enabled by the strategies 'control', 'enforce' and 'demonstrate', which can be seen as three different stages of intervention. The link between privacy protection goals, design strategies and threats is illustrated in Table 3. Two design strategies could be linked to two different protection goals: control to intervenability and transparency; minimise to unlinkability and transparency (as in LINDDUN's content awareness).

Table 3. Relationship between protection goals, design strategies and threats

Privacy protection goals	Design strategies	Threats
Unlinkability- Anonymity and Pseudonymity -Undetectability and unobservability	Aggregate, minimise, separate	Linkability – Identifiability – Detectability
Plausible deniability		Non-repudiation
Integrity	Control?	Tampering
Confidentiality	Hide	Disclosure of information
Availability		Denial of Service
Transparency	Inform Minimise?	Content unawareness - Policy and consent non-compliance
Intervenability	Control, enforce, demonstrate	Non-intervenability

The authors of LINDDUN [5] did not develop their privacy principles starting from the applicable law, but rather from Solove's list of privacy principles, which conflates privacy (i.e. private life) with data protection. As a result, there are some incongruences in their analysis. For instance, 'non-repudiation' is seen as a threat to privacy. Yet, non-repudiation could be deemed to be a threat only in the case of what the authors call hard privacy, and only when users actively pursue repudiation. In all other cases, non-repudiation is desirable because it is key to the accountability of data controllers. The problem arguably derives from conflating private life with data protection, which leads to overlooking their respective subtleties.

Danezis et al. [6] built their system based on the Data Protection Directive [28], and hence with a stronger degree of adherence to EU law. Yet, EU law has evolved since the Directive. First, new legislation has been adopted, which gives meaning to data protection not only as a statutory requirement, but also as a right, clearly independent from the right to private life. Second, both rights demand that additional requirements be taken into account when developing PbD, requirements that I illustrate in the following.

3   Legal Approaches to PbD in EU Law

In the EU, 'privacy' splits into two constitutionally protected rights: respect for private and family life, home and communications, and protection of personal data, enshrined respectively in Articles 7 and 8 of the Charter of Fundamental Rights [13]. The two rights are fully independent and tend to be mostly complementary but can also display clashes (as discussed in the conclusions).

To further complicate the matter, the requirement to implement PbD is not contained in the definition of the right, but rather comes from secondary law, i.e. Art. 25 of the General Data Protection Regulation [29] (hereafter GDPR). In the GDPR, which implements the right to the protection of personal data, PbD becomes 'data protection by design' (hereafter DPbD). Legislation addressing Art. 7 of the Charter, such as the proposed e-Privacy Regulation [30] (which will repeal the e-Privacy Directive), does not contain rules on PbD. Nevertheless, the proposed Regulation is a lex specialis of the GDPR (draft Art. 1(3)). Therefore, the obligation of the controller to implement by design approaches contained in the GDPR should arguably apply to provisions of the e-Privacy Regulation, including those addressing confidentiality of communications that fulfil Art. 7 of the Charter, at least insofar as personal data are concerned.[4] Moreover, awareness of the interplay between technical and legal approaches to the right to private life has value beyond the application of PbD requirements, as discussed in the conclusions.

Secondly, both fundamental rights are subject to 'permissible limitations', i.e. limits defined in Art. 52 (1) of the Charter. Accordingly, the exercise of privacy rights can be limited for the sake of 'objectives of general interest' which must be clearly spelled out in the law. An example is Art. 23 of the GDPR, which lists, among others, national security, the protection of judicial independence, as well as the protection of the rights and freedoms of others. Yet, the limitation of both rights cannot violate the 'essence' of the rights. There is an ongoing debate about the meaning of the essence of fundamental rights in general, and data protection in particular [14–16, 31].

As I will argue in section four, any attempt to purse 'by design' approaches in EU law needs to come to terms with the dual nature of privacy, as well as the concept of the essence, to which I turn now.

3.1   Operationalizing Legal Approaches: The Essence and Boundaries of Articles 7 and 8 of the Charter

Not only the concept of the essence contained in Art. 52(1) of the Charter is not defined, but also the Court of Justice of the European Union (hereafter CJEU) has yet to provide a univocal interpretation on the matter. In the case law of the right to the

---

[4] I am grateful to Marc van Lieshout for his comments, which prompted the clarification of this point.

protection of personal data, for instance, the CJEU seems to opt for a substantive understanding of the essence [31], that is, a specific entitlement enabled by the right; following the case law of the CJEU, this entitlement should be expressed in a rule [31].

In the absence of guidance by the CJEU to identify the essence, I have borrowed the method for selecting the 'attributes' of a right that was developed by the UN Office of the High Commissioner on Human Rights (hereafter OHCHR) in the context of work on indicators [32], a method that was also implemented by the UK Equality and Human Rights Commission on which I rely for private life [33]. Attributes are the intrinsic and distinctive substantive dimensions of a right, which define its boundary; in turn, the essence is the 'core' of an attribute [31]. In other words, appraising the intrusion into fundamental rights entails answering the question: what does that fundamental right mean? It obliges one to perform the exercise, in the abstract, of dissecting the right into its substantive characteristics or attributes. Such an exercise, in turn, allows identifying the essence of the right (through a value-based approach [31]), the intrusion into which is legally prohibited.

In detail, attributes are "a limited number of characteristics of [a given] right." (…). To the extent feasible, the attributes should be based on an exhaustive reading of the standard, starting with the provisions in the core international human rights treaties; (…) the attributes of the human right should collectively reflect the essence of its normative content (…) To the extent feasible, the attributes' scope should not overlap" [32]. Attributes represent the synthesis of what would otherwise be the 'narrative' on legal standards of a human right. Note that I borrow from the OHCHR only the method (which was supported by the Fundamental Rights Agency [34]), and not the understanding of rights, which is rooted instead in EU law.

To be sure, the attempt to identify 'principles' synthetizing the two rights is an approach followed by different commentators, and stems historically from the formulation of both rights (e.g. the fair information principles concerning data protection), as well as national and international case law on both rights [31]. Nevertheless, the scholars who have attempted the enterprise have neither singled out principles for both Art. 7 and 8 as understood in EU law, nor have they systematically identified the essence [15, 16], [35, 36], leaving an important gap in the literature. In the next two sections I summarise the steps I developed elsewhere to elaborate the attributes and essence of the right to respect for private life [12], and the protection of personal data [31]. The identification of attributes and essence is in turn instrumental to link the legal understanding of the rights with the technical approach to DPbD/PbD.

3.2   Attributes and Essence of Article 7 of the Charter

Elsewhere [12] I have distilled the attributes for the right to private and family life starting from the Human Rights Measurement Framework developed by the UK Equality and Human Rights Commission [33] duly modified to take into account the specificity of EU law. Accordingly, Art. 7 of the Charter is read in the light of Article 8 of the European Convention on Human Rights (hereafter ECHR) [37], which represents the minimum standard for the substantive understanding of the right, as well as the benchmark to assess permissible limitations (in harmony with Art. 52(3) of the Charter). I also argue that the scope of the right in EU law is different from Art.

8 ECHR; in particular, Art. 7 does neither concern the protection of personal data, nor physical integrity in the context of medicine and biology, nor environmental protection, which are covered instead by Arts. 3 and 37 of the Charter.

The specific contents of the attributes are refined on the basis of the case law of the following bodies: i) judgments of the CJEU concerning instruments of secondary law which give substance to the rights listed in Art 7; the ECHR, insofar as the scope of the two rights corresponds; and iii) the case law of the UN which, according to settled case law, supplies guidelines.

Art. 7 reads "Everyone has the right to respect for his or her private and family life, home and communications. The definition contains four prongs (private life, family life, home and communications) which lead to seven attributes and essence.

The first prong includes those elements that are relevant to develop and maintain one's identity and personality, understood as unique and worthy of equal respect. It includes three sub-attributes.

The first is physical and psychological integrity. This includes the *forum internum* of the mind, i.e. one's thoughts, feelings and emotions; the *forum internum* of the body, meaning genetic characteristics and unique physical traits, and the *forum externum* of the body, that is, the right to own one's body and protect it from undesired or forced access to it. This attribute could have as an experimental essence the *forum internum* of the mind and of the body.

The second is personal social and sexual identity, which consists in the '*forum externum*' of mental integrity, which takes substance in the coherent portrayal of one's personality and identity to the external world. It includes control over one's name, the upkeep of one's reputation, the expression of one's sexual orientation, but also the manifestation of one's beliefs and personality in the form of attitudes, behaviours and clothing. Following the case X and Others ([38], para 46), the expression of one's sexual identity is a good candidate for the essence. In Opinion 1/15 ([39], para 150), the CJEU alludes to the fact that information could constitute the essence of the right, without nevertheless providing further indications. Further candidates for the essence could be the official recognition of one's original or acquired name, and the faithful social representation of one's identity.

The third is personal development, autonomy and participation, which relates to the partaking of individuals in the democratic society, which is threefold. The first way is the development of one's personality in the spirit of self-determination; the second way is autonomy of one's movements and actions; the third way is participation in the social and political life as one sees fit. All three ways require a minimum degree of control, even if conducted in public, and embody the possibility to develop social relations of an amicable or professional nature. In this sense, this sub-attribute concerns the 'outer circle' of one's life and links with the 'inner circle' of one's family. In the absence of clear indications by the Court, a candidate for the essence could be the absence of secret external constraints.

The second prong of the right, family life, leads to one attribute expressing the 'inner circle', one's kin by blood and election, which represents the first mode of existence of individuals in society, which predates the state. It includes horizontal and vertical relationships regardless of their seal of legitimacy, and reside in emotional and material ties with individuals and surroundings. The CJEU found that, for a father, the essence of family life lies in the possibility to apply for the right to custody ([40], para 55). Other options include the continuity and recognition of a relationship of care.

The prong 'communications' lies in expressing the ability of individuals to choose with whom and how to share information, and the presumption that information shared privately should remain confidential, regardless of its content and the mode of communication. This includes the expectation that information shared privately will not be used against the individual. In the case Digital Rights Ireland [41], the CJEU found the essence to be "the content of one's [electronic] communications as such" (para 39).

The prong 'home' corresponds to the last attribute, which refers to one's settled and secure place in the community, where individuals can develop ties of an intimate nature and nurture self-determination, far away from the public gaze and undesired intrusion. The essence of this attribute could be found in a minimum zone of physical intimacy (e.g., in a home, the toilet, or the bed) (Table 4).

Table 4. Attributes and essence of Art. 7 of the Charter ('private life')

Attributes of art. 7	Core
PL(1) Physical and psychological integrity	The *forum internum* of the mind and of the body
PL(2) Personal social and sexual identity	The expression of one's sexual identity (CJEU) Official recognition of one's original or acquired name Faithful social representation of one's identity
PL(3) Personal development, autonomy and participation ('outer circle')	Absence of secret external constraints
Family	For a father, the possibility to apply for the right to custody (CJEU) Continuity of relationship of care Recognition of relationship of care
Communications	The content of one's communications (CJEU)
Home	A minimum zone of physical intimacy

3.3 Attributes and Essence of Article 8 of the Charter

Attempts to identify the attributes and the essence of Art. 8 of the Charter are scant [16] and non-conclusive, as I discuss in [31]. I propose the attributes and essence of the right to the protection of personal data on the basis of the method developed by the OHCHR, and a value-based approach to the right. Differently from the right to private life, the right to the protection of personal data does not derive from the ECHR, and should be read instead in the light of Article 52(2) of the Charter, whereby the interpretation of the CJEU of EU secondary law has preeminent importance in defining the contents of the right.[5] In this case, the case law of the ECHR on Convention 108 [43] (one of the sources of the right) 'supplies guidelines' in accordance with settled case law.

Art. 8 is composed of three paragraphs, which read: "1. Everyone has the right to the protection of personal data concerning him or her. 2. Such data must be processed fairly for specified purposes and on the basis of the consent of the person concerned or some other legitimate basis laid down by law. Everyone has the right of access to data which has been collected concerning him or her, and the right to have it rectified. 3. Compliance with these rules shall be subject to control by an independent authority." The three paragraphs contained in the formulation of the right to the protection of personal data lead to 5 attributes; the rationale is explained in [31].

The fist limb of Art. 8(2) embodies the attribute of legitimate processing. This attribute expresses the expectation for the data subject that the processing must be legitimate, which refers to three interconnected principles stemming from the rule of law, namely fairness and transparency, purpose limitation (& storage limitation), and lawful legal basis. In para 150 of Opinion 1/15 [39], the CJEU found that rules concerning purpose limitation constitute the essence of the right.

The second limb of Art. 8(2) concerns data subjects' rights, which correspond to one single attribute: data subjects' control over their personal data, enabling them to intervene in the processing. It includes the following steps, which should be seen as a range of options available to the data subject depending on the situation: (i) accessing the data and obtaining a copy; (ii) rectifying inaccurate data; (iii) objecting to processing, including profiling; (iv) restricting the processing of one's personal data. Whilst the CJEU has yet to identify the essence concerning this attribute, a candidate is the right to access. Milder options are the right to rectify incorrect data and object to profiling.

Art. 8(3), which concerns oversight, paves the way to[6] the attribute of supervisory authority, which concerns the ability of the individual to claim without hindrance the intervention of an authority for the protection of his or her right. This attribute embodies a form of legal remedy.[7]

The combination of Art. 8(3), literature and international law [31], could also support the attribute 'human intervention', whereby decisions significantly affecting an individual cannot be taken by a machine, and that a human being must be involved in the process. A potential essence of this attribute is the right to obtain human intervention on the part of the controller, to express his or her point of view and to contest the automated decision (a requirement poised to become essential with further expansions of datafication and applications of data science).

---

[5] This is because the CJEU has found, in ground 69 of *Google Spain and Google* [42], that requirements of Article 8(2) and 8 (3) of the Charter "are implemented inter alia" by provisions contained in the DPD. I justify my argument in [31].

[6] See footnote above.

[7] Note that the CJEU invalidated the Safe Harbour Agreement in *Schrems* [44] on grounds of disrespect of this requirement, which it found to be the essence of the right to effective judicial protection enshrined in Art. 47 of the Charter, with no mention to the essence of the protection of personal data.

The last attribute, data security and minimization, is found explicitly in secondary law, is an old fair information principle, and arguably it can be linked to Art. 8(1), in that it expresses essential components of the right [31]. It embodies the expectation to trust that personal information is protected against risks of a varying nature and likelihood, which could cause physical, material and non-material damage. It further includes the right to communicate the minimum amount of personal data possible for a given purpose.[8] In Digital Rights Ireland (para 40) and Opinion 1/15 (para 150) the CJEU found the essence in the provision of integrity, confidentiality and security safeguards in the legal basis relied upon for the processing of personal data.

As a last note, sensitive data should not be seen as an attribute, nor as the essence of data protection, but rather as a requirement that automatically makes the threshold of permissible interferences more severe (Table 5).[9]

Table 5. Attributes of Art. 8 of the Charter (data protection)

Attributes	Essence
Legitimate processing	Purpose limitation (CJEU)
Data subjects' rights	Access (experimental); Rectification and objecting to profiling (experimental)
Supervisory authority	
Human intervention	The right to obtain human intervention on the part of the controller, to express his or her point of view and to contest the decision (experimental)
Security and minimization	The provision of security safeguards in the legal basis relied upon for the processing of personal data (CJEU)

The identification of attributes and essence enables us to link the legal understanding of the rights with the technical understanding of privacy/data protection goals (and related threat scenarios), onto which I move next.

4 Blending Legal and Technical Approaches to Privacy

Any attempt to pursue 'by design' strategy in EU law needs to come to terms with the dual nature of privacy, as well as the concept of the essence. This is because 'by design' approaches will always be confronted with privacy and data protection not just

---

[8] In the version of this research discussed at the conference, I had proposed 'minimization and accuracy' as a separate attribute. While accuracy is very well expressed by the requirement to rectify the data, which is part of the attribute data subjects' rights, the question remains as to whether data minimization should form part of a different attribute. The importance of minimization as a prerequisite for Privacy by Design is well argued, for instance, by Gürses, Troncoso and Diaz [45].

[9] That is, by making the interference of limitations to the right automatically serious.

as statutory requirements, but as rights, too.[10] The use of personal data-driven technology, in fact, always engenders the competition between the two fundamental rights and objectives of general interests. If the data controller is a private individual, and therefore technology is used for business purposes, the protection of personal data and the right to respect for private life stand in dialogue with the objective of general interest of developing an internal market as well as the rights and freedoms of others, which find joint expression in the controller's freedom to conduct a business (Art. 16 of the Charter). If the data controller is a law enforcement official, and therefore technology is used to support the fight against crime, the protection of personal data and the right to respect for private life stand in dialogue with the objective of general interest of public security, and the rights and freedoms of others.

To answer the research question, which concerns the way how DPbD/PbD approaches can incorporate the understanding of privacy as two rights and the ensuing requirement of respecting their essence, I propose to map the interaction between protection goals and attributes. Actually, there are more connections between the legal and technical concepts than may appear at first sight: the essence is to law what protection goals are to technology, namely a boundary which cannot be crossed without violating the right.

4.1   Legal and Technical Approaches to Private Life

As for private life, Table 7 shows the correspondences between privacy protection goals and the attributes for respect for private and family life. The first column to the left lists the attributes. The second column lists the essence relating to an attribute, if any (those found by the Court are marked with the acronym 'CJEU', the ones I am proposing are marked as 'Exp.' for experimental). The third lists the privacy protection goals, or canons, corresponding to each attribute. The fourth and last column lists the corresponding design strategy.

The attribute of communications concerns the ability to share information with other individuals, under the presumption that information shared privately should remain confidential, regardless of its content and the mode of communication, and with the expectation that information shared privately will not be used against the individual. The content of communications represents, for the CJEU, an element of essence. This attribute is also of central importance for information security, and corresponds to confidentiality, which possibly carries with it the desirability of plausible deniability, for instance in the case of a whistle-blower wishing to deny her or his actions.

---

[10] I believe this reflection addresses the important point raised by Bieker et al. [10], whereby the risk management performed in the context of technology is different than that performed in the case of privacy rights, because the first enables to factor in some risks, whereas the latter does not. While in abstract this is the case, in practice, particularly in the case of Art. 8, the applicable law allows to factor in a degree of risk. This is the case, for instance, of personal data breaches, which need to be notified only when they entail an appreciable risk to the rights and freedoms of data subjects (Art. 33 GDPR). I articulate the many reasons for this in [46].

The attribute home, which refers to one's settled and secure place in the community, where individuals can develop ties of an intimate nature and nurture self-determination, far away from the public gaze and undesired intrusion, is also enhanced by confidentiality, e.g. in the case of measures of surveillance (e.g. listening devices, cameras etc.), and thus calls for the design strategy 'hide' particularly in relation to a minimum zone of physical intimacy. Unlinkability, as the strategy 'separate', would enable to discard information violating the essence (Table 6).

Table 6. Relationship between privacy canons and attributes of Article 7

Attributes of Art. 7	Core	Protection goal	Design strategy
Private life	See sub-attributes		/
i. Physical and psychological integrity	The forum internum of the mind and of the body	/	/
ii. Personal social and sexual identity	The expression of one's sexual identity (CJEU) Official recognition of one's original or acquired name; Faithful social representation of one's identity	/	/
iii. Personal development, autonomy and participation ('outer circle')	Absence of secret external constraints	/	/
Family	For a father, the possibility to apply for the right to custody (CJEU) Continuity of relationship of care; Recognition of relationship of care	/	/
Communications	The content of one's communications (CJEU)	Confidentiality [Plausible deniability] Authentication/authorization	Hide
Home	A minimum zone of physical intimacy	[Unlinkability confidentiality]	Separate Hide

4.2   Legal and Technical Approaches to the Protection of Personal Data

Table 8 shows the correspondences between protection goals and the attributes of personal data protection. The first column to the left lists the attributes of the right. The second column lists cores relating to an attribute, if any (the essence found by the Court is marked with the acronym 'CJEU', whereas the essence I proposed is marked with 'Exp.', which stands for experimental). The third lists the privacy protection goals, or canons, corresponding to each attribute, while the fourth column shows the design approach corresponding to the protection goal.

The attribute 'legitimate processing' includes three requirements, two of which relate to a canon. Fairness and transparency correspond to transparency (particularly in the LINDDUN sense of policy and consent compliance) in a self-explanatory manner. Purpose limitation, which also expresses a core of the right, relates to confidentiality and the design strategy hide, in that data which is not disclosed to unauthorized parties is less likely to be processed unlawfully. It also relates to unlinkability, in that personal data kept in separate batches, aggregated, or minimized is also less likely to be processed without authorization. Confidentiality and unlinkability would be therefore important canons to comply with the essence.

The attribute 'data subject's rights' as a whole relates to intervenability and transparency (in the LINDDUN sense of content awareness) and the design strategies 'control' and 'inform'. The step 'access' relates to intervenability (control) and availability of the data, whereas 'rectification' relates to integrity, and non-repudiation of the data. The steps objection, particularly to profiling, and rejection, concern unlinkability; objection calls, in particular, for separation. Rejection could call for minimize (e.g. anonymization of the data), or a new design strategy, e.g. 'delete'.

Oversight, expressed by two attributes, is linked to intervenability, i.e. the possibility to request and apply corrective measures and counterbalances where necessary, and the design strategy control. Note that intervenability presupposes non-repudiation, which pertains to information security and means the ability to prevent a sender from denying later that he or she sent a message or performed an action, so that liability can be attributed. Intervenability and the related strategy of control would be important requirements to satisfy the experimental notion of the essence I propose here. Note that these findings support an important lesson against believing that DPbD/PbD can be an easy fix to compliance with privacy rights, as expressed for instance by Pagallo [7], Koops and Leenes [1] and Kamara [8].

Security calls for availability, confidentiality and intervenability, and the related design strategies hide and control. Minimization relates to unlinkability (in the self-explanatory form of 'minimise').

Finally, sensitive data, which is not, per se, an attribute, but rather affects the threshold of permissible limitations, is supported by unlinkability and the design strategy separate, as well as confidentiality and the design strategy hide, for the same reasons that apply to the attributes discussed above. In addition, plausible deniability may be very important to protect sensitive data, and hence exercise other rights freely.

Table 7. Relationship between privacy canons and attributes of Article 8

	Attributes of Art. 8	Essence	Protection goals	Design strategies
Legitimate processing	Lawful legal basis			/
	Fairness and transparency		Transparency (policy & consent compliance)	Inform
	Purpose limitation	Purpose limitation [CJEU]	Confidentiality Unlinkability *Intervenability*	Hide Separate (minimize, aggregate) *Demonstrate*
Data subjects' rights			Intervenability Transparency	Control Inform
	Access Rectify	Access [Exp]	Availability Non-repudiation Integrity	
	Object	Objecting to profiling [Exp]	Unlinkability	Separate
	Restrict		Unlinkability	/
Oversight	i. Supervisory authority		Intervenability (Non-repudiation!)	Control
	ii. Human intervention	The right to obtain human intervention on the part of the controller, to express his or her point of view and to contest the decision [Exp]	Intervenability (Non-repudiation!)	Control
Security and minimization	Security Minimization	CJEU: The provision of security safeguards in the legal basis relied upon for the processing of personal data	Confidentiality Availability, Intervenability Unlinkability Transparency	Hide Control Minimize
	Sensitive data: makes interferences automatically serious		Unlinkability, confidentiality *[Plausible deniability]*	Separate

4.3   Considerations: Essence, Attributes and Obligations of the Data Controller

Based on the analysis carried out in these pages, it is possible to conclude that, first, the two design strategies hide and separate (minimize, aggregate) and the corresponding protection goals confidentiality and unlinkability seem crucial for respecting the proposed notions of the essence of both rights. In addition, respecting the essence of Art. 8 calls for the design strategy control and the protection goal intervenability.

However, in both cases, not all potential notions of the essence seem to be matched by an existing design strategy; similarly, not all attributes seem to be matched by a protection goal. The case could be different, however, if all information security canons (see Sect. 2) had been taken into account. By means of example, the information security canon 'utility', whereby the information is relevant and useful for the purpose for which it is needed [24], links both with the attributes of private life (Art. 7) and the attributes data subjects' rights and security and minimization (Art. 8). As a result, there is room for further developing privacy protection goals and design strategies.

Moreover, some design strategies described in Sect. 2, such as enforce and demonstrate, seem underrepresented. Yet, it does not follow that the missing protection goals and design strategies are superfluous. In the case of data protection, the reason why some protection goals and design strategies are missing is that they express obligations of the data controller. Such duties do not feature in the definition of the right but are actually implied by them in the form of (data protection) principles in the applicable law. For instance, the two attributes of data protection which express oversight relate to the principle of accountability, which links to the protection goal of intervenability, and the strategies 'enforce' and 'demonstrate'. Similarly, the sub-attribute 'rectify' relates to the principle of accuracy, which expresses the duty to ensure that data are adequate, relevant and not excessive, which is fulfilled by the protection goal integrity.

The conclusion is that DPbD/PbD approaches should take into account both the definition of the rights, which represents a minimum threshold, and the applicable law which implements the right and lays down corresponding duties. The mapping between protection goals, essence and attributes, should be complemented by an equivalent mapping between protection goals and the obligations of the data controller stemming from the applicable law, as exemplified in Table 8. As a result, further protection goals and design strategies could be added (e.g. to embrace the important principle of minimization [45, 48], or protect the essence).

Table 8. Comprehensive approach to PbD/DPbD

Essence	Attribute	Principles expressed in the law	Duties of data controller
Protection goal	Protection goal	Protection goal	Protection goal
Design strategy	Design strategy	Design strategy	Design strategy
Right			
	Secondary law		

5   Conclusions and Further Research

In this paper I tackled the question, currently unaddressed in the literature, of how to reconcile the technical understanding of 'privacy by design' with the nature of the rights to private life and data protection in EU law, whose essence cannot be violated. My proposition was to map the equivalences between, on the one hand, the legal understanding of the attributes and essence of the fundamental rights to private life and data protection with, on the other hand, the technical notion of privacy protection goals developed in privacy threat modelling.

The analysis unveiled hidden connections between the legal and technical concepts: the essence is to law what protection goals are to technology, namely a boundary which cannot be crossed without violating the right. As a result, the identification of the concept of the essence and subsequent linking with privacy protection goals eases the implementation of 'by design' approaches in EU. Indeed, the design strategies hide, separate (minimize, aggregate) and control, and the corresponding protection goals confidentiality, unlinkability and intervenability, seem crucial for respecting the proposed notions of the essence of the two rights.

The analysis also showed mismatches between, first, attributes and essence, and second, protection goals and design strategies, suggesting there is a need to further develop the latter, e.g. by considering other information security canons (and related threats), as well as to take a comprehensive approach to PbD/DPbD. This means taking into account both the definition of the rights, which represent a minimum threshold, and the applicable law which implements the right and lays down corresponding duties. Such a comprehensive approach could be applied beyond building privacy-compliant technology.

First, a comprehensive approach can be used to unveil existing tensions inherent in technological design, not just among protection goals, but also between and among rights. For instance, while non-repudiation can be of crucial importance for personal data protection, it can be problematic for confidential communications, because it negates plausible deniability, which is important for confidentiality (e.g. of a whistleblower). Hence, there can be a clash between personal data protection and private life (which testifies to their independence). Clashes may also appear within a right: plausible deniability may be very important to protect the meta-attribute of sensitive data, and hence exercise other rights freely, but is at odds with the other attributes of the right.

Secondly, a comprehensive DPbD/PbD approach which takes into account also information security canons/threats can underpin tensions in the fight against cyber-crimes (understood as data crimes [47]), thus informing the development of informed and sustainable approaches to cybersecurity, as I illustrate in [12] in relation to an off-the-shelf intrusion detection and prevention system for universities.

Finally, the comprehensive approach can be used to perform meaningful impact assessment of technologies (as in [10, 25]) and policies. The attribute and essence can be used as a powerful instrument to capture the granularity of the intrusiveness of technologies and policies addressing public security into any fundamental rights (hence beyond data protection, as discussed in Sect. 3), whilst protection goals and design strategies could be used as a corrective approach, as I intend to show in future research.

Acknowledgements. I wish to thank my anonymous reviewers, the participants of the APF 2018 and Martyn Egan for suggestions on how to improve this draft. An early draft of this chapter appeared in a restricted deliverable of the FP7 SURVEILLE project (grant agreement no. 284725), as well as my PhD thesis, partly funded by SURVEILLE. Completion of this chapter was funded by the EPSRC research project "Combatting cRiminals In The Cloud" (CRITiCal - EP/M020576/1).

References

1. Koops, B.-J., Leenes, R.: Privacy regulation cannot be hardcoded. A critical comment on the 'privacy by design' provision in data-protection law. Int. Rev. Law Comput. Technol. **28**, 151–171 (2014)
2. Schartum, D.W.: Making privacy by design operative. Int. J. Law Inf. Technol. **24**, 151–175 (2016)
3. International Conference of Data Protection and Privacy Commissioners: Joint Proposal for a Draft of International Standards on the Protection of Privacy with regard to the processing of Personal Data (The Madrid Resolution). 30th International Conference of Data Protection and Privacy Commissioners, Madrid (2009). https://icdppc.org/wp-content/uploads/2015/02/The-Madrid-Resolution.pdf
4. Cavoukian, A.: Privacy by Design...Take the Challenge (2010). http://www.privacybydesign.ca/content/uploads/2010/03/PrivacybyDesignBook.pdf
5. Wuyts, K., Scandariato, R., Joosen, W.: LINDDUN: a privacy threat analysis framework. https://people.cs.kuleuven.be/ ∼ kim.wuyts/LINDDUN/LINDDUN.pdf
6. Danezis, G., et al.: Privacy and data protection by design – from policy to engineering. ENISA (2014)
7. Pagallo, U.: On the principle of privacy by design and its limits. In: Gutwirth, S., Leenes, R., De Hert, P., Poullet, Y. (eds.) European Data Protection. In Good Health?, pp. 331–346. Springer, Dordrecht (2012). https://doi.org/10.1007/978-94-007-2903-2_16
8. Kamara, I.: Co-regulation in EU personal data protection: the case of technical standards and the privacy by design standardisation 'mandate'. Eur. J. Law Technol. **8** (2017)
9. Rachovitsa, A.: Engineering and lawyering privacy by design: understanding online privacy both as a technical and an international human right issues. Int. J. Law Inf. Technol. **24**, 374–399 (2016)
10. Bieker, F., Friedewald, M., Hansen, M., Obersteller, H., Rost, M.: A process for data protection impact assessment under the European general data protection regulation. In: Schiffner, S., Serna, J., Ikonomou, D., Rannenberg, K. (eds.) APF 2016. LNCS, vol. 9857, pp. 21–37. Springer, Cham (2016). https://doi.org/10.1007/978-3-319-44760-5_2
11. Tsormpatzoudi, P., Berendt, B., Coudert, F.: Privacy by design: from research and policy to practice – the challenge of multi-disciplinarity. In: Berendt, B., Engel, T., Ikonomou, D., Le Métayer, D., Schiffner, S. (eds.) APF 2015. LNCS, vol. 9484, pp. 199–212. Springer, Cham (2016). https://doi.org/10.1007/978-3-319-31456-3_12
12. Porcedda, M.G.: Cybersecurity and privacy rights in EU law. Moving beyond the trade-off model to appraise the role of technology. Ph.D. thesis. European University Institute (2017)
13. Charter of Fundamental Rights of the European Union, OJ C 303/01. Official Journal C 303/01, pp. 1–22, European Union (2007)

14. Brkan, M.: In search of the concept of essence of EU fundamental rights through the prism of data privacy. Maastricht Working Paper (2017)
15. Lynskey, O.: The Foundations of EU Data Protection Law. Oxford University Press, Oxford (2015)
16. Tzanou, M.: EU counter-terrorism measures and the question of fundamental rights: the case of personal data protection. Ph.D. thesis, European University Institute (2012)
17. ENISA: Glossary. https://www.enisa.europa.eu/topics/threat-risk-management/risk-management/current-risk/risk-management-inventory/glossary
18. Microsoft: Threat modeling. https://www.microsoft.com/en-us/sdl/adopt/threatmodeling.aspx
19. OWASP: Risk modeling. https://www.owasp.org/index.php/Threat_Risk_Modeling
20. OWASP: Threat modeling. https://www.owasp.org/index.php/Application_Threat_Modeling
21. Jouinia, M., Rabaia, L.B.A., Aissab, A.B.: Classification of security threats in information systems. In: 5th International Conference on Ambient Systems, Networks and Technologies (ANT-2014). Procedia Computer Science, pp. 489–496 (2014)
22. Microsoft: The STRIDE threat model. https://msdn.microsoft.com/en-us/library/ee823878(v=cs.20).aspx
23. Microsoft: Applying STRIDE. https://msdn.microsoft.com/en-us/library/ee798544%28v=cs.20%29.aspx
24. International Telecommunication Union: Security in Telecommunications and Information Technology. An overview of issues and the deployment of existing ITU-T Recommendations for secure telecommunications (2015). https://www.itu.int/dms_pub/itu-t/opb/tut/T-TUT-SEC-2015-PDF-E.pdf
25. Berendt, B.: Better data protection by design through multicriteria decision making: on false tradeoffs between privacy and utility. In: Schweighofer, E., Leitold, H., Mitrakas, A., Rannenberg, K. (eds.) Privacy Technologies and Policy, pp. 210–230. Springer, Heidelberg (2017). https://doi.org/10.1007/978-3-319-67280-9_12
26. Hansen, M., Jensen, M., Rost, M.: Protection goals for privacy engineering. In: Security and Privacy Workshops (SPW). IEEE (2015)
27. Hoepman, J.-H.: Privacy design strategies. In: 2013 Privacy Law Scholars Conference (PLSC), Cornell University, Ithaca, NY, USA (2013)
28. Directive 95/46/EC of the European Parliament and of the Council of 24 October 1995 on the Protection of Individuals with regard to the Processing of Personal Data and on the Free Movement of such Data (Data Protection Directive) OJ L 281, vol. OJ L 281, pp. 31–50 (1995)
29. Regulation 2016/679/EU of the European Parliament and of the Council of 27 April 2016 on the Protection of Natural Persons with Regard to the Processing of Personal Data and on the Free Movement of such data, and Repealing Directive 95/46/EC (General Data Protection Regulation), OJ L 119/1 (2016)
30. European Commission: Proposal for a Regulation of the European Parliament and of the Council concerning the respect for private life and the protection of personal data in electronic communications and repealing Directive 2002/58/EC (Regulation on Privacy and Electronic Communications) (2017)
31. Porcedda, M.G.: On boundaries. In search for the essence of the right to the protection of personal data. In: de Hert, P., van Brakel, R., Leenes, R. (eds.) Proceedings of the 11th Computers, Privacy and Data Protection Conference, Hart (forthcoming)
32. United Nations, High Commissioner for Human Rights (OHCHR): Human Rights Indicators. A Guide to Measurement and Implementation (2012)

33. Candler, J., Holder, H., Hosali, S., Payne, A.M., Tsang, T., Vizard, P.: Human Rights Measurement Framework: Prototype Panels, Indicator Set and Evidence Base. Equality and Human Rights Commission, London (2011)
34. Fundamental Rights Agency: Using indicators to measure fundamental rights in the EU: challenges and solutions (2011)
35. Koops, B.-J., Clayton Newel, B., Timan, T., Skorvanek, I., Chokrevski, T., Galic, M.: A typology of privacy. Univ. Penn. J. Int. Law **38**, 483 (2017)
36. Finn, R.L., Wright, D., Friedewald, M.: Seven types of privacy. In: Gutwirth, S., Leenes, R., de Hert, P., Poullet, Y. (eds.) European Data Protection: Coming of Age, pp. 3–32. Springer, Dordrecht (2013). https://doi.org/10.1007/978-94-007-5170-5_1
37. Convention for the Protection of Human Rights and Fundamental Freedoms (as amended by Protocols No 11 and 14), Council of Europe, ETS no 005, 4 November 1950, Rome (1950)
38. X and Others v. Austria, no. 19010/07 CE:ECHR:2013:0219JUD001901007 (2013)
39. Opinion 1/15 of the Court (Grand Chamber), ECLI:EU:C:2017:592 (2017)
40. Judgment of 5 October 2010 in McB, C-400/10 PPU, ECLI:EU:C:2010:582, (2010)
41. Judgment of 8 April 2014 in Digital Rights Ireland and Seitlinger and Others, Joined cases C-293/12 and C-594/12, ECLI:EU:C:2014:238 (2014)
42. Judgment of 13 May 2014 in Google Spain and Google, C-131/12, ECLI:EU:C:2014:317 (2014)
43. Convention for the Protection of Individuals with regard to automatic processing of personal data, Council of Europe, CETS n. 108, 28 January 1981. In: Europe, C.o. (ed.) vol. CETS No. 108, Strasbourg (1981)
44. Judgment of 6 October 2015 in Schrems, C-362/14, ECLI:EU:C:2015:650 (2015)
45. Gürses, S., Troncoso, C., Diaz, C., Engineering privacy by design. In: Paper Discussed at the 4th Computers, Privacy & Data Protection Conference, Brussels (2011)
46. Porcedda, M.G.: Patching the patchwork: appraising the EU regulatory framework on cyber security breaches. Comput. Law Secur. Rev. **34**, 1077–1098 (2018)
47. Porcedda, M.G., Wall, D.S.: Data science, data crime and the law. In: Berlee, A., Mak, V., Tjong Tijn Tai, E. (eds.) Research Handbook on Data Science and Law. Edwar Elgar, Cheltenham (2018, forthcoming)
48. Gürses, S., Troncoso, C., Diaz, C., Engineering privacy by design reloaded. http://carmelatroncoso.com/papers/Gurses-APC15.pdf

Author Index

Printed in the United States
By Bookmasters